CAMEL SPIT & CORK TREES

A YEAR OF SLOW TRAVEL THROUGH PORTUGAL

Jack Montgomery

First Published in 2020
www.buzztrips.co.uk
Email:jack@buzztrips.co.uk
Twitter: @buzztrips
Facebook: @Buzztrips.co
Copyright ©2020 Jack Montgomery
Cover illustrations ©2020 Emily Flanagan

ISBN:9798662833
ISBN-13: 9798662833890

CHAPTERS

Winter

Spring

CAMEL SPIT & CORK TREES – THE PHOTO ALBUM

As a pictorial accompaniment to Camel Spit & Cork Trees: A Year of Slow Travel Through Portugal, there is an online photo album with images related to chapters in the book. This album includes some of the places and incidents referenced in the following pages and can be viewed at:

www.flickr.com/photos/buzztrips/albums/72157715861535168

SPRING

We lounge on the bench behind our temporary abode drinking Bohemian craft ale. Two bears masquerading as dogs, Caracol and Cookie, lie slumped on the grass at our feet whilst an enormous golden sun which reminds me of the poster for Apocalypse Now slips towards a not-so-distant horizon.

DEPARTURE

The ship dearly wants to be a cruise liner, even though it's
not much bigger than the ferries which regularly transported us
the relatively short distances to other Canary Islands. A DJ plays
jaunty Latino music whilst a troupe of dancers twirl, swirl and
wave at passengers from their stage - the edge of a swimming
pool barely bigger than the average bath tub. Dotted around
the deck are mainly Spanish passengers wearing tee-shirts and
shorts who sit at tables nursing plastic beakers of amber liquid.
Beyond the stern the distinctive white cobra hood of the Tenerife
Auditorium recedes into the distance under typically blue skies.

Departure.

It feels surreal. The party atmosphere makes it seem like a
celebration of our time, more than a decade, on Tenerife. Any
sadness at leaving the island we came to know and love is erased
by the thrill of excitement at undertaking a voyage of discovery.
There are 36 hours until we dock at Huelva; time in which to
reflect, chill-out, notch up a lot of reading, talk about our plans,
and just enjoy the journey with no regrets, no tears goodbye.
Our cabin in the bow of the ship is cramped but cosy, the sea is
calm, and the sunset spectacular. All feels good with the world.
Tomorrow, a new and exciting day dawns.

We'd arrived in the Canary Islands as naive Tenerife virgins
without a clue as to what living abroad actually entailed. After a
roller-coaster fourteen years we're more than ready to move on,
this time armed with bulging bag loads of experience as well as
Cindy, our trusty Fiat Punto, packed to capacity with the items
we consider most essential. Ensconced in the ferry's lounge,
we sip at a couple of *cervezas* and chat about what our new life
in Portugal might be like. It's all supposition as we've no idea
where we'll be staying in the long-term.

"Why Portugal?" friends and family have asked, some
bemused why we'd swap an island with a near perfect climate

1

for anywhere else.

There are a variety of reasons. We've been writing about Tenerife and the Canary Islands for years, we're jaded. Whilst there will always be something new to discover, much of the time we feel like we're going over the same old ground we've covered on many previous occasions. Travels in various countries around Europe in recent years have awoken a desire to experience somewhere new on a longer-term basis. There's also a need to reconnect with the outside world in a broader sense. Island life can be inward looking; I knew that from growing up on a small Scottish island and Tenerife was no different. If anything it was more insular, especially the traditional parts. That's partly what made the Canaries such an appealing place to live, until the realisation dawned that we had gradually become outsiders in the wider cultural loop. That's not necessarily always a bad thing; we've no idea who friends and family in the UK are talking about when they mention reality TV celebrities; although, we do know who their Spanish counterparts are. But neither do we recognise the musicians they listen to, or have read the books they reference. That might sound strange, but life in the north of Tenerife isn't what many who typecast the whole island as being a 'holiday resort' might think. It has its own unique culture and traditions, and these can be culturally all-consuming. Additionally, life on the island lost some of its shiny gloss thanks to events which unfolded in our later years there. Portugal feels like the logical next step. We like what we've already seen of it, and it's a mainland European country where there are enough similarities to help ease a smoother transition into the groove of life, but also enough differences so everything feels all fresh and new. Language is a huge factor. We know from the dual language grocery products we've been buying for years (Spanish on one side, Portuguese on the other), written Portuguese can be very close to written Spanish, so we'll already recognise many words. This has to be an advantage. Spoken Portuguese is obviously a different matter, we're not kidding ourselves about our ability to understand or be able to speak it quickly. Then there's the weather. The southern half of

Portugal may not share the same climate as the Canary Islands, but it doesn't look half bad and shouldn't be too much of a shock to bodies which have been pampered by years of an almost perfect climate. And finally there's ease of travel, an essential in our line of work. Countless flights from numerous destinations arrive on and depart from Tenerife on a daily basis. We could fly to lots of Spanish destinations from Tenerife's North Airport and many main cities around Europe from Tenerife South Airport. On the downside, it's a longish flight to travel most places and, when it comes down to it, international destinations we could actually fly direct to from Tenerife were limited to those which send plane load after plane load of sun-seeking tourists the island's way. The idea of being able to jump on a train, or in the car, and cross border after border, discovering off-the-beaten-track places without the need to step on a plane is an enticing one. Talking about all the potential new experiences we have to look forward to makes us feel slightly intoxicated. But not as intoxicated as some. We see one man who's spent too long at the pool bar being escorted to his cabin by a member of the crew. Although the sea is mirror-calm, the man lurches from side to side as if the ship is being tossed around by tumultuous waves. It makes me wonder if the sea was choppy would he be the only one walking in a straight line?

Dinner on the Naviera Armas ferry pops the party balloon. The buffet is cheap and the selection is... is what exactly? Not totally depressing is the nicest thing I can say about it. It is completely uninspiring. I wander up and down the row of sad, tired, dry-looking dishes on offer, like a disappointed sergeant inspecting his troops, trying to decide what to choose using a method of elimination, discarding the most unappealing meals first. To add insult to injury the food isn't even lukewarm, it's cold. Tellingly, there is a microwave in the dining room. It's a classy ship where you have to heat up your own food. A boisterous extended Spanish family seem wise to the ferry's culinary flaws, they've brought their own food stash and hog the microwave. We "*permiso, por favor*" our way into their midst and make a grab for the metal box. I can't even figure out how to open it (we're still microwave rookies, mainly because we simply prefer cooking using oven, grill, and hob). Andy has a go and also fails. The Spanish family's 'head cook', a whip-thin young man wearing a baseball cap back to front, a vest tee-shirt, and loops of gold chains around his neck, smiles at our pathetic efforts, leans over and presses a button. The door pops open. Without speaking a word he takes my plate, puts it inside and sets the dial. At least we know enough to understand the ping means the contents are hot. Being warm makes the food edible... just.

Overnight we sail into rough seas. Our cabin is at the prow, right at the highest point of an arc when the ship rises into the air, pauses and then crashes violently back into the waves, making the most terrifying screams. It sounds as though Poseidon himself is tearing at the hull with a can opener. The stormy weather has set in for the duration. Surprisingly, we manage to grab a few hours of sleep without nausea engulfing us completely. But the second we leave the relative stability of our bunks in the morning, the lurching motion causes conflicting signals to career anarchically around the brain. There's a limited time between leaving the bunk and getting out of the cabin before sea-sickness takes a firm hold. Moving from our cabin to the less violent rear of the ship involves a bruise-inducing journey of silly walks as the floor disappears below our feet with every other step.

The lounge at the stern of the ferry becomes our sanctuary, the only place we're not thrown around like rag dolls in a shaggy dog's mouth. There are far fewer voyagers in the lounge than the previous day. It is a ghost ship. Many passengers are ill and stay in their cabins. Maybe many passengers are ill *because* they stay in their cabins. I bet quite a few are regretting the amount of *cervezas* they downed during the ship's *fiesta*-like departure. Reading anything is completely out of the question. We sit, subdued, like extras in *One Flew Over the Cuckoo's Nest*, wishing the hours away. It's a long, long day. Only the ever-bubbly entertainment team provide relief from the irritated sea and depressing selection of mediocre food. Still, we console ourselves with the knowledge we will be on terra firma by early evening, with hearty food in a proper Spanish restaurant to refuel deflated spirits.

At 19:50 (an hour from docking) there's still no land at all in sight. There have been no announcements about any delays, but something clearly isn't right. We should be halfway along an estuary by my reckoning. I silly-walk my way to the information desk.

"Rough weather has delayed us four hours," I'm told when I ask why there's no dry land outside the portholes.

I'm not sure when the crew planned on sharing this important piece of information. I'm gutted. At least the sea has calmed, but the delay means we have another meal on board to not look forward to instead of dining in Huelva. We agree the food was so poor we can't face another rematch at dinner. Instead, I head outside to the the pool bar, the domain of serious drinkers and heavy smokers, to check if they have anything at all as an alternative. Anything junky will suffice - crisps, nuts, donuts. Not only do they have snacks, they have burgers and pizzas which look far more appetising than the tired offerings in the dining room. The man in front of me is served with a generous-sized beefburger which looks delicious. If only I'd ventured outside previously we may have eaten if not like kings at least not like paupers. I order two burgers and try to avoid drooling.

"Sorry, that was the last one," the barman informs me.

My misery is complete.

At midnight we finally reach the Spanish mainland and with immense relief escape our temporary prison. Now the next chapter can really begin.

A Pause in Azeitão

We lounge on the bench behind our temporary abode drinking Bohemian craft ale. Two bears masquerading as dogs, Caracol and Cookie, lie slumped on the grass at our feet whilst an enormous golden sun which reminds me of the poster for *Apocalypse Now* slips towards a not-so-distant horizon. About forty misty kilometres away, on the other side of the Tagus, the lights of Lisbon add their magical twinkle to the scene. Views in the opposite direction are of the lush valleys and curved *serras* of Arrábida Natural Park. This might only be an Airbnb house we've rented for two weeks until we get sorted, but it feels as though we've arrived; a new life in Portugal has begun... and we're nowhere near prepared.

It occurs to us we've done exactly the same as with Tenerife fourteen years previously. There, we chose where to stay based on an instant feeling. During a brief recce two months ago, we immediately decided somewhere close to Setúbal was where we wanted to be based in Portugal. We know little about the area save for the fact it felt right to us. One of the places we identified as a strong possibility was here, Vila Nogueira de Azeitão.

Although we knew Lisbon was only a thirty minute drive away, actually being able to see the sun glinting on a tributary off the Tagus in the warm early evening rams home just how close we are to one of Europe's most exciting cities. We wanted to feel more connected to the European mainland, emerging from a cultural desert in a way, and being a stone's throw from Lisbon feels as though we might have achieved it. I don't mean that in a disparaging way, just that Canarian culture can be very, well, Canarian. A few years ago, for a magazine article, we interviewed Tenerife's newly elected Carnival Queen and had asked her what music she liked to listen to. She reeled off a list of Spanish and South American musicians. Few English speaking readers would recognise them so we pushed her for the names of any American or

British musicians she liked, or even knew. She looked blank for a few moments and then her face lit up as she thought of one.

"Supertramp," she shouted triumphantly, adding. "My father has one of their albums."

At fiestas and music festivals, the sounds we heard were mostly Latino, reggaeton and Spanish pop. By the time we left Tenerife we had no idea who the big names in American and British music were, but we could tell you who was hot on the Spanish music scene.

Even with the glow of a friendly sun warming our faces, and strong beer coursing through our veins, there's a growing realisation that in some ways we're back where we were when we first touched down on Tenerife. There, on the first night, we had the shock of discovering the Castilian Spanish we'd spent a year learning at night school in Manchester's Cervante's Institute wasn't the same unintelligible Spanish being spoken to us as we tried to pick up the keys for the house we'd rented; the Spanish spoken in the Canary Islands has more in common with South American than it does with mainland Spain. This time it's the discovery that being able to speak Spanish isn't going to help us much when it comes to attempting Portuguese. Seeing Portuguese written down on the back of a packet of Special K is one thing, hearing it spoken is another. After a handful of interactions with the locals we know that being able to read and speak Spanish might be somewhat of a double-edged sword. Thankfully, so far most people respond in excellent English when our attempts stutter or fail. At worst, they try their best to communicate in English, surpassing our pathetic attempts at Portuguese. This isn't new; in language terms, we regularly blunder our way about in the dark in various countries. Our inability to communicate in Portuguese is far more frustrating though. We can recognise many words when they're written down. But when we attempt to speak them we're met with blank stares. Possibly it's that familiarity, virtually useless so far, which is at the root of our frustration. We're not in Kansas anymore that's for sure. Arriving at our temporary accommodation opened our eyes to that little fact. Our landlady,

Barbara (a German married to a Brazilian, José), had told us we'd struggle to find the *quinta* (a type of estate/farm) so had met us in the car park of a nearby supermarket. The *quinta* is located atop a hill about three kilometres from Azeitão's centre, a kilometre and a half of which is on a dirt track, the final uphill section being seriously rutted and not the sort of terrain our little Canarian Fiat Punto was designed to tackle. Spotting the shock on our faces in her rear-view mirror as we gingerly followed her, Barbara told us these country 'roads' were common, but I wasn't a happy bunny at the idea of having to drive up and down what seemed little more than a walking track on a regular basis.

My disappointment at the awkwardness of the approach dissipated when I saw our temporary hilltop abode; a pretty, little traditional farmhouse outbuilding with hydrangeas and lilies outside of it. It has one bedroom, a living room, and a dining room kitchen with views to Lisbon; just perfect for a short stay. It's also clearly built for Hobbit-sized inhabitants. The work surfaces are ridiculously low. When Andy chops food or washes up she looks like Gandalf visiting Bilbo Baggins. Whenever I cook on the mini-me cooker, I invariably smack my head on its extractor hood. And I'm not what you'd call tall. However, these doll's house-sized features make the place even more charming. Barbara and José live in a large house opposite, although we rarely see them, whilst another part of the outbuilding we're in is occupied by Gene, the *quinta's* Brazilian gardener/handyman. It feels like belonging to a small, friendly community, which is rather nice. One morning, Gene brings a tray of bread rolls to our cottage, indicating they need to be baked before we eat them. They are *pão de queijo*; deliciously addictive Brazilian cheesy rolls. I want to tell Gene how much we like them so use Google translate to come up with "*Gostamos muito do pão, obrigado,*" trying to make it sound Portuguese by pronouncing every S as "sh". I have a theory that to speak Portuguese the way Sean Connery's James Bond would might help people understand me more. Who knows if Gene understands, but he gives me the thumbs up. This thumbs up has become our way of communicating.

Each morning we open our door to be faced by Caracol and Cookie, the two bear-like dogs belonging to José and Barbara. Caracol and Cookie turn up at the door for a hug and a head scratch in the morning, afternoon and early evening when we crack a Portuguese IPA. We quickly grow very fond of these gentle bear-dogs and look forward to hearing Caracol's 'get up I'm waiting for a pat' bark each day.

When our first weekend on Portuguese soil arrives, we stroll into the village along the unsurfaced country lane to spend the afternoon at a small gastronomic fair in the main square. We work our way around the various wine and food stalls lining the *praça*, starting our gastro-journey with *bifanas* which are warm, seasoned pork fillets in bread rolls. The rolls are soft (unlike their Spanish counterparts) and freshly baked, ideal for warm meaty fillings. They remind me of the rolls they still make at the Electric Bakery in Bute, the Scottish island where I grew up. After scoffing the *bifanas* we move on to bite-sized *empadas* (pies); one has chicken inside, the other shrimp. These are followed up by sweet pastries whose fillings we can't identify. Noticing a crowd swarming one stall, we follow suit and, like everyone else but with far less ease, buy a slab of dense fig cake. As we sit, chewing our way through the sweet slab of fig, a woman passes holding a tray of something in white-chocolate shot glasses. Andy makes a comment about how good they look to which the woman smiles and replies in perfect English "they are delicious, you should try some."

So we do – knocking back a syrupy cherry liqueur called *ginja* before eating the white chocolate glass it's served in. Impressed with the drink, we buy a *castanha* (chestnut) flavoured bottle of the stuff and two mini bottles of Moscatel, whose labels confirm they're '*Moscatelitos*' – little Moscatels. The afternoon slips easily past as we eat, drink and listen to music which switches from *saudade* (melancholic Portuguese songs) to UK and US hits from the 80s and 90s; sounds which unlock waves of warm nostalgic memories. Each visit to a different stall represents a challenge, even when it comes to ordering beer. Because the beer kiosk has Super Bock signs all over I ask for two Super Bocks.

"*Imperial*?" asks the barman, completely confusing me as there's no reference to Imperial lager anywhere, not even on the pump he has his hands on.

"*Nao, Superbock, por favor,*" I insist as I've never tried '*Imperial*' noticing a look of increasing bemusement on his face.

It transpires that '*imperial*' means draught. The barman is asking if we want draught or bottled lager. Just to confuse the issue more when it comes to ordering draught lager in Portugal, in Porto the word used is '*fino*'. Although attempts at communication are occasionally stuttering, to a person everyone is incredibly friendly; something which makes us feel very welcome. Elated with our first experiences of life in Portugal, we stroll home along a road which would be completely dark if it weren't for the dots of light from fireflies and Lisbon's soft, orange glow. The air is perfumed and filled with the faint sound of music coming from the *festa* which is just hitting its stride. We knew Azeitão would be a good fit.

Although a small town, Azeitão boasts a rich history and two famous *adegas* (wineries); José Maria da Fonseca in the town centre and Bacalhôa just a short walk from the main square. Whether it's the presence of these *adegas*, or because it's become a popular place to live with well-to-do Lisboans, it's a sophisticated, cultural and relatively lively town with a youthful vibe. Subsequently, Azeitão has a number of very good restaurants, ranging from down-to-earth cafes selling *caracóis* (snails, apparently very popular in these parts as we spot a number of restaurants with signs proclaiming '*há caracóis*' – we have snails) to stylish, but not expensive, restaurants. We work our way around as many as we can in the time we have available.

Casa Nobre D'Azeitao, located on the main *praça*, has a menu which features a selection of game, including wild boar and my favourite meat, venison, which I order whilst Andy ends up with a family-sized pot of seafood rice. We keep forgetting portions tend to be bigger than we're used to, and the Canarian portions we're used to are not what you'd call meagre. The meal introduces an aspect of Portuguese dining that seems strange to us. What is listed on the menu as 'chips' is actually what us Brits call 'crisps'. A plate of venison arriving with a side serving of crisps looks bizarre. The venison is really good, but I'm left with an unanswered question. How, exactly, am I supposed to eat venison and crisps? I pop a chunk of meat into my mouth and then pick at the crisps... it feels like a mismatched pairing.

Every time we eat out, which is a lot as cooking over the Hobbit stove is a backbreaking business, we discover something new about Portuguese gastronomy in this area. At the Jardim do Moscatel we learn that even though the opening hours show a restaurant is officially open, if you roll up early you might walk in to find all the staff eating their dinner. Seeing the chefs tuck into their dinner, we apologise and walk straight out again. But they call us back and urge us to take a seat. We also discover there that *bife à portuguesa* is a steak topped with an egg.

We find it's virtually impossible to walk past a restaurant called Casa das Tortas without being enticed in by an aroma of grilled fish from the barbecue on their shack-like terrace. And we also discover, through thorough first hand research, that the dodgy-named Casa Negrito serves the best *tortas de Azeitão* in town. These are local specialities which are made with egg and sugar, have a Swiss roll-shaped outer casing, and a runny, creamy, cinnamon-rich filling.

Azeitão a small town, but it's one which punches above its weight gastronomically.

The Reality of House Rentals

There's little time to explore further afield as we have two pressing tasks to complete. One is to finish writing a mini travel guide and walking directions for two Slow Travel holidays in the west of Crete. Modern travel writing can come in various forms; one aspect of our work involves helping create walking holidays for UK specialist Slow Travel company Inntravel. We were on Crete just over a week before we bade *adios* to Tenerife and the deadline for completing the work is bearing down on us like a runaway juggernaut. Subsequently, mornings are spent typing furiously on our laptops and listening to recordings of ourselves bickering over which way we should go when creating walking routes on a Greek island where signposts are still few and far between. The other task is equally pressing; get registered with as many accommodation rental agencies as possible.

We laid the foundation during our recce visit, but few *inmobiliarias* (real estate agents) showed much enthusiasm toward a couple of foreigners who may or may not return. This time we expect a different attitude as we've now relocated, which, hopefully, will prove we're serious.

House hunting turns out to be more problematic than we anticipated. *Inmobiliaria* websites show a decent amount of potential homes, but when we contact them online to try to make appointments to view the properties we like the look of, there's no response. When we turn up in person at *inmobiliaria* offices in the locations we're interested in, their actual portfolio of available accommodation for rent isn't as comprehensive as their websites suggest. When we ask to view those which might have potential, estate agents say they'll make an appointment with owners and get back to us. Not a single one does. Rental prices are also high; surprisingly so for a country where average earnings are low when compared to many northern European ones. High-earning, middle class Lisboans are partly the cause in the Azeitão area. But there's a bigger issue. Even though the Setúbal Peninsula is virtually unknown in Britain and other countries, Portuguese holidaymakers descend in their thousands between mid-June and mid-September. As a result, the rental market is predominately a holiday one. Even out of season rental prices reflect what people pay during summer months. There's no adjustment at all for low season. Our Airbnb host Barbara tries her best to help us find somewhere locally. She knows a woman in the village who is interested in renting out a house in her *quinta* on a longer-term basis and arranges for us to meet her at the property. Whereas Barbara and José's *quinta* is more of a casual farm, this one is most definitely at the stately mansion end of the *quinta* definition spectrum, and is reached via a long, elegant avenue of cypress trees. The regal house has been in the same family for some years, centuries in fact; this is an estate which belongs to a family referenced in books about Portugal's history, the Fonsecas. The owner is amiably aristocratic and speaks perfect English, casually mentioning Portuguese luminaries, including José Saramago, who've stayed at the mansion. She shows us around two houses she has for rent, both in former outbuildings. It looks as though we could be, yet again, destined to live where animals once were bedded down (our house in Tenerife was a converted cowshed). One house is far too small, but we're tempted by the other which looks just the right size for working and living. The idea of residing somewhere famous Portuguese writers have laid their heads is appealing, maybe some of their talent might have oozed into the bricks and mortar and might ooze back out again and into us.

After observing the polite formalities of casual chit chat we eventually get around to the crass business of asking "how much?" Surprisingly, the owner doesn't have a figure in mind. She grabs a piece of paper, does some calculations and shows us the result. We almost physically stagger when we see what she has written; two thousand Euros a month. Two thousand Euros for a small house with virtually no privacy. Outdoor spaces, which are extensive to be fair, are all communal. We throw a white lie her way and tell her we'll think about it even though we've already thought about it. It's crazy money.

We're more honest with Barbara when she asks how we

got on, and tell her the house is way overpriced. We've figured out why. Houses in this area are rented out as holiday homes throughout summer and the owner simply calculated a monthly rent based on what she charged for her summer holiday rentals. She made no adjustment at all for long-term occupancy. We had been warned about this by a real estate agent in nearby Palmela who'd also advised that, as foreigners, rental costs we're quoted could be substantially higher than if we were Portuguese accommodation-hunters.

Time is running out and we have made not one iota of progress in securing somewhere in the area to rent long-term. Once again Barbara does her best to come to our rescue. She offers to rent the cottage to us for a longer period as we've fitted into life at the *quinta* so well. Barbara and José like us, Gene likes us, and the dogs like us. The feelings are mutual. We adore staying in the quaint little cottage at the *quinta*. But it is simply too small for longer-term living, especially for people like us who a) work from home and b) for whom cooking is important. But with no options on the table regarding moving into accommodation in the Setúbal area, we seriously mull over the enticing prospect of staying on. It has so much going for it; it's a serenely lovely place to live and it's in the perfect location, save for the rutted dirt track road approach. We are deliriously happy here. But heads have to rule hearts in this instance and we reluctantly tell Barbara we have to decline her kind offer. Possibly if we didn't have 'stand-in' accommodation already arranged we might have decided differently. But we have a safety net in deepest Alentejo.

When the decision to move to Portugal had been finalised, our good friend and work colleague James, Inntravel's project manager for Spain and Portugal, put us in touch with an English couple, Ken and Carole, who have lived in Portugal for decades. They run a guest-house on the border with Spain in the Serra de São Mamede Natural Park which Inntravel use for some Slow Travel holidays. Ken and Carole also own a second house in the area which is currently lying empty and up for sale. They offered it to us as a temporary summer abode at a far more bank account-friendly rate than the shocking rental prices in Azeitão. It isn't in an area we'd considered relocating to as it is too remote for us to spend time there in the longer term; the aspect of our work which involves travel wouldn't be easy. But it is a much appreciated and needed safety net. We'd agreed to rent it for a couple of months, looking after its upkeep until we found accommodation near Setúbal. As the days in Barbara and José's cottage rapidly shoot past we realise just how much of a lifesaver this arrangement has turned out to be.

We're very, very sorry to have to leave Azeitão, but it's a sadness countered by a growing excitement at heading off to pastures that are completely new to us. Who knows what life beyond the back of beyond will be like?

SUMMER

It is not a good night for smuggling. The full moon bathes the land in a ghostly white light. I can see the clear, sharp outline of the hills around me. I can even see moon shadows cast by cork trees 200m away. Smugglers would be easy pickings for border guards on a night like this.

Where is the Petrol Station?

Two weeks living on a hilltop south of the Tagus has been far too short, but still long enough to know this is where we want to be. It feels like a snug and comfy fit and we're reluctant to leave Barbara, Jose, Gene, Cookie and Caracol, all of whom we've developed a bond with. But the idea of being able to settle into one place for a decent, if unknown, length of time is appealing as there's an unsettling sense of still being in transit. Additionally, we know absolutely diddly-squat about Alentejo, so having the opportunity to become familiar with life in the remote Portuguese wilderness near the Spanish border is an exciting prospect.

We let Google Maps plan our route, avoiding toll roads as we want to take our time to enjoy the journey. Initially, we tackle the commuter belt on the opposite side of the river from Lisbon before heading west and through Vendas Novas, birthplace of the savoury *bifana*. It's not the prettiest of towns, it has a military base and subsequently roundabouts reflect its presence. An artillery gun on one doesn't say 'welcome to the town' in quite the same way as Azeitao's wine-themed roundabouts did. But it does have a lot of *Casas das Bifanas* selling the town's famous snack.

West of Vendas Novas, the countryside becomes more rural. Small, urban settlements are replaced by sprawling thirsty plains broken by rare conical hills with castles perched on the soft curves of their summits. At one point we pass a band of pigs, their hides the same colour as that of a rhinoceros, happily snuffling around in the dappled shade provided by cork trees. They are *porco preto ibérico* - Iberian black pigs.

Town names on the map act as checkpoints to be ticked off along the way, each tick a step closer to our new home. The road dissects Montemor-O-Novo, a place we looked at as a potential base during our reconnaissance trip earlier in the year. There's a Michelin star restaurant in Montemor-O-Novo, something which made us think it might have an interesting gastronomic scene. But an explore of depressingly ghostly streets in its older quarter on a grey March day had it quickly erased from our list of potentials. Next checkpoint is Évora, another town we'd checked out. Évora is a different prospect altogether; a pretty-as-a-postcard hill town and UNESCO World Heritage Centre. We spent three nights in heart of the old town and were charmed by its historic streets, diverse restaurants and youthful personality. It's home to the morbid quirk that is the *Capela dos Ossos*, a chapel whose walls and ceilings are decorated with the bones and skulls from 5000 cadavers. There's also a direct rail link with Lisbon, a huge plus point when your job involves frequent forays into other lands. Évora didn't make it onto our shortlist because, although the town itself ticked many boxes, we were completely uninspired by the surrounding countryside. Ideally we wanted a location with relatively easy access to a few varied walking routes and weren't convinced Évora could offer us this, especially after an enquiry in the town's tourist office about walking in the area resulted in us being handed a leaflet with three routes, one of which seemed excessive in length.

"One of these is 70km long and this suggests we do it in a day."

"Yes, in a day," the girl who handed us the leaflet smiled and replied.

"Walk 70 kilometres… in a day?"

"Yes."

"You're not a walker are you?"

It turned out the routes were recommended driving itineraries.

The final town before the road veers sharply north east is Estremoz, a name we've never heard before. Yet an impressive castle and fortified town identifies it as somewhere which was clearly important at some point in the past. The road passes through the newer part of Estremoz, where some large supermarkets are located, before we emerge into a landscape of low flat plains again. It has a big country beauty to it, an immense canvas of endless golden fields broken only by the neat mushroom-shaped tops of emerald-coloured stone pines. Over

the course of a couple of hours there hasn't been much variation
in the scenery. I don't want to admit it to myself at such an early
point in our new relationship with Portugal; however, I know
not so deep down this is a landscape I could become bored with
quite quickly.

The plan is to stop for lunch at any quaint, roadside restaurant
that catches our eye at just the right time. But 12:30 comes and
goes, as does 13:00 then 13:30, and 14:00 before we realise our
flawed plan was reliant on us actually passing a quaint, roadside
restaurant. At 14:30, as we arrive at the outskirts of Portalegre
on the edge of Sao Mamede Natural Park, we decide if we want
to eat at all we need to stop. Portalegre's leafy main *praça* looks
promising and pretty. On one side, the vibrant lilac blossom
of mature jacaranda trees compliment elegant old buildings
whose blinding, whitewashed walls are broken by sunny
yellow strips around windows. Lining the other side is a row of
shops, bars and restaurants. We're immediately drawn to one
which promises gourmet *petiscos* (small dishes which are like
the Portuguese version of tapas). The basement-level interior
looks more 'heavy metal bar after a wild night' than creative
petisco palace and we decide to pass, especially as there's only
one weary patron propping up the bar and no evidence at all
that any food, gourmet or otherwise, is on offer or has been in
recent memory. A bar on the corner of the square has a handful
of external tables and looks more inviting. A menu scrawled on
a blackboard inside reveals it serves snacks. Result. I catch the
barman's eye and order a couple of *bifanas* and beers.

"Sorry, we stopped serving food at three."

I look at my watch, it's 15:05.

With time and lunch options running out, we pin fading
hopes on a fast food pizza joint; not exactly what we had
envisioned. But even there we're thwarted. They stopped serving
at three also. By this time I'm in full chunter mode. On Tenerife,
with its Spanish dining patterns, this would still be lunch
time. We're not used to there being limits on when we can eat.
Stomachs in mutinous mood, and with me still grumbling about
not being able to eat lunch at lunchtime, we leave Portalegre and

immediately enter a world which lifts our hungry spirits. The dry flatlands are replaced by green scenes of undulating hills and, annoyingly too late, quaint-looking, roadside restaurants - we're in Sao Mamede Natural Park. This is our sort of landscape. This happy campers feeling is short-lived. As we wind up and over hill and dale, an orange circle on the dashboard catches my eye.

"How are we doing for petrol?" I ask Andy.

"Oops, shit, not good," Andy grimaces. "We're almost out."

"Didn't it occur to you to keep an eye on the gauge?"

Thereafter follows a short, sharp, viscous exchange of accusations and recriminations and soon we're sitting stony-faced and not talking to each other. We have no idea how far it is to the next petrol station, and the point where it would have made sense to turn back to Portalegre has passed. The scenery might be beautiful, but all we're interested in is spotting a petrol station sign. Pretty, petrol-station-free hamlets come and go as the dial drops ever closer to empty. Finally, as we reach the outskirts of Portagem, we see the blue sign we've been praying for. It shows a petrol pump, 3km, and an arrow pointing us away from the town we should be passing through. We can relax. Three kilometres later and we're parked beside a lone, finger-in-its-ear pump which looks like it belongs in a museum.

"This can't be it," I'm convinced this is the 'former' petrol station and a new shiny replacement lies just along the road. Andy thinks otherwise.

We drive on further to the centre of a village whose name we don't even know. There's not a lot here; no shops... and no petrol station. But there is a bar which two men wearing checked shirts and flat caps have just left. This is no time to be embarrassed about appalling attempts at trying to speak Portuguese. In a stuttering mix of English, Spanish (our default foreign language), and bad Portuguese I ask them where the nearest petrol station is. They nod, seeming to understand the question, before one replies.

"*Espanha.*"

"Spain? The nearest petrol station is in Spain?" Both our jaws hit the floor.

"*Sim, Espanha,*" the other man nods and then adds, thankfully, in English. "Follow us."

They jump into a car and take off at a speed we struggle to keep up with as our overfull car groans to negotiate the steep, narrow and winding road whilst Google's directions woman assertively informs us we're going in completely the wrong direction. We have no idea where we are. We'll worry about that when, or if, we find petrol. The road levels out and then descends to join a main road where our saviours wait in a lay-by. We pull in behind them. The driver leans out the window and points along the road.

"Petrol ten minutes."

Eight minutes later and we're at the Portuguese/Spanish border; an oddity of a location where a large concrete building straddles the centre of the road. There is nobody around, it's deserted. Large black birds circling above add to what is a post-apocalyptic vibe - they are vultures. It's eerie and quite unsettling. We drive across the border, half expecting a guard to suddenly appear, machine gun raised because we haven't stopped to show our papers. There's still no sign of a petrol station.

Two minutes later, or an hour and two minutes as we've swapped countries and time zones, and we see a most welcome man-made oasis - a petrol station which is open and buzzing with activity.

Now we can relax, even though we don't know where we are in relation to where we want to be. All we do know for sure is that we are in the wrong country entirely.

A Marvellous Mansion

Crença is like the abodes featured on *A Place in the Sun* we used to fantasise about living in; a big old building with bags of character and many intriguing nooks and crannies. It's the sort of place retired house-in-the-sun hunters from Bury would gush about how perfect it was, before they drove us mad by opting for an 1980s apartment overlooking a pool in an anonymous beach resort. Without any planning on our part, and thanks to both contacts and the generosity of strangers, we have landed on our feet. All our certainty about wanting to be based near Azeitão is blown to smithereens from the second we cross a former smugglers' path which separates the rough car park from the old house. We have to pass through two low, iron gates on either side of the path - in place to prevent incursions by the local goat herd which passes this way twice a day and who have their slitty eyes on the lookout for any forbidden fruit along the way.

To people like us, who have been used to living in a converted animal shed eighty metres square for 14 years, Crença is a massive mansion - a sturdy, blinding-white, rectangular farmhouse building with exposed honey-coloured stones around its small windows. The house nestles into a hillside whose summit is in Spain. It is such a part of the hillside that the uneven tips of large boulders embedded in the earth form some of the steps into the kitchen and also from the kitchen into one of the three bathrooms. Their are two staircases; one leads from the front door, dissecting the house, to the main bathroom and two bedrooms. The other leads from the kitchen to a dining room and the master bedroom. The downstairs living room's aged, wood-plank ceiling is also the floor of the bedroom above - which there are glimpses of through splits in the warped wood. The kitchen is not massive, not much bigger than the one in our small house on Tenerife, but has sufficient counter surface to keep enthusiastic amateur cooks like us happy, and it's well stocked with pots, pans, crockery, and cooking utensils. The place oozes character. Personality-rich as the interior of the house is, it's the outside spaces which elevate it into dream property status. A front terrace (beside another, detached, one-bedroomed house which is currently being used as storage space) looks across a gently rolling valley of golden fields and copses of cork trees. There are only a couple of other houses in the frame; these are our nearest neighbours, located between us and one of the most picturesque hilltop towns in Portugal, Marvão, just ten kilometres away. It is an inspirational view; a view that holds our eyes firmly in its grasp, refusing to let us look away.

A door from the kitchen leads to a multi-levelled area with a swimming pool, and a slate terrace shaded by a combination of canes and billowing, pastel curtains. Beyond this terrace is a vine-covered arbour above a curved stone bench set into a dry stone wall. This has the best views of all - Marvão atop a hill to the west, and to the north an endless Alentejo savanna of wheat-coloured fields populated by a handful of copper-coloured cows. Beyond these lies a vast, empty wilderness. We are on the very eastern edge of Portugal, and it *does* feel like we're perched on the outer fringes of a country. Portagem, the nearest town, looked like a remote outpost whereas Galegos, a hamlet with bumpy cobbles and a ridiculously narrow 'main street' we nervously drove through to get to Crença, had the air of a forgotten community hidden away from the outside world. Crença is nearly 3km beyond Galegos. The Spanish petrol station which saved our bacon and allowed us to complete our journey is only an eight minute drive away.

A friend who knew the area described its location as being beyond the back of beyond. Now we know exactly what he meant. It is the sort of place I can imagine setting up the laptop facing an artist's dream of a landscape and letting the views caress my imagination, setting it running like a hare across the fields. It's perfect. Crença means belief and we're rapidly becoming believers.

Carole and Ken welcome us to our gorgeous new abode by cracking open a couple of bottles of fresh, crisp, and far-too-easy-to drink *vinho verde* from northern Portugal. We sit on the cane and curtain terrace drinking the slightly fizzy wine whilst

they bombard us with helpful pointers about local life and
the essentials of living in a hamlet on the Portuguese/Spanish
border. There's a fountain in Castelo do Vide 20 minutes drive
away where we can stock up on drinkable spring water. The
stuff coming out from the taps is from a bore hole so purity
unknown - we later discover it leaves nicotine stains on clothes
after they've been through the washing machine. The nearest
supermarket is also in Castelo de Vide, but there are a couple
of shops in Portagem, a sleepy village ten minutes away which
becomes a lively village at weekends in summer when Spanish
from across the border descend in their hordes thanks to it
having a *fluvial* - a river swimming pool. Portagem also boasts
a handful of traditional restaurants, making it a good place for
becoming acquainted with Alentejano cuisine. Our biggest
centre, where there's out of town shopping, is at Portalegre,
around a 35min drive away. There's a farmers' market every
Monday at Valencia de Alcántara, the nearest town across the
border. The goats which pass twice daily have a tendency to try
to eat the garden... and so on.

Then there's the maintenance of house and pool. Keeping
the plants/fruit trees fed with water sounds easy peasy, there
are strategically placed hoses and taps. Finding out that if the
water stops it might be because the pump has tripped starts the
descent into the more complicated aspects of house and garden
maintenance. The water is pumped up from a bore-hole so there
are a couple of 'actions' to take if things go wonky and the water
from the well literally dries up. This having to be potentially
proactive to ensure we have running water is a whole new ball
game for us. But the thing that has my head spinning most,
nothing to do with *vinho verde*, is the sequence of lever settings
required to perform various aspects of pool maintenance.
There's no way I'll remember them. I ask Ken, a tousle-headed
Evertonian with the typically sharp and cutting wit associated
with that part of England, to show me each sequence over and
over again as I sketch out six different diagrams.

Suddenly, responsibility weighs heavily.

Pool Settings

Clean, automatic or manual

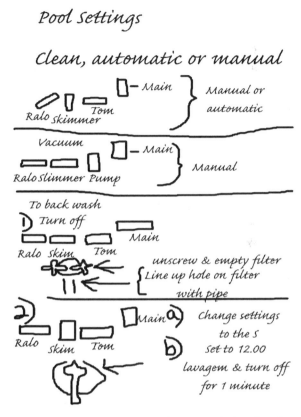

When Ken and Carole return home to their other 'mansion' just outside Galegos, we wander wide-eyed like children set loose in a sweetshop, sitting for minutes at various stone benches, testing each for comfort and views. We decide which terrace will be used for breakfast and which will be used for lunch and dinner as well as the general sipping of Portuguese wine whilst basking in the warm embrace of Idyllville. We learn that it's easy to lose touch with each other whilst exploring the house – the peril of having two staircases – but, thanks to the wooden floorboard/ceiling situation, that we can communicate clearly from just about anywhere in the big house, including from inside closed bathrooms. Acoustics could potentially be embarrassing if we have visitors, an unlikely prospect out in the

Alentejo wilds. Other discoveries are that a person can easily come a cropper on the uneven rock steps, and the stone lintel on the kitchen doorway leading to the outside terrace isn't anything like as high as the beaded curtain which covers it suggests... ouch, ouch, and ouch again. That one will take some time and many bumps to remember.

Unpacking doesn't take very long. All we have are a couple of suitcases and those 'essentials' we could fit into the back of Cindy. Too excited to settle, we decide to burn off some excess energy by going for a walk along the country road which runs below the house. Despite the scorching heat, the landscape is surprisingly lush, with small forests of evergreen trees contrasting against golden meadows. Over the course of two kilometres we pass no other people, four houses (all little farms), and a herd of bovines squeezed together in the shade of the lone tree in their field. This is farming country, a place where the thatched roofs of shepherd's huts are shaped like a wizard's hat.

It is unnervingly remote, but we're not totally cut off from the outside world. There is no ADSL line, but we picked up a Vodafone mobile hotspot when we were in Azeitão; it's essential for our work. We couldn't contemplate living here if we had no internet connection - no internet means no work. The signal is surprisingly decent, certainly fast enough for us to be able to work online. In fact, it seems far quicker than the download speed we had in our house in Tenerife. There, whilst it was sufficient for work purposes up to a point, it wasn't speedy enough to get us the whole way through a streamed movie on Netflix without numerous annoying pauses. Even when there were no interruptions, the picture on the screen was mostly poor quality. We set up our Apple TV box, just to have a quick look – the image is sharp, beautifully clear and characters on screen move seamlessly rather than jerkily. There are obviously going to be many, many delights to living in such a special location, being able to watch Netflix programmes streamed in almost HD quality is one of them. If we can ever drag ourselves away from the views.

I Didn't Realise We'd Moved to the Amazon

"What's that?" Andy jerks her knees back and something orange-brown drops to the tiles. I'm on it with the designated 'insect glass' and a postcard (combined they make a good temporary insect prison) in a flash and it's rapidly cast out into the black Alentejo night.

"What was it?" she asks again.

"Nothing, just a little bug," I lie.

I lie because I really don't want her to know what was creeping up her bare leg. If I did we'd be moving out again that night, our first. The last time I saw anything like it was in a jungle toilet in Sri Lanka... and in *Indian Jones and the Temple of Doom*. It was a centipede the thickness of my finger, but longer. Its feet didn't look like feet either, they looked like talons. It was not the sort of thing I expected to see in Portugal and subsequently it wasn't a difficult beastie to track down on the internet. The Megarian banded centipede grows to 20cm. I was right about those feet, the first ones also double as venomous fangs.

"There's something in the room," the words spin around a black void in my head. "There's something flying about the room." "What?" I realise it's not a dream and sit up.

Andy switches on the light, then pulls the covers over her head. "It nearly touched my head."

The 'something' is a bat, and now it's clinging to a wooden door frame. If I wasn't half asleep I probably wouldn't have known what to do. Instead, I drowsily stand up, grab a discarded tee-shirt, and gently wrap it around the rigid bat. The bat doesn't struggle. I walk to the window, hold the tee-shirt outside and shake it. The bat flies off into the night.

"Wow, that was impressive," Andy appears from below the sheets looking, well, impressed.

It's still our first night in the house and I've had to evict a giant centipede and a flying mouse. I'm hoping these are just two rare glitches.

There are spiders galore; leggy ones with spindly bodies who colonise every corner, recess, door and window frame. It's a big house which hasn't been lived in for a long time and the spiders have taken over. They're not the sort which freak either of us out, but they do create palatial webs overnight. For a few weeks we have to eject twenty a day until the house has been reclaimed. I don't really mind the spiders, not these ones at least.

Outside the front door is a no-go area. Where the spiders had taken over the house, a small swarm of wasps have set up home in a bush. We're 'live and let live' sort of people and are happy to co-exist with the wasps. They, unfortunately, are not of similar accord. We discover this the "ouch" way. Andy makes a mistake early on of watering the wasp bush, causing the small community to swarm and chase her out of the front gate. I regularly forget about them as I head past their bush to the shed until a sharp pain, somewhere flesh is exposed, has me evacuating the area at speed, spraying the air with expletives. Another wasp family keeps attempting to set up home in a lamp at one end of the swimming pool. That one we do try to deter. We've already been confined to one part of the pool by bullish wasps who like to use it as a watering hole.

It quickly becomes evident that insects in remote Alentejo are going to be a part of life whether we like it or not. Despite having lived on Tenerife for fourteen years, this is not something we're used to. Although subtropical, Tenerife is not an insecty sort of place. The big insect magnet here is the swimming pool, there's such a variety of species to be found there that David Attenborough could narrate an episode of a wildlife programme based on wildlife around the pool alone. Each morning there's a motley crew of drowned and half-drowned insects and other creatures waiting to be scooped out of its crystalline blueness. On any one day it might be an army of refugee ants clinging to a leaf; a few dead lizards; a handful of large hoppers; and large red beetles with long aardvark-like snouts. We thought they were rather pretty until I posted a photo of one on Facebook and a friend who's knowledgeable in such things pointed out they were palm weevils, responsible for the destruction of thousands of palm trees across Southern Europe. Other victims include various large black beetles with long antennae, the occasional praying mantis, and a sodden mouse or two.

When we sit outside at night, essential in the oppressive summer heat, watching life around the pool light is compelling viewing. The circle cast by the pool lamp reveals a black wall of insects where a white one should be. One night, something big and dark sweeps through this insect wall like a Dyson, leaving a wide, neat white runway in its wake. I'm compelled to investigate. The culprit is a spider, a really big one. Thankfully he only ever appears at night, and only in this spot. I suspect he lives in the hole where the control lever for the swimming pool is, something I try not to think about as I have to stick my hand in there twice daily.

The most curious insect has the appearance of a mini hobo porcupine which pulls itself across the slabs in front of us as we grab an hour of sunbathing at the end of the day when the fierceness has gone from an unrelenting sun. It's a bagworm, an insect which constructs a portable house from bits of plants. On another day, a miniature snake with beautiful arrow markings slithers past our gaze at a speed I didn't realise snakes were capable of. By the time this happens we've acclimatised to our surroundings and watch it without the hysterics which might have accompanied it a couple of weeks previously. The insects and their friends are simply part of our environment and we've become used to them. This more relaxed approach does not apply to the Megarian banded centipede.

GETTING TO GRIPS WITH SHOPPING IN ALENTEJO

Here's the image some people might have of life abroad - an overly-tanned couple sitting on a sunny, whitewashed balcony overlooking a sparkling jewel of an ocean with equally sparkling G&T cupped in their bronzed hands. In our case, a social media image may show a happy-looking couple clinking Champagne flutes (filled with Cava not Champagne) as they gaze out across their slate terrace to a softly rolling landscape of wheat-coloured fields and twisted cork oaks under an intensely blue sky. It's living the dream.

Our reality *does* involve the clinking of glasses... in celebration of finding out where to pick up the everyday items we need to exist. Tranquil idylls are all well and good, but one aspect of the reality of living and working somewhere you're completely unfamiliar with involves investing a significant amount of time finding out where to do basic things we normally take for granted in locations we know well. Beyond the back of beyond, that's not always easy.

It takes two months for me to get my hair cut, and even then it's at a hipster barbers in Cáceres, an hour and a half drive into Extremadura. By this time my hair has gone into full-on, floppy Quentin Crisp mode; a style which might have made *The Naked Civil Servant* look flamboyant and interesting but which gives me the appearance of an old tramp. There is a hairdresser in Portalegre thirty minutes away, and I did make one pathetic attempt to have it cut there, hovering with intent at the doorway. But as the place was shoe box-sized and filled with women of a certain age being given the Portuguese equivalent of a blue rinse, I completely bottled it. Now I tell friends, "It's so rural here we have to travel to another country to get haircuts."

Adjusting to shopping and the quirks that come with living in such a rural setting can be illuminating. You pick up a lot relating to local culture just from people's shopping habits. Particularly interesting is where we stock up on drinking water.

Another gem of a tip from Carole and Ken relates to the existence of a rather lovely, honey-stone fountain tucked away in a dead end street in Castelo de Vide. Pure and drinkable spring water pours from the mouths of four ornate lion heads, emanating from the same source which feeds the water factory next door. Every couple of weeks we roll up laden with a bulging batch of empty 6 litre bottles to fill up with the sweet *agua*. Having access to free water on ornate tap proves a money saver, especially as the water at Crença comes from a bore-hole and has a tendency to add unattractive and difficult-to-remove nicotine stains to clothes during washing. We're not keen on putting anything in our bodies which could do something like that, so the fountain's pure water is used for drinking, cooking, making tea and coffee - anything that involves water entering our mouths.

Castelo de Vide, 15km away, is our preferred choice for the weekly shop because a) it is the closest town with a decent supermarket and b) that supermarket is a Pingo Doce, which has quickly become one of our favourites of the supermarkets commonly found in Portuguese towns. We've not taken to Continente or Intermarche at all. I often confuse both their names and end up calling one or the other 'Intercontinente' (it works for me as they seem virtually interchangeable anyway). Every time I spot an E.LeClerc supermarket I can't stop myself thinking, "It is I, LeClerc." So we avoid them altogether to keep cheesy scenes from the old Brit sitcom *Allo Allo* from flooding my thoughts. As for Aldi and Lidl, we've never been in a branch in Spain or Portugal we liked, so they don't get a look-in even though friends tell us they stock decent gin.

Pingo Doce is our favourite because it has a wider range of the sort of things we like to eat. As well as having Portuguese products which pique our interest, it stocks other goodies we particularly enjoy – tubs of hummus and guacamole, decent Greek yoghurt, and feta cheese. Pingo Doce is the first place we pick up *empadas*, chunky little Portuguese pies filled with chicken, meat, or spinach. It also stocks the firm but soft Portuguese bread rolls which remind me of the ones from my home Isle of Bute rather than that mass produced rubbish with the texture of cotton wool. These are proper rolls, the sort which go perfectly with square slice (lorne) sausages in Scotland, and seasoned pork *bifanas* in Portugal. We decide the Portuguese are far better at bread rolls and pies than the Spanish. Curiously, one of the most popular sauces on the supermarket shelves is *molho inglês* (English sauce) which is basically Portuguese Worcester sauce. There are loads of different brands. Why Worcester sauce is so popular in Portugal is something we haven't managed to find out yet. Surprising evidence of a British influence from days gone by is beginning to stock up.

Then there's also the weekly *poupe* which, apart from having schoolboy snigger potential, tends to have us leaving the supermarket feeling good about the place. *Poupe* is short for *poupança*, which means 'discounts'. Locals at Castelo de Vide thoroughly scan the weekly *poupe* brochure like punters studying race form, before taking to the store's narrow aisles to throw what's on offer into their carts. Strategic shopping like this makes one hell of a difference to the bill. We do it more randomly, not knowing where the *poupe* applies. There's a sad little thrill in finding out how much is taken off the bill thanks to the power of the *poupe* - 60 cents off for bananas, a saving of €1.50 on beer, and so on. Overall it usually works out at around €12; a figure not to be sniffed at.

In some ways Pingo Doce in Castelo de Vide is like a throwback to another age and even another country. The aisles are filled with lots of wee men in bunnets (flat caps for anyone who doesn't hail from Scotland). I never associated flat caps with Portugal, but nearly every man we pass wears one. I'm guessing it's traditional and not because the area just happens to be populated by a load of septuagenarian hipsters. The bunnet-wearing men don't seem to know what to do with themselves as their wives drag them reluctantly around the aisles; these are a generation of men who have yet to hear the word metrosexual. Two or three of them hang around the fruit and vegetable aisle, chatting and basically getting in the way of anyone who's actually trying to shop. Others stand with their trolleys blocking aisles that are already on the too slender side, looking like rabbits caught in the headlights and waiting for instructions from equally diminutive wives, many of whom wear patterned housecoats. Every so often, combined husband and wife teams completely block our way forward. "*Com licença*" one of us tentatively tries. In the Canary Islands the equivalent would have been a "*permiso*" which would have been met with an apologetic smile and an instant moving of the trolley. In Castelo de Vide our words are met with a scowl from the female half of the blockade whilst the man stares ahead blankly, waiting for instructions from his spouse. Then there might be a mutter and eventually, maybe after a second "*com licença*", the trolley will be moved just enough for us to squeeze past.

They're not downright hostile, but neither would I call them friendly. Having spent over a decade on an island known for its amiable population, this apparent sullenness comes as a bit of a shock. The Canary Islands stood at the crossroads of the world, the descendants of the Canarios were all incomers at one point. Throughout their history, since the conquest of the islands, they have been used to the comings and goings of strangers of various nationalities. Places on historic travel routes anywhere are possibly more open to new faces, whereas there can occasionally be a 'this is a local shop, for local people' attitude in rural, inland communities. I come from a small Scottish island, I recognise the signs only too well. My father classed people who'd moved to the island thirty years previously as being 'newcomers'.

There's one bar in Galegos, the hamlet closest to us, and there are always a couple of patrons sitting in the shade of the steps outside its entrance. It's a narrow street and we wave a greeting every single time we drive past almost close enough to reach out and shake hands. Sometimes they respond, sometimes they don't. Mostly it's the latter, which doesn't exactly give us the urge to venture inside even though it is technically our local.

Being Scottish, I'm okay with the general dourness of shoppers at Pingo Doce. The staff themselves are friendly, and it's a super little supermarket where we can pick up exactly the sort of ingredients we use to create our favourite dishes. But I'm disappointed that people don't seem as welcoming as I'd hoped.

For serious shopping we drive to the out-of-town business park at Portalegre where there are branches of all the supermarkets we're not so keen on. There's also a Worten, decent for all things electronic, and an Intermarche Bricolage, a DIY type store, which helps us tick off all the household/outdoor items we need to make us feel more at home.

Closer to home, five minutes away in Portagem, is Terrius, a former mill beside the River Sever which has been turned into a showcase for Aletejano produce, especially those from the surrounding hills and valleys. This is the place we visit to pick up quality local goods. On our first visit we come away with a bottle of artisan olive oil; pumpkin and walnut jam; a jar of pepper mustard; and an artistic tin of *filetes de carapau* (horse mackerel). There are two interesting aspects to the tin of fish. The first is that I learn from the back of the tin that horse mackerel in German is called *bastard mackerel*. The other is the brand is called *Good Boy*. Everything else on the lid is in Portuguese except the brand name. We stumble across this a lot in Portugal, an English phrase suddenly appears out of the blue surrounded by a jumble of Portuguese words we struggle to make sense of.

It's four weeks before we discover Portagem actually has a supermarket. The reason this vital piece of information eluded us is there is no sign at all outside it to identify it as being a supermarket. There is a sign which shows that behind an anonymous metal, fly curtain across the door of what looks like any other cottage is a *chouriço* specialist. I've fancied buying some locally made *chouriço* for weeks but lacked the courage to try and enter into a conversation which might result in any in-depth debate about Portuguese cured sausages. Finally, I work up the courage and push my way through the metal strands into the darkness beyond... and find a rather large supermarket. It's not the best stocked supermarket in the universe, but it's handy for essentials. Right inside the door is the *chouriço* and *morcela* (blood sausage) counter. Luckily a man in a bunnet is having exactly the conversation with the butcher I feared, an

in-depth one about *chouriço*. When my turn comes I point to
a cannonball-shaped *morcela* and one of the *chouriço* strings
the previous customer bought. A scrap of paper with writing
scrawled across it identifies it as *chouriço de osso*. The word
osso rings a faint, niggling bell. But if it's good enough for the
chouriço aficionado, then it's good enough for us. It's only as
we're driving home I remember where I've seen it before. It was
in Évora. In a chapel in Évora to be more precise, the *Capela
dos Ossos* – the Chapel of the Bones. It can't really be bone
chorizo, I hope. It is. And it's pretty rank.

CASTLES IN THE AIR

Despite numerous jaunts around Europe in recent years, the reality of living on the European mainland after over a decade of being confined by the obvious natural boundaries of island life is a tad overwhelming. As well as the remoteness of Galegos itself proving a jolt of a culture shock, the sheer scale of Alentejo with its endless golden plains intimidates us.

Alentejo is the largest and least populated of Portugal's regions. To put this into perspective, where the population of Scotland is around 65 inhabitants per square kilometre, in Alentejo it is 23. The land beyond the Tagus (the name Alentejo originated from '*Além-Tejo*' - beyond the River Tejo. Tejo is Tagus in English) is a huge expanse of countryside where there are more cattle and pigs than people. Ironically, in a way we feel more cut off from the sophisticated civilisation we yearned and hoped for than we did in the middle of a banana plantation in the north of Tenerife. That in itself is initially exciting. Galegos is not a place we'd planned on relocating to, even on a temporary basis. Our ideal abode is in rural surrounds but within easy reach of the amenities (cultural, gastronomical, practical, and materialistic) offered by largish towns. We have the same feelings about remote living as we do toward children; we enjoy spending time with them, but it can be a relief to say goodbye to them at the end of the day. Our friend Jo lives in an isolated valley on the edge of Garajonay National Park on the Canary Island of La Gomera. There are around eight other families in the valley; it takes her about forty-five minutes to drive to the nearest shop; she still can't access ADSL; and she has to go outside to get to her bathroom. It is idyllic, a rural retreat where mornings consist of sitting on her terrace gazing trance-like across a forest canopy to the breast-shaped magnificence of Mount Teide on neighbouring Tenerife. We adore visiting her, and spending time in what is a supremely special spot, but we couldn't live there. The idea of spending a longer period of time in a similarly remote area is intriguing and, the prospect

of getting a decent insight into what life is like in and around
the hamlets, villages and towns of São Mamede Natural Park is
appealing.

Galegos

The closest settlement is Galegos about 2.5km away. The
postbox we share lies on the outskirts of the hamlet. That in itself
puts rural life in Portugal into perspective. Although we used
a P.O. box in Puerto de la Cruz on Tenerife, we did have a sort
of letterbox at the reception of the golf course where our house
was located. In Galegos, like much of rural Portugal, there aren't
individual letterboxes. Mail is left in a 'tower block' of boxes at
the end of a road.

Galegos is a tiny settlement with the bar we never set foot
in and an Olive Mill which we refuse to visit out of principle;
the cost of a tour is ridiculously expensive. A small river runs
through the hamlet, gurgling past one of nature's curios, the
Marmitas de Gigante – the Giant's Pots; large smooth cavities
created from being pounded by rocks and boulders dragged
downriver by the force of the water. After an initial exploration,
Galegos becomes a place we drive through to get somewhere
else.

Portagem

Portagem, a ten minute drive away, is the gastronomic centre
of the area as it's where the best restaurants are to be found.
Although not a particularly pretty town architecturally speaking,
Portagem quickly becomes somewhere we enjoy spending
time in. It sits at the base of the rock which has Marvão atop
it, making it a good location from which to enjoy views of the
aloof beauty. It also boasts a Medieval bridge known locally
as the Roman Bridge even though it's likely it was constructed
toward the end of the 16th century. The Roman moniker is said
to be due to it being built from stones salvaged from either an
earlier Roman bridge upstream, or from other Roman ruins in
the vicinity. On one side of the bridge is the toll tower which
earned the town the name Portagem – toll (anyone who's driven

Portugal's motorways will be familiar with seeing the word
portagem). The toll gate operated from around 1416, exacting
payment on merchandise passing between Portugal and Spain.
It's a serene part of town, even though it's only a hundred metres
downstream of the attraction which brings Portuguese and
Spanish families flocking to Portagem during summer months.
Look one way from the River Sever and you get a scene of
multitudinous families enjoying summer by the river. Look in
the other direction and the picture is of sunlight dancing across
the water whilst the old bridge remains quietly cool, shaded by
poplar and chestnut trees.

The people magnet in town is the *Praia Fluvial de Portagem*
– the river beach. In this case it's not so much a beach as grassy
banks in the dappled shade of the protective trees lining the
river. The *fluvial* itself is a one hundred and fifty metre section
of the Sever which has been partially dammed at both ends to
create a river swimming pool. We've never seen one of these
before, it is damned (dammed) ingenious. Children get to
enjoy the exhilaration of jumping into a river on a sizzling day
combined with the safety that comes with bathing in a swimming
pool. There is also a conventional swimming pool complex
right beside the river which, if anything, is even more popular.
Personally, I can't see the attraction of the concrete pool when
there's river swimming, albeit a sanitised version, on offer. It's
fascinating to wander along the river bank early morning when
the *fluvial* section of the river has been 'emptied', watching a
mini dumper truck with a roller brush attached to its front drive
up and down the man-made riverbed. It's not only us who find it
fascinating, most of the retired male population of the town turn
out on a daily basis to watch the river being cleaned.

There are a couple of cafe/restaurants beside the *fluvial*,
perfect for a lazy lunch by the water. At Maruan Miragem, part
of the 'proper' swimming pool complex, we discover two things
about the Portuguese version of a cheese and ham toastie (*tosta
mixta*). The first is that these can be huge – one portion comes
in double-decker form (four slices of chunky bread) and is a
hefty snack for two let alone one. The other is the *tosta mixta*

is far superior to its British cousin. The bread is spread with butter or drizzled with oil and tastes more fried than toasted. It's then sprinkled with herbs. Both these touches help ramp up the flavour. It's also a cheap eat.

One of our other favourite parts of town is also a natural feature, the *estrada dos freixos cintados* on the road to Castelo de Vide. It's considered by some to be the most beautiful stretch of road in all of Portugal, consisting of a kilometre-long avenue of ash trees with white bands painted around their bases; the *freixos cintados* (belted buckle). It's a long, mostly straight, avenue which curves just before it ends (if driving from Portagem). This curve makes it look as though it's an endless, tree-lined avenue; a magical road which leads to another dimension. The *estrada dos freixos cintados* is barely wide enough for two cars, a fact which can lead to some serious breathing in when there's a juggernaut bearing down on us. There are passing places along its long stretch, but they're infrequent, so luck and timing has to be on our side if there's something big coming from the opposite direction. Every so often I stand in the centre of the narrow road to try to capture a hint of its magic with my camera, Andy keeping a watchful eye for any metal monsters heading my way. The road seduces my gaze but I don't want to end up, like some unfortunate roadkill, as part of it.

Castelo de Vide

Runner up for the award of most picturesque town in the area is Castelo de Vide, an historic hill town which isn't quite as perched as many of the other Alentejo hilltop towns and villages. The castle which gave the settlement its name is typically atop a hill, but the town itself lies nestled, safe and sound, in the undulating folds which spread out from the base of the fortification.

Although clearly occupying a strategic position (any hill in Alentejo is a strategic position) nobody really knows why a town was built on this particular spot. Even though the inhabitants cultivated vines, flax, olive trees, fruit and cereals, Castelo de

Vide was especially known for grain milling and wool-spinning, the latter to such an extent the residents were called *cardadores* (wool weavers). One of the particularly interesting things about Castelo de Vide is that, thanks to its proximity to the border, it had a sizeable Jewish community, originally made up with Spanish Jews expelled from Castile and Aragon.

By one of those weird coincidences which occur every now and again, we find we have a contact in Castelo de Vide. Good friends of ours from the North West of England had spoken regularly about a relation, Phil, who lived in a remote part of Portugal. We never thought for a second we'd end up staying just a handful of miles away from him.

Phil offers to be our guide for our first proper exploration of the town. On a hot Friday morning, market stalls fill the cobbled streets around the *Igreja de Santa Maria da Devesa*. It doesn't take long to realise this isn't one of those markets we're going to come away from laden down with local goodies; floral housecoats, nylon bedlinen, and industrial strength bras not being high on our shopping list. We arrange to meet Phil at his house, not easy to find as it's located in the oldest quarter of town; a maze of winding, narrow, cobbled streets lined by old cottages and town-houses whose whitewashed façades are fronted by rows of terracotta pots brimming with scarlet geraniums. It's a tad reminiscent of a Greek village. We take to Phil immediately; within minutes of meeting him we're listening to fascinating stories which twist and weave like the streets around his house. His knowledge of Portugal and Spain is encyclopedic, skipping from historic snippets to amusing quirks. As we sip a steaming mug of coffee, a women wanders in off the street and asks if she can buy his house. Phil doesn't blink an eye and, acting as it's the most normal thing in the world for a stranger to ask to buy his house, chats to her for a few minutes before directing her to another resident of the street who might actually be interested in selling.

Where we're dressed in urban wear, the sort of gear you throw on for strolling a town's streets, Phil looks like he's ready for a decent trek in the countryside – hiking shorts, tee-shirt, cap with neck flap, a crook. As the streets are steep, there's not a cloud in the sky, and the temperature is stuck in the mid 30s, his is the far more sensible dress-wear. After just a few steps Andy and I are sweaty messes. Phil's route climbs past rows of stepped houses squeezed tightly together on the steep slope, and through the Gothic arch of the former town hall to a position on one of the fortified walls where there are expansive views across the town's tangerine-coloured rooftops to Marvão. It's far too hot to linger long in open ground, so we quickly retreat through one of the original arched gates, seeking protection in the shaded streets of the *Judaria*, the Jewish quarter, where an ornate fountain is the centrepiece of a small square surrounded by a ramshackle collection of humble abodes.

Castelo de Vide is water rich, a town of springs and fountains of which *Fonte da Vila* is the most interesting. Built in the 16th century, it consists of a central fountain protected by a stone pyramid-shaped roof supported on six marble columns. Next to the fountain is a stone trough - drinking water for livestock. The story goes that following the expulsion of the Jews, Jewish women who were supposed to be *conversos* (converts to Christianity) met in this spot to fetch water and to wash clothes whilst also secretly passing on the teachings of Judaism to their children. One house doorway has an image of a fish carved on it to show the family who lived inside were *conversos*, the carving representing the eating of fish on Friday; a symbol of Christianity.

Food being used as a means for identifying who was and wasn't Jewish led to the creation of one of Portugal's most popular sausages, the *alheira*. In the 15th century, during the Inquisition, anyone who wasn't spotted regularly munching on local sausages fell under suspicion of being a Jew. To try to blend in with everyone else and avoid persecution, some creative chefs among the Jewish population in northern Portugal came up with an *alheira*, a sausage that looked like a chorizo but was made with just about every other meat under the sun except pork. Chicken, beef, partridge and, or, quail were mixed with wheat bread, garlic, olive oil and a secret mix of spices and made into a horseshoe-shaped sausage which could be fried, grilled or barbecued. Ironically, the *alheira* tasted so good it was adopted by non-Jews as well and is now immensely popular across Portugal. I like *alheira* a lot, but Andy is less keen; it has a quite distinctive gamey, smoky flavour. As well as traditional sausage shape it turns up in various guises – as meatballs, in croquettes, in burger form. However, out of all the supposedly sausage-shaped ones I've eaten there's only been one which would have fooled me into believing it was a sausage; the reason being most *alheiras* look more like, and there's no delicate way to put this, a turd. This is possibly why Andy isn't as big a fan of them as I am.

By the time we leave the *Fonte da Vila*, the sun's fierceness defeats us and we take refuge in A Confraria where the food is traditional but with contemporary touches. Phil enjoys A Confraria's food so much he keeps ordering more and our lunch lasts so long it overlaps with the lunch of the family who own the charming restaurant.

By the time we emerge into daylight again the sun has calmed down and it's time for us to head for home. We say our farewells to our new friend and agree we'll meet up again in Marvão and that next time, as Phil picked up the bill, lunch will be on us.

Marvão

Marvão is quite simply one of the most alluring towns I've set eyes upon. Even from a distance it hypnotises, demanding our gaze. We are privileged to be able to wallow in views of this marvellous castle in the sky every time we step outside the front door. At night, illuminated by lamps on the cliff face below, its golden features make it even more mythical looking. On many nights music flows from Marvão across the valley. Sometimes it can be classical, at others lively rock. The classical fits the serene landscape just that little bit better.

Considered one of Portugal's prettiest towns, Marvão is virtually on our doorstep, around 10km and a 15 minute drive away. Yet after four weeks of living with it as a neighbour we knew we really ought to pop round to see, we haven't done so. It's hard to say why. Even from a distance it's easy to see how it has earned a reputation as one of the most picturesque villages in the land. Maybe that's part of the problem. Over days and nights of admiring its obvious beauty from our terrace, expectation is as high as Marvao castle lording it over the Alentejo countryside. Higher, too high possibly.

It has also been the sort of summer where it is so hot we tend to spend the day huddled in the shadiest of spots in a bid to stay, whilst not cool, at least alive. Any venturing into direct sunlight (e.g. essential shopping) is done as quickly as possible, like commando raids, with no hanging around in case we spontaneously combust. Sightseeing trips have been shelved until more bearable weather arrives.

On the last day in June the heat abates to the point we actually need to wear light fleeces, so we finally take to the country road which leads to the castle in the sky, climbing past small farms, cork trees and shepherd's huts with thatched roofs shaped like wizards' hats. Ken told us we can drive right into the walled centre, but the huge and empty car park outside the town's walls appeals far more than the idea of negotiating an archway entrance which is less wide than a condor's wingspan, nor the equally narrow cobbled streets beyond. It's a good call. Anyway, this is a town to be discovered on foot.

Despite the picturesque town tag, the old centre is virtually deserted as we step through a portal into what had once been a Moorish stronghold but which is now a peaceful paradise in the sky. Cobbled streets spread outward in a V, narrowly twisting their way past pretty, white cottages with burnt orange-tiled roofs. It's immediately evident Marvão is as much of a stunner up close as it is from a distance. Expectations have been well and truly exceeded. There are many ways to climb to the castle; one soars upwards along the protective walls, reminiscent of the surprisingly steep steps of sections of the Great Wall of China. Other routes wind gently upwards through the town. For some masochistic reason we opt to huff and puff our way along the wall, ducking every so often to avoid low flying swifts doing that Star Wars Death Star run they tend to do.

With each step, the views of the town and countryside way below just get better and better. The old stone wall is an excellent vantage point for spotting nooks worth exploring later. At one point we pause for breath, taking the opportunity to try to pick out Crença tucked into the valley folds before the Alentejo plains stretch to infinity. As there aren't that many houses in those valleys, it's not as difficult a task as it might sound. As we reach the summit (aka the castle entrance) we're treated to a completely unexpected surprise; an immaculate, Italian style garden with neat dwarf hedges and scented blooms lies between the castle and the town's church, the *Igreja de Santiago*. The vista across the little garden and pretty town to golden plains and green hills beyond is of the sort to make a heart soar as high as the kamikaze birds which had insisted on playing chicken with us as we'd scaled the walls. It is an exuberant natural high.

Marvão is designed for meandering, we duck down alleys and through arches whenever anything interesting catches our eyes. We make a mental note to return after dark to a wine bar, O Castelo, with what must be the best bar views in Alentejo; memorise the most interesting sounding dishes (piglet's pastry) on menus in the handful of restaurants within the walled town; laugh at doors a Hobbit would have to bend to get through; admire contemporary and imaginative handicrafts made from cork; and pop into a tiny supermarket which sells local cheese, honey, wine and dried mushrooms.

I'd previously read remarks which dismissed Marvao as being an overrated, over-priced tourist trap. When I pop into O Castelo cafe lounge it's not just tourists I stand behind. Hogging the bar area are two Alentejano men in flat caps, sipping coffees and nosily picking up the receipts left by non-local patrons. One shows the other one a receipt left by a girl who bought a bottle of water and there's a sharp intake of breath accompanied by a shake of the head – some prices are obviously higher than you'd pay in the towns and villages in the valley below, but I also suspect these two are Marvao's answer to *Still Game's* Victor and Jack. For a tourist trap there are surprisingly few tourists.

Two days later we return to eat at one of the town's restaurants. There are even fewer tourists; none to be exact. There is a gathering of people outside the Cultural Centre in *Largo de Olivença*, locals congregating around a rusty old drum on which rows of sardines are being grilled. We have visited plenty of picturesque towns and villages in our time, too many of which where the balance had slipped from being residential to just tourist attraction. As well as being one of the most beautiful small towns we've visited, Marvao still feels like a real place and is all the more charming for it.

Portalegre

"That could easily be Robinson's Brewery in Stockport," Andy points to a large rectangular building from which two Northern England-style, red brick chimneys pierce the blue sky. As we walk closer, we notice white writing down the side of one of the chimneys. What it says is unclear until we work our way to the front of the old building R-O-B-I-N...

"Bloody hell," I splutter, adding in best Victor Meldrew fashion. "I don't believe it."

The chimney does actually have Robinson written on it. Finding a Robinson's chimney stack in a town in rural Alentejo is on the surreal side to say the least. It would be too much to discover it is actually the same Robinson. It's not. Stockport's Robinsons were born and bred Stopfordians, the brewery coming into existence after William Robinson purchased The Unicorn pub on Lower Hillgate in 1838. Portalegre's Robinson was George William Robinson from Halifax, who bought a small cork factory in the town in the 1840s. As demand grew, he expanded by buying part of an adjacent convent. In its heyday Robinson's cork factory employed more than 1000 workers, by far the biggest source of employment in the town. Incredibly, despite its Victorian appearance, it was still functioning as a factory up until 2009. There are examples of British entrepreneurs all over Portugal, the Port producers of the Douro being the most famous.

As it boasts an out-of-town shopping centre with

supermarkets, electrical, and DIY stores, we have had many 'functional' visits to Portalegre. This is the first time we've taken the time to have a wander around the old town itself. I can't imagine it's much of a tourist magnet, it doesn't have that knock-you-off-your-feet impact of towns like Marvao and Évora; its attractions are more hidden away, requiring a lot of walking. But the historic streets are riddled with baroque churches, palaces, convents and town-houses. 13th century portals arch across narrow streets whilst *azulejo* murals depict agricultural practices in the area. It's not pretty as such, but it is an interesting town with a certain down-to-earth charm. There are intimate *largos* and grand *praças* such as *Praça da República*, traditionally the venue for anything interesting in the town. Markets, fairs and bullfights were held here in the past. Now, it's all manner of cultural events from Medieval fairs to summer festivals. What tickles us is one side of the square is lined with bars, the other is where the police station is located, which has got to be a deterrent to over enthusiastic revelling getting out of hand.

Santo António das Areias

In many locations Santo António das Areias might be considered a reasonably pretty town, but with such sparkling jewels such as Marvão and Castelo de Vide as neighbours it is completely overshadowed. Despite being the closest town to us, we treat it as something of a plain wallflower, especially as there doesn't seem to be anything in the place to draw us back to it after an initial recce. Mostly we only pass through it when we use the quiet back roads to get to Marvão. However, one Saturday night after a meal in Marvão, Santo António das Areias springs a surprise. Every time we drive through it in daylight hours it is a ghost town. At 11pm on this particular Saturday night we find ourselves at a standstill in the centre of the small town, our car entrenched in a sea of people. Hundreds, if not thousands, fill the streets, and there are cars queueing in all directions. Being stuck in a traffic jam close to midnight in a town which has around 1000 residents is not something we foresaw. We've completely underestimated the draw of one of the town's buildings which hadn't interested us in the slightest, the bullring. There's a bullfight about to take place and it's attracted hordes of Alentejanos from miles around.

We'd been surprised when we first saw the bullring as we didn't even realise there *was* bullfighting in Portugal. Where Spain gets all the flack for bullfighting, Portugal flies under the radar when it comes to attracting criticism for cruel sports. There are those who say Portuguese bullfights (*touradas* or *corridas de touros*) aren't the same as Spanish bullfighting as bulls aren't killed; dealing a death blow to the bull has been illegal in Portugal since 1928. In 2001, one of the country's most famous *toureiros* (matadors) was given a hefty fine after breaking the law by, urged on by a frenzied crowd, killing a bull during a bullfight. However, participating bulls are still stabbed with *bandarilhas* (small spears) during the savage spectacle. Additionally, campaigners who oppose bullfighting claim the fact that bulls aren't killed in public in the ring is just a meaningless sham as most bulls die, or are slaughtered, after the fight. It's said that around 4,000 bulls die each year in Portugal following bullfights. Whichever way anyone tries to dress it up, Portuguese bullfighting is a violent and cruel sport which deserves to be consigned to history's dustbin. There remains a relative lack of knowledge among non-Portuguese that *touradas* continue to be a popular past-time in Portugal, there's even a ring in the centre of Lisbon. But the tide has been turning for some time; statistics show more than half of the Portuguese surveyed want an end to it, but these figures are only just over 50%. There's still a long way to go, as the sheer volume of people we encounter in Santo António das Areias illustrates.

Valencia de Alcántara

The nearest Spanish town is Valencia de Alcántara, 13km and a 20 minute drive away in the Cáceres province. There are a few curios and historic sites in and around this workaday town which at various times in the past was Portuguese and at others Spanish. In 1762, Portuguese-British troops under John Burgoyne attacked and captured the town, a Spanish supply base at the time. The Spanish defeat at the Battle of Valencia de Alcántara put a dent in the planned invasion of Portugal. It's a bustling little town and convenient for banking, given that it's in Spain and we still have a Spanish bank account. It's also good for picking up Spanish products. There are some differences between what you can buy in Spanish and Portuguese supermarkets; getting hold of a bottle of sherry isn't easy in Portugal even though we're right on the border. Ken tells us you can even find fresh cod in the town, unheard of in lands which worship the salted version, but that's something we haven't managed. After painful attempts at trying to communicate in Portuguese, speaking Spanish again is almost easy. It isn't, and there are huge gaps in our knowledge of the language, but it feels comfortable to slip back into the familiarity of Castilian words. There are a few restaurants (none that have a different enough menu to tempt us though), and a decent amount of bars and cafes, one curiously called, in English, The Cousins Corner. Valencia de Alcántara is just not the sort of town you'd expect to find a coffee house with an English name. The big draw at Valencia de Alcántara is its Monday market, especially the food stalls which circle the town's bullring. We stock up on *jamón ibérico*, Manchego cheese and intoxicating smoked paprika which lends an extra punch of flavour to dishes; once used there's no going back to plain old paprika.

LARD FROM HEAVEN AND DRUNKEN PRAWNS

Sarapatel - the very name conjures up visions of far-flung places. It's a dish which sounds as though it was concocted in a steamy kitchen in Mumbai. Indeed, this spicy and savoury blend of lamb's liver, lungs, heart, garlic, onion, mint, paprika, cloves, and parsley *is* popular in parts of India, and in Brazil. But it's resolutely Portuguese, carried with explorers to distant corners of the globe during their voyages of discoveries. A bowl of steaming offal might sound, well, awful to some. Being Scottish, *sarapatel* was like meeting the foreign cousin of the haggis, something I devour with relish whenever the opportunity arises. *Sarapatel* was also, thanks to a recommendation from Ken, the first Alentejana dish we try in a restaurant in the frontier village of Portagem. Its unexpected composition is responsible for getting our taste-buds prematurely excited about what might lie ahead on our meandering path through Alentejo's cuisine. The restaurant we eat it at was also recommended by friends as being one of the best in the area.

Mil Homens sits above the River Sever on the eastern outskirts of the village; a friendly restaurant which is especially popular at weekends when the hordes of Spanish make the journey across the border. On a sultry Saturday night the trick is to nab a table before Spanish dining hours kicked in, so arriving at 20:00 means we are able to squeeze in at the end of a long table before the Castilian-speaking masses arrive. The proximity to the border with Spain has an unexpected bonus, just about everyone speaks Spanish. After fourteen years living in the Canary Islands, it's our fall-back language. An odd thing happens when we're confronted by people who don't speak English, we start speaking Spanish. Don't ask me why, it just happens. I know it doesn't make any sense at all, but we do it whether we're travelling in France, Italy, or German. I immediately cringe afterwards, sometimes during. I can often see confusion in folks' eyes at the time; the bemused Bavarian villager wondering why this strange British couple are jabbering away at him in

Spanish. But in a village on the border with Spain it partially solves communication problems. It also means we hardly learn any Portuguese during our time here.

Following the *sarapatel* is a platter (plate wouldn't do the size of it justice) of juicy *javali* (wild boar) chunks with homemade French fries (lots of traditional Portuguese restaurants do great homemade French fries) and then a *pudim molotov*, ordered purely because of the name. It's often how I choose food in new destinations - "I've no idea what this is, but it sounds interesting." It's the Russian roulette method of ordering. This particular *molotov* is a light-as-a-cloud sweet soufflé drenched in caramel sauce. Overall it's a promising start.

Our second foray into the world of Alentejano cuisine is at another recommended restaurant in Portagem, J.J. Videira's, where we descend into Monty Python *Meaning of Life* territory. For anyone who doesn't know, Portuguese meals begin with the *couvert*, a selection of small nibbles to get the juices flowing. I regularly read reviews on Tripadvisor where people complain about being duped after being charged for something they didn't ask for, assuming the *couvert* is complimentary. There's no duping going on, it's the way things are done. If you don't want it, just say so; nobody is going to be offended. At J.J.'s the selection on offer all looks too good to refuse. So we kick the meal off with a plate of cured goat/sheep/cow cheese, a basket of doorstep-thick bread, a bowl of olives, and sardine pate - a standard *couvert* selection. When the starters arrive we are already borderline full. At least Andy has been relatively sensible by opting for a simple tuna, tomato and onion salad. I, on the other hand, decide to try *sopa de tomate Alentejana*. A word of warning for anyone who ventures into Alentejo, *sopa de tomate Alentejana* isn't a soup at all, despite being on the *sopa* section of menus. It's a hearty stew which *does* involve tomatoes, but also various other ingredients including more bread, which is steeped in the soup to bulk it out. Topping things off are a couple of poached eggs sprinkled with herbs. It is possibly the best tomato soup I've eaten, but it is so filling I involuntarily groan as I squeeze in the final mouthful. This prompts a boisterous Spanish family at the next table who've been singing their way through their meal (it's another Saturday night) to misunderstand the reason for the groan and apologise for being so noisy… before they start singing again. No amount of washing things down with glasses of red *vinho* is going to help create any space for our main courses, especially when one is a mountain of *porco preto* (Iberian black pig) with chestnuts and chipped potatoes, and the other is an even bigger mountain of sweet potato *migas* (a filling accompaniment made from leftover bread, garlic and olive oil) with grilled meats and sausages. It's enough food to feed four people. We can't manage more than a couple of mouthfuls, earning us an accusing, "what's wrong with the food?" from a waiter who doesn't seem convinced by our whimpering replies that we are both just too stuffed to eat another mouthful. The hard lesson learned from this experience is that in Alentejo restaurants order half of what we think we want.

By the time we notch up our third Portagem eatery we are starting to become a tad jaded with menu choices. The freshness of any travel location generally adds extra flavour to the most simplistic food. Traditional restaurants with cut and paste decor; jaunty paper tablecloths; napkins which wouldn't cover your modesty let alone protect your lap from wayward saucy drips; and menus featuring main courses which involve variations of meat, meat and more meat might initially seem engagingly different just because they are new to us. Subsequently first meals tend to be devoured with gusto and lots of lip-smacking praise in a culinary world which feels all shiny and new. It's just that, as is the case with rural locations in so many places around the world, things can quickly became monotonously samey. Over the course of a week or two there might be sufficient culinary interest to be explored in menus which vary little from restaurant to restaurant. However, over the long haul it's a different kettle of fish, especially when there's a noticeable lack of said fish. The part of Alentejo hugging the Portuguese border is as far from the coast as you can get without venturing into Spain. It's not a place for fish and seafood, and we'll opt for fish or seafood before meat any day of the week. We have a general rule when it comes to eating out in traditional restaurants anywhere - eat meat in the mountains and fish at the coast. *Parque Natural da Serra de São Mamede* is most definitely meat country. We also like to maintain a balance when we dine out; sometimes we fancy good traditional regional fare at other times we have a yen for something a bit more sophisticated. Our favourite restaurants tend to be run by chefs who like to give traditional dishes a kick up the backside with a contemporary makeover. There are none of these within miles of where we are staying. We've scoured menu after menu looking for signs of innovation without success. As a result, we soon become bored with the choice of main courses on offer. When you enjoy the food you create at home far more than the food you pay for in restaurants then why bother dining out? This is the conclusion we reach after a month of living in Galegos. The food is generally just too heavy for us. Instead of eating out once a week, restaurant visits became increasingly rare. Saying that, we still enjoy various individual dishes in specific restaurants, as well as the overall experience of dining out, both for good and not so good reasons. It's all grist to the mill.

The menu at the Sever Restaurant, located romantically right on the banks of the river, involves the usual meaty subjects, including *veado* (venison). When it comes to meat I can usually take it or leave it, but show me a menu with venison or wild boar and it's a different matter. A chef in Hay-on-Wye once told me if it was up to him he'd strip all steak from his menu and replace it with far more tender and flavoursome venison instead. I'm with him on that view. The Sever's menu also features *silarca*, flat-headed mushrooms which are so popular in parts of Alentejo there's a *silarca* festival in Beja in March.

Our most surreal dining experience is at Ze Calha, a sprawling restaurant with a large outdoor terrace beside the *fluvial* in Portagem. Opposite the restaurant a mini gastro-festival is taking place at Terrius, a former mill that had been converted into a centre for promoting the best regional artisan produce. The chatter and laughter from the mill combined with the buzz from diners on the open air terrace adds to a convivial atmosphere which is perfect for our wedding anniversary dinner. The surreal element is provided by a girl at the adjoining table who has brought an over-sized white rabbit to dinner with her. Whilst she eats, her rabbit happily nibbles at the grass under her chair. The odd thing is we are the only people who are distracted by the sight of a rabbit in a restaurant (one that isn't actually on a diner's plate). Maybe girl and rabbit are regulars. Ze Calha serves a mean *camarões fritos com cerveja* - a messy mix of fried prawns in beer flavoured with bay leaves, garlic, and chillies. They also have salmon and trout on the menu. Unfortunately both confirm our rule about sticking to meat in the mountains and fish at the coast - they are overcooked and bland, despite the chef's best attempts at covering this fact up by smothering them in salt.

Dinner at El Rei Dom Manuel in Marvão turns out to be immensely educational regarding Portuguese desserts. With its summer programme of classical and rock concerts, Marvão is the sophisticated centre of our universe. Sadly, the restaurants within its walls don't quite match that sophistication. But the seductive lure of the place after dark is so strong we decide to try one of them anyway, choosing El Rei Dom Manuel as it has the most potentially interesting menu. Apart from its picture postcard prettiness, Marvão's attraction is that it lords it over the Alentejo plains; from its elevated position you can see forever in every direction. Not from El Rei Dom Manuel you can't. In a village renowned for its vistas, El Rei Dom Manuel's dining room doesn't have any windows you can see out of. It's a trick missed. There are only two other diners; a Portuguese couple. At first we think the woman diner is suffering from a sore throat as her voice is little more than an imagined whisper in the air. She doesn't have a sore throat at all, she is actually whispering her way through the meal as though any noise is forbidden. It's an unnerving contrast to the lively conversation we are used to courtesy of the Spanish weekenders in Portagem in the valley below. It makes the whole experience feel as though we've sneaked food into a library. If anything, we talk louder to try to break the oppressiveness. The meal itself is unremarkable apart from two things. It's my first taste of a classic Alentejana dish, *carne de porco à Alentejana*; a tasty surf and turf combo consisting of pork and clams marinaded in white wine, garlic, bay leaves, cilantro, and hot paprika. The other is an interesting piece of information we find out thanks to the restaurant's *sobremesa* menu which includes *sericaia*, a cake made from eggs, flour, sugar, milk, lemon zest, and cinnamon which is traditionally topped with a syrupy Elvas plum. More interesting is *toucinho do ceu*, which translates as lard from heaven; not something which automatically has you licking your lips thinking 'yum, I must try that'. But the name is so bizarre it falls into the category of dishes labelled 'those which must be experienced'. *Toucinho do ceu* is also a cake made from eggs, sugar, flour, and cinnamon. But this time with almonds as well. Lard did once feature, hence the name, but not any more. El Rei Dom Manuel's *toucinho do ceu* is so dense it could successfully double as an airplane chock. I post a photograph on Facebook to which a journalist friend from La Palma comments, "that's one of those famous Portuguese conventual desserts."

Conventual desserts are so-called because they are desserts concocted by nuns. Whilst it's interesting in itself to think that a country's dessert menus are dominated by puddings created by nuns, the reason why is even more interesting. After using egg whites to starch their wimples, nuns were left with an excess of yolks. Instead of just dumping them they used these leftover yolks to make pastries and cakes, many of which became sought after across Portugal. Some, like *toucinho do ceu*, have rather bizarre names. Another favourite oddity is *barrigas de freira* (nuns' bellies). After a few times asking waters what various unfamiliar sounding Portuguese puds on their menus consist of we soon know what the answer is likely to be - egg yolks, flour, sugar, cinnamon…

The most WOW dish we are presented with in rural Alentejo is at A Confraria in Castelo do Vide, another ridiculously picturesque Alentejo hill town. We'd spent an enjoyable and entertaining morning in the company of Phil, the cousin of a friend and it's time for lunch. His first choice restaurant is packed with a mix of soot-blackened firefighters and equally black-faced cork workers; peeling the bark from cork trees is clearly a grimy business. It's a fascinating mix and it would have been an illuminating afternoon to spend it in the company of both. But there's no room at the inn. So, after a cooling *cerveja*, we decamp to A Confraria where we are served with an obligatory lesson in Portuguese by a spunky, funny waitress with a big personality - "unless you ask in Portuguese, you don't get any food," - as well as the most refreshing, delicious and surprising gazpacho. A Confraria's *gazpacho* is unlike any we'd sipped - a chilled, salty, fruity, sweet broth which positively zings its way around the mouth. Excellent on its own, its flavours are boosted further by a slate plate filled with *presunto* (dry-cured ham similar to Spanish jamón Serrano).

The most insightful observations I've read regarding traditional food in rural Alentejo were in a *Guardian* travel article titled '*A foodie tour of Portugal's Alentejo*'. These weren't actually part of the travel piece, which tried its best to convince readers (after obviously successfully persuading the paper's commissioning editor) Alentejo was being touted as the new Tuscany in gastronomic terms. The first person to comment on the article questioned its assertions with a gently contrasting, "Knowing the region well, I'm non-too-convinced by the idea of Alentejo as a foodie or gourmet destination." Before adding, somewhat acerbically, "… perhaps the best tip about 'foodie-worthy' fine-dining in the Alentejo is this: Extremadura is a short drive away."

To fans of Alentejo cuisine, that might sound on the harsh side. However, after squaring up to mountainous portions of simply cooked Alentejana cuisine in a bevy of restaurants beyond the back of beyond, it's a view which I wouldn't necessarily disagree with. The most sophisticated food we eat during out time in Galegos is during a trip to Cáceres in Extremadura to celebrate Andy's birthday.

Don't misunderstand me, I like Alentejo cuisine in much the same way I like Scottish tablet. I lap it up in small doses but I don't want eat it day after day. Additionally, you may or may not have noticed that I've used the term 'rural' Alentejo when talking about the food. Alentejo is a huge region, and the cuisine we had encountered at the coast during a reconnaissance visit in March was more in line with the sort of gastronomy which gets our juices flowing.

Vicente and Life at the Frontier Petrol Station

The border makes me feel uneasy. Even though the days when it was manned are long gone, there's a niggle that I could be grabbed by two sturdy border police at any moment, guilty of a cultural *faux pas* I didn't know I'd committed, and dragged off to an underground cell never to be seen again. Crazy though it may sound, there's a sense of relief every time we successfully drive past the large, austere, bunker-esque complex which separates Portugal from Spain. We drive the route a lot as the only garage for miles is on the other side of the border, a six minute journey from our house.

It's also a fascinating place. Architecturally the border's buildings have an appearance I mentally associate with Cold War, Eastern Bloc military/police installations; a low, squat grey building consisting of different-sized rectangular blocks. All austere angles and straight lines, it oozes serious business. There's no softness to it at all. The building dominates the middle of the road, it's deserted, and there are often vultures circling above. All of which lends the scene an unsettling post-apocalyptic *28 Days Later* vibe. The 'everybody has died' aura isn't helped by a poster plastered to the window of a long-time closed cafe/restaurant unimaginatively named A Fronteira. The poster features photographs of a woman and has "*Desaparecida*" written across it - Disappeared.

Despite the apparent emptiness of the building (I'm sure I see a vague shape moving behind glass doors at one point when I wander closer than feels comfortable), we slow down considerably whenever we drive across the border. Just in case. Large billboards on both sides make sure you know you're swapping one country from another. On the Portuguese side, a sign informs drivers they should drive at 50kph in residential areas, 90 outside of residential areas, 120kph on motorways and 100kph when... well I'm not too sure what a car inside a blue rectangle means. On the Spanish side, a green sign shows you've entered Extremadura before a blue traffic sign informs you about speed limits in Spain (the same as Portugal but with different icons). One kilometre further on is the petrol station.

Where the border crossing has the feel of the world after a deadly virus has swept through it, the border petrol station has the bustle and vivacity of a frontier trading post, circa Wild West 1868. There are only three buildings, all joined together, but there's more life in the place than in many of the small Alentejo towns and villages we pass through. People are drawn to it for all sorts of reasons. It is always busy. Despite being miles from anywhere, and having a big area in which to park, it's not always easy finding a vacant parking spot, especially at weekends when the traffic passing through increases significantly thanks to Spanish heading to Portagem's river swimming pool. Petrol is the obvious reason for its popularity - petrol/diesel is cheaper on the Spanish side of the border, as are the *butano* bottles which everyone uses in these parts. But we discover quickly there's far more to 'Los Pinos' than just being the place to fill-up on fuel. There's a decent restaurant which is popular with firemen, Spanish policemen in khaki uniforms, forest rangers, and smartly dressed office workers. Where the latter group come from I have no idea. There's also an *Aladdin's Cave* of a supermarket; one of those places which at first perusal looks as though it has a limited stock in relation to food products, but which actually turns out to have everything we need that we didn't know we needed, until we needed it. Sacks of fruit and vegetables are piled up against the door whilst inside, as well as basic food supplies and lots of sweet things, are tools, kitchenware, boots with steel toe caps, hunting gear, bits for fixing pipes, barbecues, a haberdashery section, and just about anything you'd need to build a house from scratch. It reminds me of some of the supermarkets we saw when driving the Carretera Austral in Chile. They were also frontier supermarkets. The wine selection is interesting and illuminating. Even though it's located on the border with the biggest wine-producing area in Portugal, the supermarket stocks only one bottle of Portuguese wine. The rest is Spanish. To be fair, it's the opposite in supermarkets on the

Portuguese side.

The biggest jewel in this little tiara of a place is Vicente's garage. Carole and Ken put us on to Vicente as the go-to person for anything concerning cars. Our first experience was after a tyre exploded on the motorway driving back to Galegos from Setúbal. It happened just before we reached Estremoz, and we had to limp home for 80km. Ken had told us to introduce ourselves as being friends of his, asking us to pass on a message, a personal joke from him in Portuguese. We should have Google-translated first because, whatever it was, Vicente didn't laugh or look in the least amused when we passed on Ken's words. Thankfully, he still agreed to change the tyre there and then, charging us a ridiculously low amount for doing so. We've come to learn Vicente looking unamused is a rare sight. He has a permanent smile fixed to his face and a mischievous twinkle in his eye. Looking a bit like a Spanish Ian McShane, he's instantly likable; one of those people who make you feel like a friend from the second you meet them. He has time for everyone who passes through the petrol station, pausing whatever he's doing to share a few moments with anyone who stops to fill up their cars, or to admire motorbikes (he's a passionate collector himself) and any car which stands out from the crowd. Vicente is a super-efficient mechanic, which is just as well as his amiability and chatty personality slow him down somewhat. On one occasion, after he'd interrupted repairs to Cindy quite a few times to chat to old and new friends, the smile slipped from his face momentarily to be replaced by an earnest expression.

"All these people want to speak to me, I can never get any work done," he sighed. Then someone else he knew pulled into the petrol station and he was off again to say "*hola*", leaving me shaking my head and laughing.

His greatest rescue act came on the eve of us heading off on a work trip taking in Lisbon, Porto, and Coimbra. We'd popped out to get some essentials, opening the car windows in the hope there'd be at least a hint of coolish air. But when we returned home, the passenger window refused to slide shut. As we'd planned to leave the car in Évora train station for two weeks, a window which was stuck open was a bit of a minor disaster. Despite being busier than usual, cars were queued up waiting for his magic touch, Vicente, on hearing our dilemma, agreed to try to fix the problem there and then. The electric motor which operated the window had gone, so he had to order another to fix it, but he managed a temporary fix that kept the window lodged shut until we returned from our trip. He was a hero, not for the first time, and we were able to leave the car in Évora train station car park without worrying whether she'd still be there when we returned. As it happens the station car park in Évora is right next to the police station, so she might have been fine anyway, but we'd still have fretted.

If it wasn't for Vicente, life beyond the back of beyond would be a lot more difficult.

WALKING IN SMUGGLERS' FOOTSTEPS

It is not a good night for smuggling. The full moon bathes the land with a ghostly white light. I can see the clear, sharp outline of the hills around me. I can even see moon shadows cast by cork trees 200m away. Smugglers would be easy pickings for border guards on a night like this.

It's easy to get caught up in imagined skirmishes with border patrols when paths lead into the hills all around us, paths that were used by smugglers plying their trade between villages and towns either side of the Portuguese Spanish border. The term 'border country' itself conjures up thoughts of an untamed land where life isn't quite the same as elsewhere. And it's not inaccurate. I can walk a few hundred metres up the hill and jump forward in time an hour. When you're never entirely sure what country you're in, or what the time is, it can be a tad unsettling.

During the less atmospheric hours of daylight, on a day when the searing heat isn't quite as oppressive, we follow one of these trails, a *rota de contrabanda do café* - a route carefully tread by light-footed coffee smugglers. From the tiny hamlet of Galegos we climb a stony path which takes us past a flock of squawking azure-winged magpies into hills which mark the border between Portugal and Spain. In this place, between the 1940s and 1970s, two dictators, Franco and Salazar, erected a glass wall which caused suffering to the residents of both countries and which forced some to take up smuggling. These smugglers weren't dangerous *desperados*, they were usually women transporting goods, albeit illegally, we now take for granted – coffee, food, sugar, medicines, fabrics, sewing threads, sausage skins. Basic essentials. Take away the smuggling tag and the two dictators and what you have is a trading route of the sort which once existed between towns and villages all across Europe. Smugglers were more often than not ordinary people taking risks in order to survive. That's not to say there weren't those who exploited the situation. As well as everyday household goods, sometimes silks, furs, perfume and stockings made their way under the cover of darkness between the two countries.

Knowing this adds spice to the route, even in daylight hours and in the absence of border patrols. The first sighting of a wooden post with the word *contrabando* etched into it is quite thrilling, prompting thoughts about the people who walked these illicit paths, some of whom still live in the neat white houses nestled into the valleys around us. The path climbs through a cork forest, their trunks stripped of precious bark leaving them looking naked and slightly, but not unattractively, odd; they have the appearance of fingerless gloves. Above our heads the blue magpies are replaced by bigger birds with colossal wingspans; vultures. A land of smugglers and vultures – Indiana Jones eat your heart out.

As we reach a ridge, the shaded path veers into the outskirts of a tiny hamlet. Beside a fountain are two stone basins with one side ridged for scrubbing clothes. They look as though they belong in the 1950s, but a bottle of washing up liquid and a scrubbing brush show they're still being used. On a wall are two posters, one advertises a *sardinhada* (a small festival involving music, dancing and grilled sardines) the other a bullfight. We pass a small, pretty cottage where a woman hangs out her washing whilst her husband sits in a chair amongst pink roses, supervising no doubt. He bids us 'good morning' in what sounds like Spanish. I'm confused.

"Where are we?" I ask, embarrassed at having to seek clarification about which country I'm in. "Portugal or Spain?"

"Portugal," he confirms... in Spanish.

We continue on our way, passing more *contrabando* signs, before arriving at a crossroads where a notice warns us there are bees in the vicinity and a small, stone pyramid with a P on our side and an E on the other tells us we're about to step into *España*. Uncannily, with the change of country comes a change of terrain. In front of us, stretching as far as we can see, are sprawling wheat-coloured plains. It's an immense landscape where not many people live. The only humans we've seen were the Spanish-speaking Portuguese couple in the hamlet. There are animals though - sheep, goats, cows and a herd of stocky white bullocks who engage us in a staring competition. Their nerve breaks before ours and one of them freaks out, leading to a mini stampede. The herd takes off at speed, the noise of their hooves thundering across the dry plains reverberates around us. It's an impressive sound.

The path continues across a thirsty and rather epic landscape where there are little signs of civilisation. It could be unnerving if it weren't for the fact we know it to be misleading. We're not far from the end of our smugglers' route and we know we should be nearing the small village of La Fontañera. Sure enough, our stony path breaks free from the wilderness to emerge onto a tarmac road. 500m later we arrive at the outskirts of the village. It's a curious place, bigger than expected. There are no shops or bars, only a line of houses bordering one street; bordering being the appropriate word as the Spanish/Portuguese border, marked by another stone pyramid, cuts right through its southern edge. One rogue house lies on the Portuguese side of town, a footstep away from another country. Its existence provokes many questions; do the inhabitants speak Portuguese whilst the rest of the village speaks Spanish? Is there really an hour's time difference between houses metres apart? Will the people on the Spanish side be watching the new season of *Game of Thrones* whilst the people in the Portuguese house stare across the border enviously? (Spain has HBO at this time, Portugal doesn't). Do the people in the Portuguese house get out of bed an hour before their Spanish neighbours. I want to knock on doors and assault residents with these questions. Borders are bizarre places.

No Escaping the Tenerife Wideboys

Tenerife with its amiable islanders will forever hold a special place in our hearts, but there were aspects to the island we never warmed to. One was whenever we had dealings with some ex-pat businesses in the south of the island. Not all, I hasten to add. There are people who were instrumental in helping us move forward, and showing us opportunities we might otherwise have missed. Travel writer Joe Cawley was one. His informed mentoring and editorial advice was priceless during our first stuttering steps into travel writing. Joe gave us our first break, which came about after he mistook me for the Honorary Irish Consul to Tenerife at a wine awards dinner shortly after we moved to the island. Another was John Beckley, a bright-eyed South African with endless optimism and enthusiasm, who saw the future power of social media long before it became mainstream, and who was like a zealous missionary when it came to spreading the social media/power of the internet message from the pulpit of his website-design business. Not many businesses on Tenerife listened to him initially, a forward-looking approach isn't commonplace there, but he never stopped banging that drum. He was 100% right about the future, as we all know now. John remains at the forefront of the latest developments in social media, still enthusiastically spreading the word, whilst many of those who didn't take heed are no longer in business. In the Tenerife ex-pat business world, too many of the people we had dealings with were transparent bullshitters, so those who we met who really did know their stuff stood out like a lighthouse beacon on a foggy night. We took note of every valuable piece of advice John fed us and benefited immensely from his sage words.

Often we came away from business encounters with ex-pats feeling many were trying to screw us in one way or another. After the third time we ended up not being paid for work we'd carried out, we made the decision to, save for the people we already knew and trusted, stop working with businesses based in the Canary Islands. It was a necessary case of self preservation. In the worst example, we invested half a year in a job. The substantial amount owed to us was never paid, leaving us financially up shit creek and nearly ended our living abroad adventure.

When trying to arrange the transport of our belongings from Tenerife to Portugal we couldn't find a Canarian firm to do the job, and so were left with choosing between two ex-pat removal companies based in the south of Tenerife. Both appeared to know their stuff, and there were plenty of decent customer reviews, so we picked the one with the most favourable quote.

The Tenerife side of the operation went smoothly enough, even though we had concerns about the flimsiness of cardboard boxes they supplied to be used as packaging; in retrospect, evident signs of corner cutting. However, after four weeks in Portugal and no sign of our belongings, nor any correspondence from the removal company we'd used, alarm bells started clanging loudly. Memories of the container with our worldly goods going missing when we moved to Tenerife resurfaced. Then, they'd taken a wee detour to spend some time in an African country. Knowing it could be a sluggish business, we weren't unduly worried until a month passed and there was no correspondence from the Tenerife removal company. A 'slightly concerned email was sent to try to prompt action:

20 June

Hi Dave,

How are you?

Jack and I were just wondering where our belongings are at the moment. Do you have a date yet for delivery to us in Portugal?

Thanks,

Andrea

To be fair, they replied after a couple of days:

22 June

Hi Andrea

Just received the following from the agent in Portugal.

Sobre esta expedición a Portugal no podemos contactar con esta mujer, para que pague los gastos de la aduana y entregar la mercancia. Disponéis de otro teléfono ¿? (translated - about this expedition to Portugal we can not contact this woman, so that you pay the customs costs and deliver the goods. Other phone available?) Please advise. Do you have another number they can contact you on?

Best Regards

Dave

More alarm bells. This little trick of companies saying they tried to contact us might have worked in the past but these days, when emails and smartphones are records of when any contact has been attempted, it's an excuse which can be easily exposed. Nobody had made any attempt to contact us.

22 June

Hi Dave,

I hope they're not trying to use our Tenerife landline number...!

My mobile number is still the same (see below) and there has been no contact, no missed calls, no text messages, nada. The best way for them to contact me would be by email.

Cheers,

Andrea

PS What gastos de la aduana? Aren't those covered in the total cost?

22 June

Hi Andrea

I will forward your email to them. The import duty is an extra, as you may recall this was discussed on my first visit.

Best Regards

Dave

22 June

Cheers, Dave.

No, I don't remember but I don't doubt you, we talked about a lot of stuff on that first visit. What sort of sum are we looking at?
Andrea

22 June

Minimal amount as we only declared a low value....
Dave

23 June

Hi Dave,

We've just had a phone call from a guy named Paulo who tells us our stuff has been in Customs in Lisbon for weeks and he did not have a contact for me. He says he contacted you for my number weeks ago! He also says our goods may now 'be lost' if this isn't sorted by Monday or Tuesday. The issue is that I don't have a Portuguese VAT number which apparently is required in order to release the goods. It all sounds a bit of a cock-up doesn't it?!

Can you do anything to try to sort it? Paulo is contacting Customs again to try to sort it but needless to say, we're now very concerned!
Andrea

26 June

Hi Andrea
My mainland guy is on the case.............

26 June

Cheers, Dave.
Andrea

After this, communications switch to the 'mainland guy', Paulo.

27 June

Hello Andrea,

Has per our phone call from this morning. We gonna need the following info for make the invoice:

Complete Name + Complete adress + VAT number

After this I gonna send you copy of invoice and ask to send bank transfer.

We need also your complete adress in Galegos (just to confirm the delivery place)

Wait your soon reply.

Regards,

Paulo

27 June

We will make the bank transfer as soon as we receive your invoice. When can we expect delivery?

Best regards,

Andrea

27 June

Hello Andrea,

My contability departement is asking me, if its possible you send me a copy of the NIE (VAT) document, please.

Wait y/soon reply

Thanks & Regards,

Paulo

27 June

Hi Paulo,

We do not have a VAT document. In Spain, we use the NIE for tax and IGIC (VAT) purposes. Here is a copy.

Andrea

After a few more emails and phone calls to Paulo we finally supply all the information to make the ransom, err.. , I mean payment to have our goods released. Dave is an absent figure in all this; another email is sent.

28 June

Hi Dave,

We finally have the invoice for Customs Duty from Paulo and it's a whopping €402.26, half of which is 'customs warehousing'. Given that we could have taken delivery of our goods any time from 4th June but heard nothing until I chased last week, we're not very happy. I think communications need tightening up in future.

Cheers,

Andrea

29 June

Hello Andrea,

Customs finished. We gonna ship today to Alentejo. I think they gonna deliver to you between tomorrow & Monday. Give you the phone number from the distribution company on the South, so you can confirm with them from tomorrow (if you wish):

Regards,

Paulo

At this point Dave re-enters the picture

30 June

Hi Andrea

I am working on the charges, will get back to you next week.

Best Regards

Dave

30 June

Hi Dave,

That's good to know.

We've been notified that our goods are finally out of Customs and are going to be delivered on Monday. I'll confirm once they've arrived safely.

Cheers,

Andrea

On 3 July I receive a phone call from the delivery driver
who is in the vicinity but can't find the house. He can't speak
any English at all so I have to attempt to 'talk him in' using bad
Portuguese mixed with decently good Spanish. I'm amazed,
and quite proud of myself, when, after five minutes, I see a van
coming toward the house along the country road. It's a bit of a
logistical exercise, but the driver manages to reverse the van up
the narrow entrance, taking out a few tree branches as he does.
He has no assistant. It quickly becomes apparent that it's not a
removals van, it's simply a delivery van. He dumps a load of
palettes containing familiar items on the rough ground, asks
me to sign some documents, and then he's off. It's down to us
to unwrap everything and shift the lot from their delivery spot
in the searing sun to inside the house 50m away. In 34C heat
it's a killer of a task which takes us the rest of the day. Still,
it's a relief to see all of our belongings (we hope) safe, sound
and in our hands at last. There was a moment during our initial
communications with Paulo when it seemed there was a real
possibility all our belongings were going to be impounded by
Portuguese customs. If we had waited a week longer before
chasing up their whereabouts we would have lost the lot.
Another email is sent whizzing Dave's way.

Hi Dave,
Our goods were delivered on Monday afternoon. As I said in
my earlier email, we paid the invoice straight away as directed
by the Portuguese agent who told us our goods could not be
released from Customs without evidence of payment. We haven't
heard anything about a refund.
It might be useful for you to know, if you undertake any
more moves to Portugal, that the delivery was done a bit like a
parcel would be delivered. There was just one man in a van who
unloaded the three palettes onto the driveway and left everything
else to us. There is some damage to the desks (some scratches
and chips on the surfaces) but other than that, it's all here safe
and sound.
The other thing I noticed was that, according to the

paperwork he left with us, the goods appeared to have been in Customs since 5th June but no attempt was made to contact us until I followed up with you. I also noted that my mobile phone number was attached to every individual box and item of furniture so the "we didn't have a contact number for the customer" line is crap (technical term!).

I look forward to receiving a refund.

Cheers,

Andrea

And that's the last communication between us. No refund is forthcoming. We've been here before with Tenerife cowboys and know that attempts to get anywhere will be time consuming, stressful, frustrating and ultimately fruitless. It is far better for our collective state of mind to simply suck it up, cut the cord and put the experience down to just another life lesson in dealings with an unavoidable side of the Tenerife ex-pat scene. We did our best to avoid having dealings with these sort of people when we lived there, made easier by living in the north of the island, but it still feels good to know they're now consigned to history. We want to concentrate on what's ahead rather than behind.

THE SUMMER PORTUGAL BURNED

There hasn't been a cloud in the sky all day. Hours and hours of unbroken blueness until an ugly nicotine stain taints it at around 6pm. An hour later and Marvão doesn't look like one of Portugal's prettiest villages any more, it looks like Mordor. The hill town and surrounding plains have become shrouded in a sinister black cloak, an ash cloud which has drifted across the sky. The normally pure air becomes acrid, the smell of a singed landscape fills our nostrils and small, white flakes float on the breeze. The same thing has been happening for days, and it's frightening. Each evening we wonder whether it's drifted across from a raging forest fire far, far away, or from a new wildfire which is ravaging the land just beyond the next range of hills.

One of the things people don't tell you when you move abroad, especially to rural areas and hotter climes, is how nature can seem a hell of a lot closer, dangerous and more unpredictable when you're not living in the relative embrace of an urban jungle in Britain where the weather might often be depressingly grey and damp, but rarely feels life-threatening. The first, destructive, subtropical storm we experienced on Tenerife soon put us straight to that little oversight. Then, after experiencing the devastation of serious storms, sitting on our terrace watching flames out of control dance across the Tigaiga ridge barely 10km away made us realise the long, hot, dry days of summer brought their own natural problems. Or maybe not so natural as humans are the cause of most forest fires, either through maliciousness or stupidity. On one occasion, at a small agricultural fare in the Teno hills on Tenerife, we watched a helicopter pass overhead, a bulging bucket of water collected from a nearby reservoir swinging below it. There was a small forest fire in the next valley. The little *fiesta* involved displays of traditional methods of wheat threshing, using horses and teams of oxen, which meant there was tinder-dry straw everywhere. Even as we watched the fire-fighting copter pass overhead, a local farmer next to us grabbed the cigar from his mouth and threw it into the undergrowth. Another time, we stood on a hillside and watched a huge section of forest explode in a ball of flame. It was sobering and provided a far-too-close insight into the impossible task forest firefighters have. No amount of personnel and firefighting vehicles can hold back a force like that. On yet another occasion, we made a very good friend after we took her in when she was evacuated by the Guardia Civil in the middle of the night as flames raced across the valley behind the one where her house was located. Experiencing these violent acts gave us a respect for nature's power we hadn't had before we moved abroad.

Summer in Portugal is on a completely different scale. One we couldn't have imagined.

It became deadly serious in June 2017 when a series of wildfires devastated Pedrógão Grande, between the centre and the north of Portugal, leaving 66 people dead, hundreds injured, tens of thousands of hectares of forest destroyed and hundreds of homes burnt to the ground. Of those killed by the wildfires, two thirds were trapped in their cars, trying to escape. Portuguese television was dominated by shocking scenes of the destruction and the ongoing attempts by firefighters to try to tame an out of control monster. It was terrifying, but at that time seemed a tragedy which was happening to other people, like so many news reports of tragic events. You watch quietly, and then get on with your life as normal. However, as the summer draws on and fire after fire breaks out it becomes evident that this time they aren't occurring in a land on the other side of an ocean, this time they're knocking on our door.

By mid-July I have an app, fogos.pt, which informs where fires have started, how many firefighters are tackling them, and what state the fire is currently at. These range from a green flame, which shows the fire has been extinguished (good), to a red one, which shows it's still raging (bad). The app's map of Portugal is covered in red flames. The whole country is on fire. It's a fabulous app and every country should have similar, if they don't already. It's not something you know you need until you need it. One of its best features is it sends an alert to your phone if a fire breaks out near to you. This is highly sensible, potentially life-saving and, at the same time, terrifying. My phone pings a lot with these alerts.

Mostly they turn out to be small outbreaks. Having learnt quickly from what happened at Pedrógão Grande, firefighters tackle any flare-ups as soon as they're reported. On the fogos app we watch red flames turn to blue and then, with relief, green.

One afternoon, I see a plume of smoke on the hillside directly below Marvão. I don't hesitate, I immediately call 112 and hope the person on the other end of the phone speaks English. They do. Despite the fire having just broken out they've already been informed, the *bombeiros* are on their way. We spend the afternoon watching the fire being fought; the smoke billowing darker and higher before finally it concedes defeat and we can breathe sighs of relief. It is completely distracting.

We don't sleep well. From a distance this might sound like paranoia, but each night we go to bed wondering whether a fire might break out on the hillside behind the house and we'll wake, if we're lucky, to find orange fingers tapping on the glass of the bedroom windows. I work out where the best place is to jump from to reduce the chance of breaking an ankle. One morning, as we tuck into warm croissants filled with pumpkin jam, I notice the copse across the valley, about 500 metres away, is looking a lot blacker than it did the previous day.

"Does that look burnt to you?" I ask Andy.

We didn't hear or see a thing. Was it put out or did it just not spread? We'll never know.

What we do know is we can't wait for the end of days where the temperature doesn't drop below the mid 30s centigrade, for cooling clouds to roll across the sky and for decent rainfall to calm down the parched earth. The heat is oppressive, the air lacks oxygen. Being outside without shade for any length of time is simply unbearable. It's not so much the searing skin, it's more the feeling that nature is trying to strangle the life out of you. We know what scientists meant when they referred to the Canary Islands as having almost the perfect climate. It isn't what many think, that the days are generally hot and sunny. It is because they have the perfect climate for living and working, they are temperate all year. It is difficult to achieve anything when day after day the shade temperature is 34/35C. We don't explore anything like as much as we'd like. On the hottest days, forays outside (such as stocking up on water from the fountain in Castelo de Vide) are planned like commando raids – getting in, achieving our objective, and scuttling back to the shade sanctuary of home as quickly as possible, keeping being machine-gunned by the sun's rays to a minimum.

For the first time ever we desperately want summer to end.

Northern Soul and Faded Grandeur

There's a saying in Portugal which describes the personality of each of its main cities:- "*Porto works, Coimbra studies, Braga prays and Lisbon shows off*"

We have to vacate Crença for a couple of weeks from the end of July due to a long-standing arrangement Carole and Ken have with a Lisboan friend who brings his family for some rural Alentejo time each summer. It's potentially inconvenient – who wants to go anywhere when the sun makes it too hot to do anything but huddle in the shade? But we knew about our temporary eviction before we agreed to rent Crença. With perfect timing, our buddies at Inntravel come up with a proposal which creates a win-win situation. Their *On the Waterfront* Slow Travel holiday, a train journey taking in Porto, Lisbon and Coimbra, needs updating and we are in the perfect place to do it... well, the same country at least; it's a 1hr 40min drive to the nearest train station at Évora.

The journey is an introduction to the common sense and environmentally sound approach the Portuguese have to car parks at train stations. Many are free. We leave our car at Évora's and jump on the train to Lisbon. I'd booked tickets for all our train journeys - Évora to Lisbon, Lisbon to Porto, Porto to Lisbon, Lisbon to Coimbra, Coimbra to Lisbon, and Lisbon back to Évora – online. It's hassle-free travel and a relaxing way to see the country, especially as trains are clean and comfortable with plenty of empty seats. It's also a treat for us as the closest thing to rail travel in the Canary Islands had been trips on the tram between La Laguna and Santa Cruz de Tenerife.

It's late afternoon by the time we arrive in Porto and check into our hotel just off *Praça da Liberdade*. We've stayed at the Hotel Internacional before and know it's a decent city centre hotel in a superb location for accessing the Porto city routes we have to update/create.

We dump our bags and head to Cafe Aviz to finalise plans,

helped by a flight of Super Bock 1927 craft ales (1927 being the date the Super Bock company was established). There's a general rule when it comes to drinking beer in Portugal's cities. In Porto it's Super Bock, in Lisbon it's Sagres. Cafe Aviz was the first place we ate in Porto a few years previously. Arriving in the city late one chilly December night Aviz was a brightly lit, welcoming oasis of people still eating when restaurants all around were winding down. It wasn't the quaint, atmospheric restaurant we'd hoped for, we'd never have darkened its doorway had we arrived when other restaurants were in full serving flow, but it turned out to be fortuitous. The place was packed with young Portuenses eating something that looked as though it was covered in custard – the *francesinha*, one of the world's great sandwiches.

The *francesinha* isn't going to win any awards for sophistication. It has the appearance of a square brick covered in melted cheese that's floating in a sea of tomato sauce. This is no sandwich you can pick up with your hands… unless you've got some sort of fetish that involves being covered in cheesy, tomato sauce. It's the only sandwich I've ever eaten that was served in a soup bowl, giving a whole new meaning to 'soup and a sarnie'. In the Avis Café they add chips to the sauce (women diners get their chips separate as it's more ladylike), just in case it wasn't already a big enough carb hit. The *francesinha* holds a Pandora's Box of surprises. The first being the tomato sauce doesn't taste of tomatoes, some sauces have a kick like Bruce Lee. Apart from tomatoes, hot spices and beer also figure in the sauce's ingredients. Then there are the contents of the 'brick.' Two, inch-thick slices of bread make up the floor and ceiling of the *francesinha*. Between these slabs are slices of thick, cured ham; a savoury Portuguese sausage called a *linguiça*; a juicy piece of steak; and a fillet of pork. To finish it off, the cheese sauce hides a domed ceiling consisting of a poached egg with a runny yolk (more scope for making a right old mess). This delicious, belly-busting mess of a dish was created by Daniel David da Silva in the 1950s who picked up the idea from eating *croque-monsieurs* and *croque-madames* in France. It's claimed he named it in honour of the spiciest woman he knew, a young French girl. Possibly because of this, it was originally considered out of bounds to Porto's female population. One urban myth was that eating *francesinhas* would actually cause behavioural changes in women.

We were introduced to two north Portuguese specialities that first night in Aviz; our waitress recommended *vinho verde* as an accompaniment. We were blown away by the idea of 'green wine', believing it actually was green. The *verde* of the name is in fact a reference to it being a young wine rather than the colour. You also get *vinho verde tinto*, something which initially blew my mind - "would you like red, green wine?"

Porto is possibly our favourite Portuguese city. I say 'possibly' because comparing Portuguese cities isn't comparing like with like, hence the whole '*Porto works, Coimbra studies, Braga prays and Lisbon shows off*' saying. There's an honest, down-to-earth, working class vibe to Porto that doesn't exist in quite the same way in the other cities. It does faded grandeur very well, but then so does much of Portugal. If Porto were a person it would be Dickens' Miss Havisham. There's also a strong, no nonsense northern air about the city, one of the reasons we like it so much. We toyed with the idea of basing ourselves near Porto when we moved from the Canaries, but two factors turned our gaze further south. One was the weather, the other was the area around Lisbon is far more multicultural than in northern parts, and we like living in places where we can enjoy the benefits multiculturalism brings.

The city has changed significantly since our last visit. Not fundamentally; the earthy personality is evident by the bucket load, as is the faded grandeur – there are still lines of washing decorating the tiled facades of riverfront dwellings. But areas have been spruced up. The last time we stood on *Rua das Flores* it was borderline seedy, lined by abandoned and derelict buildings. Now it's buzzing, the busiest street in Porto. The buildings which seemed on the point of collapsing with weariness are now all perky and fresh, having been given a new lease of life. Where, not so long ago, there were broken window panes and cracked tiles, there are smart cafes, independent shops, and boutique hostels. The street looks fabulous, reinvigorated, if a tad gentrified. The city is also a hell of a lot busier than our last visit. The famous Livraria Lello & Irmão, the alleged Harry Potter book store, illustrates just how popular Porto has become. In 2012 we walked straight through the front door. Now, from before it opens in the morning, there's a queue stretching around the block and it costs €4 to get in (redeemed if you buy a book, something I'm willing to bet most of those queueing for that essential Instagram shot of the interior won't be doing).

However, despite its growing popularity, Porto hasn't lost the charm which had us mulling over whether to relocate there. Like every city we've visited, there are still plenty of attractive crowd-free spots, or places where we stumble across those little quirks which are unique to a specific destination. As we hoof it around the city, we record everything which catches our interest. Some things are obvious and everyone knows about them, others that pique our interest are less well known.

Lisbon might be better known for its trams, but old *electricos* trundle around Porto's streets. Whereas Lisbon's trams are brightly coloured, Porto's are more muted, brown and nicotine in colour; none of that Lisbon show-off business. These *carros americanos* were introduced in 1872 and there are three lines currently in operation. We take Line 18 which runs between Massarelos and Carmo, covering a small part of the riverside route. For €3.50 it's a good value way of seeing a part of the city which is too far for some visitors to walk. The manner in which the tram's direction is changed at the halfway point is a delightful hoot; I won't spoil it by describing what it involves. Line 18 is an effortless way to get to the Crystal Palace Gardens, named after the original glass and iron palace constructed in 1865 for Porto's World Exhibition. It's a green sanctuary away from the urban bustle, featuring gardens with various themes like a rose garden overlooked by a balcony, where we re-enact the 'wherefore art thou' scene from *Romeo and Juliet*; and a Garden of Feelings with a viewpoint over the Douro. Paths lead past fountains, sculptures, and lily ponds to the Romantic Museum, a collection of paintings from the Romantic school, before arriving at the lake where a glass-domed structure now stands in place of the original Crystal Palace. As gardens go I've seen better, but you do get very different views of the city from its elevated position, and it's hard to beat reclining with a Super Bock on a cushion-covered palette at the cafe beside an arty little lake.

Close to the square where Line 18 sets off from are the laughing men. I'm a fan of sculptures. Not so much those grand, pompous, military affairs involving some member of the nobility on a horse atop a plinth. No, I mean the more eclectic off-the-wall kind, or ones whose messages evoke emotions of one sort or another. The area around Jardim da Cordoaria has a couple of intriguing examples. Along the park's impressive avenue of plane trees are four sculptures which put smiles on our faces. Each depicts a man tumbling down steps while his companions roar with laughter. It's titled *13 Laughing At Each Other* (say what you see) and is the work of Madrid sculptor Juan Muñoz. Nearby, outside the Photography Museum (formerly a prison), is another intriguing and controversial sculpture of a fully clothed man embracing a naked woman. *Amor de Perdição* (Doomed Love) depicts Camilo Castelo Branco, a famous 19th century novelist who was incarcerated in the jail for having an affair with a married woman. It's interesting as this is a sculpture which divides opinions. As Camilo Castelo Branco is clothed and the woman isn't, some see it as another example of women being treated as sexual objects.

People head to Vila Nova de Guia mainly to visit the Port cellars, but it's increasingly becoming worth a wander in its own right. Apart from the opportunity to quaff a glass or two of Port, I like to get closer to those gorgeous *rabelo* boats which used to transport barrels, goods and people down the once fast-flowing Douro. This visit we turn our meanderings into a city route, crossing the lower deck of the Dom Luis I Bridge, a 395m long forged iron masterpiece of engineering. It's a trek and a climb to Graham's Lodge, but it gives us the opportunity to get a feel for

Vila Nova de Guia. Compared to the opposite side of the Douro, it's decidedly sleepy with some urban art surprises in its back streets – like a giant rabbit made from rubbish. It's a thing these days, I've spotted mutant rubbish animals in Lisbon as well as in off-the-beaten-track towns in Alentejo. Taking a tour of a Port cellar is essential to understand the city. Port is part of its fabric and cellar tours help put Porto, and Portugal's connections with Britain, into context. We chose Graham's Lodge partly because it's still a working cellar, and partly because it occupies a commanding position above the Douro.

The visit turns out to be multi-faceted; fascinating, emotive, educational, and gives a glimpse into a past that hasn't quite disappeared. I had never appreciated just how much the Port industry came about as a result of Scottish entrepreneurs (and a couple of English ones). Graham's, Symington, Cockburn, Churchill's, Sandeman – all Scottish. Watching a film about life further up river in the Douro Valley makes us yearn to visit, and by the time we get to the tasting part we're Port converts. The barman at the Hotel Internacional had told us only old folk drank Port these days. After sipping generous glasses of various ruby and tawny ports we don't care if we're old fogeys, we're hooked on Port. We leave Graham's feeling merry in more ways than one.

From Graham's Lodge we take the easy option to get to the Serra do Pilar monastery, the cable car (€6). It's far busier at monastery level than river level because of the classic Porto and Douro views you get from the south side of the Dom Luis I Bridge. It's also a good spot for witnessing tourist stupidity – from selfie-takers perching dangerously on walls which have signs warning about the dangers of perching on walls, to folk standing with their backs to oncoming trams on the upper level of the bridge. This is what we call 'holiday head', people who leave their brains at home and behave completely differently in the places they visit than they would do at home. Visiting friends' fourteen-year-old daughter and her mate once accompanied us around an out-of-town shopping centre in the north of Tenerife wearing only shorts and bikini tops. After a few minutes, and a lot of stares, they complained about feeling uncomfortable amid locals dressed in jumpers and jeans. I asked them if they would walk around the Arndale in Manchester in a bikini top. They physically cringed with embarrassment at the very thought.

Everybody knows about the *azulejo*-covered entrance hall at the São Bento Railway Station, but we always pop in whenever we visit Porto. There are 20,000 tiles in total, dating from 1905-1916; the work of Jorge Colaço, the most renowned *azulejo* painter of his time. The name of the station derives from a Benedictine monastery built on this spot in the 16th century. The monastery was destroyed by fire in 1783 and was later rebuilt, but was in a grave state of disrepair by the end of the C19th when it was decided to expand the railway system. There's a decent little cafe just off the entrance hall. Rather than elbow our way through the crowds, getting in the way of people actually using the station to travel, we grab a coffee and enjoy the elegant entrance hall from the comfort of a seat. The station is a good starting point war a stroll along Porto's best street for shopping, Santa Catarina, and for having a coffee in the most elegant surroundings.

Beginning life in 1921 as the Elite Café, its Art Nouveau decoration, leather seating, ornate plaster ceiling and endless Flemish mirrors brought style and panache to Porto's high street. Initially patronised by bohemians and high society women, its name did not sit well with the Republican government of the day so it was changed to Café Majestic. Like Livraria Lello & Irmão, Café Majestic has become a victim of Instagram success and now there's a perpetual line of folk waiting to get in. Although Santa Catarina is the city's main shopping artery, there are some worthy sights to see along it for those who aren't turned on by window browsing. As we traverse it, Andy takes the opportunity to buy new jeans when she spots a Levi's shop. One of the things we find appealing about Portugal is the people are not only intrinsically friendly, they like to share information. We're always picking up snippets from the most unlikely sources, e.g. the best spot for wild camping and warm swimming courtesy of a bank clerk. I've no interest in jeans, I have short legs and jeans make them look even shorter. As a Brazilian shop assistant looks for Levi's for Andy, the other, a Portuense, asks me questions about how we're enjoying Porto. When I mention I like *francesinhas*, he tells me where his favourite places are. Then he asks me where I'm from.

"Scotland," I reply.

"Like McGregor?"

"That's right."

"Nobody likes McGregor, he's not very nice."

"What?" I'm taken aback by this. "I thought everybody loved Ewan."

"Who's Ewan?" The assistant now looks confused. "I'm talking about Conor."

"Conor McGregor is Irish," an amused, disembodied voice with a lyrical Brazilian lilt shouts from the changing rooms.

The Portuense shop assistant might not know his McGregors but he does know his Levis. When I tell him I don't wear jeans because of the vertically challenged leg issue, he grabs a pair and says, "try these, they'll make your legs look longer."

Bugger me, he's right, and they are ultra comfortable – THE best jeans I've ever owned. I leave with a smile on my face, even though we've forked out a couple of hundred Euros for two pairs of Levis.

Prado do Repouso isn't on our itinerary of places to check out. However, our way of getting to know a city is to walk and walk and walk some more. That's when we tend to find out the 'little things' that we enjoy so much. In this case our hoofing it around leads us to the gated entrance to *Prado do Repouso Cemetery* and a morbid tale from the 19th century involving Henriqueta, a high class Porto prostitute, and the death of her lover, Teresa Maria de Jesus. It's interesting that when describing Henriqueta, the word 'eccentric' is sometimes used as a way of saying she was attracted to the same sex without actually saying so. On the day of her lover's funeral, Henriqueta made off with Teresa's head. She was tried for the 'crime' but found innocent as the judge considered it a distraught act of love. Henriqueta arranged for Teresa to be laid to rest in a tomb in *Prado do Repouso*; a tomb on which fresh flowers regularly appear. Nobody knows who puts them there. Cemeteries always have stories to tell. Ironically, the past lives on in death, and strolls around cemeteries can paint a far more vivid picture of a place than some reference books.

Although Lisbon and Porto are both cities beside a river, there's a huge difference in the relationship each has with their respective waterways. Lisbon's feels slightly detached, maybe because of the width of the Tagus. In Lisbon the river is something to be crossed to get to work rather than a fun part of the city. In Porto the Douro is like a pal to spend time with. Subsequently there's more of a riverside scene, with bars and restaurants lining the northern bank. Unsurprisingly Port is the de rigueur drink on sunny evenings down by the Douro, but not the ruby/tawny-coloured, warming Port we tasted in the cellars opposite. We're talking a far-too-drinkable concoction called *Porto tónico* - a blend of white Port, tonic water, lemon/lime, a sprig of mint, and lots of ice. We were introduced to it by Ken and Carole in Alentejo, who make a mean *Porto tónico*; better than the ones we sip by the Douro. But drinking something in situ always adds extra fizz, and the people-watching in Porto is far superior to rural Alentejo.

A Taste of Porto

Finding good places to eat in any city or big town can be hit and miss, even with the range of tools we have at hand. Tripadvisor is flawed, but it's still useful when it comes to identifying potential places to eat. However, there can be certain trends which make some recommendations less than reliable. Restaurants near hotel areas can rate higher purely because many visitors don't walk far from their hotels to eat dinner. These restaurants get more reviews than ones which require effort to reach. In locations which play host to hordes of day-trippers, cafes and fast food joints are elevated to undeserved positions on TA's best restaurants lists.

Before we became travel writers we'd scour favoured guidebooks looking for restaurants that rang our culinary bells. But sometimes the reality didn't live up to descriptions. Restaurants with dishes which were enthused about, having been handed down from granny's recipe (how come every granny in the world except mine was an excellent cook?), had menus featuring dishes that were done equally well in any number of other places. What I now know is why some restaurants find their way onto recommended lists in travel articles, and others don't. Compare a handful of travel articles covering the same destination and it's not uncommon to find the same restaurants referenced. Often that's because they're the ones promoted by tourist boards. Restaurants not affiliated with their local tourist board don't get a look in, irrespective of how good they are. That doesn't mean recommended restaurants aren't good; they have to be to be 'pushed' to visiting travel writers. But neither does it mean they're necessarily the best.

Subsequently, where we end up eating is determined by checking recommendations on Tripadvisor and from trusted fellow travel writers; asking questions whilst in a destination; and stumbling across places which catch the eye. Sometimes we strike gastronomic gold, at others we end up somewhere fine but forgettable, and occasionally we land in a dud of a joint.

When visiting anywhere under our own steam we simply try restaurants that appeal the most. However, when working we look for a range of choices to suit people with differing preferences, i.e. traditional, fish & seafood, contemporary, snack food, and restaurants with decent vegetarian options.

Following weeks of Alentejo cuisine we're desperate for a break from hearty, meaty fare and so, on our first night, pop around the corner from our hotel to a cosy and stylish Italian restaurant, Presto Pizza Baixo, for a comfort hit in the shape of a brace of pizzas. It's not what visitors seeking a Portuguese culinary experience are looking for, but after spending a lot of time in rural Portugal this is nirvana for us. The work part of finding restaurants can start tomorrow.

Sampling gastronomic specialities is essential when putting together a destination guide, or it should be. Porto's earned its residents the nickname of '*Tripeiros*' (tripe-eaters). The story goes that in 1415 Prince Henry the Navigator visited Porto's shipyards to check the progress of ships being built for a campaign to capture Ceuta in Africa. He wasn't impressed with what he found. To prove the city's commitment, the officer in charge pledged the people of Porto would donate all their meat to the cause, and would keep only animal guts for themselves until success was achieved. They've been known as *Tripeiros* ever since, the city's signature dish being tripas à moda do Porto. Thankfully, I've already tried it during a previous visit, so don't have to notch this particular speciality up again. It wasn't unpleasant, just a bit 'blah'; no surprise for a dish created out of sacrifice.

Whereas I'm happy to give tripe a body swerve, I've no problem having a rematch with a *francesinha*, so when we pass a restaurant called Santa Francesinha on *Praça dos Poveiros* just as we're in the lunchtime zone, there's no way I'm walking by without worshipping. Their special *francesinha* is decent enough, even though they serve it the posh way; chips come in a bucket rather than in the sauce. The restaurant feels a wee bit like a fast food joint and lacks the authentic charm of

Cafe Aviz. Eating a hefty francesinha at lunch turns out to be a huge mistake. It lurks heavily in my stomach for the rest of the afternoon, no amount of hoofing it around Porto's streets can work it off. By the time there's even the slightest space in my stomach, the restaurants along the river are full; I couldn't handle a big meal anyway.

Thankfully, restaurants serving small dishes are common in Portugal. As well as places serving serving *petiscos* (Portuguese tapas), there is an increasing number of restaurants in Portuguese cities which offer tapas menus, presumably because tapas is more recognisable than petiscos. We find a bustling, tiny tapas joint, Casinha São João set into the old wall near the Dom Luis I Bridge, and manage to down a couple of dishes, including superb clams in white wine and coriander. We can tick off a suitable *petisco* place from our list.

Seeking restaurants offering an upmarket, contemporary dining experience, we decide on two we hope will give the taste-buds something to remember. The first is Flow in the arty downtown area. The décor is colonial meets urban cool and hits it off. It's elegant, modern and unstuffy. The food is creative but not avant-garde, and they immediately get on our good sides by serving a selection of flavoured butters with chunky breads (always a winner with us). Tuna ceviche, steak tartare, tuna taco with tempura rice, sea bass on an asparagus and champagne risotto all hit the mark. It's a winner.

Even more upmarket is Ode Porto Wine House, set just back from the riverside, which has rave reviews for tasting menus that feature 'the best local ingredients.' We opt for the cheapest (€48) which includes Portuguese sardine; red cabbage, celery, pea, and asparagus; veal broth with a low temperature egg; Iceland cod, Savoy cabbage and violet potato; duck with textures of beetroot; pre-dessert (usually code for sorbet of some sort); and *Abade de Priscos* pudding. The bread to get the juices flowing is stingy but that's okay, this is a marathon. The sardine tastes like a sardine but nothing more. The red cabbage dish is bland. The broth with an egg is broth with an egg. The cod and duck dishes save the menu before the dessert descends back into nothing special territory. Overall Ode leaves our taste-buds a tad underwhelmed.

In any guide there should be somewhere that ticks the 'romantic dining' box. Raiz, located in an atmospheric town house near the uptown end of *Rua das Flores*, consists of a series of bijou dining rooms on each floor of the old house which makes it feel intimate, as though there are only a handful of diners around you. We bag prime spot, a window table on one of the uppermost floors, with views of *Torre dos Clerigos*. The menu is a blend of contemporary Portuguese and international dishes - caramelized Chevre cheese with Port and macerated apple; skewered black pork with rosemary and laurel - so should suit a variety of tastes. The setting is fabulous, and the food is good. Tick.

The only culinary low point is at 31 Porto, just off *Avenida dos Aliados*. It earns rave reviews on Tripadvisor, yet the food we're served is clumsily put together - a Champagne sauce has the appearance of lumpy custard; the berries in another sauce have the consistency of jam; and an accompanying beef tomato has a black circle on its skin. Nothing tastes freshly made and the mix of flavours in both our dishes don't work, as though all the ingredients have had an argument and fallen out. This is one of those intances we're left scratching our heads at why there are glowing accounts on Tripadvisor. Needless to say, it won't make the Porto guide.

Although we generally prefer a long leisurely lunch to dinner, when working we usually grab something as we hoof it around the streets. Portugal's a great destination for people who enjoy grazing on savoury street food. These include *pataniscas* (salt cod patties), *pastéis de bacalhau* (salt cod fritters), *rissóis* (crescent-shaped, breaded bites filled with chicken, ham, shrimp), *empanadas* (pies), Scotch eggs (for some reason these are popular in Portugal), and the potentially confusing *lanche*, which is ham and cheese encased in a cross between bread and pastry. It's potentially confusing because the word for snack in Portugal is also *lanche*.

In this way, we add to our knowledge of the flavours of Porto's culinary scene.

Eating around the world in Mouraria

"You're late. I didn't know where you were."

"Sorry, it took us a lot longer to get here than we estimated."

"I didn't know where you were," Maria repeats, a mix of confusion and irritation in her voice.

Maria is responsible for managing the apartment where we're staying in Lisbon and lives in the same block. There's something about her (small frame, Elfin features, big eyes) that makes me think of a Beatrix Potter construct. She's not wearing an apron over a striped petticoat but if she were she'd be able to carry it off. The slight American lilt to her English (like many Portuguese, picked up from American TV series screened in their original language with Portuguese subtitles) adds to the feeling we're being told off by a character from a Pixar movie.

We'd arrived at Lisbon Oriente train station more or less as estimated, and then got lost in a vortex of confusion where our travel saviness totally deserted us and we lost confidence in making a decision about which train at which platform would take us on the final leg to Santa Apolonia, the closest station to the apartment in the hilly Mouraria *bairro* (neighbourhood). We shared the vortex with a Brazilian couple trying to 'eenie meenie' trains in the hope of reaching Sintra. Somehow we managed to lose an awful lot of time at Oriente.

Google directions showed it was a 1.5km trek from Santa Apolonia to the apartment, winding and climbing through both Alfama and Mouraria's maze of cobbled streets – a task in itself even when unencumbered by luggage. Thankfully we had a couple of diamond tips from Ken and Carole – the location of public elevators which by-passed some of Lisbon's steep streets with the minimum of effort. The first was in an anonymous building on *Rua dos Fanqueiros* where a poster featuring an image of basil leaves warned of unscrupulous dealers trying to pass off the herb as marijuana. Seriously? Who's going to mistake basil for weed? The second is tucked away at the back of a Pingo Doce supermarket, almost opposite where we emerge from the first. These were superb tips for ascending Lisbon's various levels without punishing thigh muscles, but not enough to help us to claw back sufficient time to keep Maria happy.

She shows us to the apartment – an exquisite affair with high ceilings, three bedrooms, one bathroom, a dining room kitchen, living room and a Lisbon apartment rarity; a small terrace with garden. Its décor is right up our street, a blend of contemporary and timeless traditional pieces with prints from the Gulbenkian Museum adding a classy artistic touch to lemon-coloured walls. We declare it the perfect base, dump our luggage and take to the streets in search of nourishment.

Mouraria is so called because it was the neighbourhood outside the city walls where Muslims were allowed to continue to live following the reconquest in the 12th century. Throughout its history it has been an area where different nationalities set up home and traded, and where numerous religions are practised. In the 1970s, emigrants from Portugal's African and Asian colonies settled in Mouraria, helping shape a personality that makes it quite different from other Lisbon neighbourhoods.

The first time we experienced Mouraria had been three years previously, to visit a prostitute's house in fact. The prostitute in question was Maria de Mouraria, Lisbon's first female *fadisto*. At that time the area was just beginning to get a nip and tuck in an effort to erase a seedy and dangerous reputation. It's a reputation which was unfounded, one which often gets attached to multi-cultural areas. Having lived and worked in inner city Manchester, I don't view multicultural areas as places to avoid, quite the opposite. I still remember the thrill of moving from an island where the only black person was called Jenny the Darkie (now it sounds shockingly offensive, but it was never meant in a derogatory way) to a place where there was a riot of colour and aromas on the shelves of ethnic supermarkets, each one filled with exotic products of the sort I'd never encountered before. I lapped up the diversity. It felt deliciously cosmopolitan to a young lad from a small Scottish island. In many ways it still does.

When we emerged from below ground at Martim Moniz

Metro station, the square of the same name was dimly lit and there were no other tourists around as we negotiated dark alleys to reach Maria de Mouraria's house on *Rua Capelão,* which had just re-opened as an intimate and authentic venue in which to listen to contemporary fado singers. It was a night full of superb traditional food, haunting music, and a fascinating chat with a modern fadista, Margarida Soeiro, who most definitely wasn't a prostitute. Mouraria felt like a magical place which was still below the radar of most visitors.

Three years down the road and Mouraria has changed dramatically. The likes of Airbnb has partially transformed it, there are now plenty of fellow tourists in streets which seem just a little bit brighter. I say partially because it's evident there's still a solid sense of community in Mouraria's labyrinth of streets and alleys. Lisboans (or Alfacinhas to give them their nickname – it means little lettuces) with glasses of *vinho* in hands mingle outside bars rather than inside them; dogs are tied to drainpipes whilst their owners pop into a tasca for a *petisco*. Tourists are in the minority, just, and the multicultural vibe which made it so attractive still dominates.

We stroll along narrow streets where, as well as Portuguese cantinhos, there are restaurants serving Cape Verdean, Goan, Nepalese, Mozambican, and Pakistani cuisine. Outside a small bar on the *Escadinhas de São Cristóvão*, location of the best mural in Lisbon, people lounge on stained, wide, cobbled steps listening to a band whilst sipping beer from plastic beakers. Every restaurant looks inviting and, at 9.30pm on a Thursday night in July, everywhere is full.

An aroma of baked bread and melted cheese draws us to a darkened doorway and a dimly lit room full of people tucking into pizzas – the Cantina Baldracca. We try our luck and are squeezed into the last available table. Within minutes there's a queue of people outside. The Cantina is tiny, dark, infectiously lively and our first proper taste of the life which makes Mouraria a seductive place to stay. The pizzas have thin bases and tasty toppings, the wine is served in chunky tumblers. My view is of a window with bars which looks onto an alley where black and white photos chronicle the lives of the people who live here. Simple, colourful, fun and friendly. In a way a reflection of the neighbourhood itself. It's our latest introduction to Mouraria's wildly diverse restaurants, each one providing a different dining experience with flavours linked to countries colonised by the Portuguese.

A few years ago I was criticised for writing about enjoying a burger on Tenerife. "When in Spain you should eat Spanish food," came the accusation. I countered with a "Do you only eat British food where you live in Britain?"

The menu at the Cantina Baldracca may have been Italian, but the people around us spoke Portuguese. Visitors seek out traditional eateries, that's what we do when we visit somewhere new, but on this occasion we're interested in places that reflect the residents of the neighbourhood.

We're drawn to *Largo dos Trigueros* by the Mozambican menu at Cantinho do Aziz. Once again we haven't reserved. Once again we get lucky and end up with the last available table squeezed into a recess in the cobbled alley. And once again the atmosphere is buzzing. We order *chamuças* (samosas), yam chips, crab curry (pliers as an accompaniment), spicy *frango* (chicken) with coconut rice. The samosas come with a sauce which is blow-your-head-off spicy. "That sauce is very hot," the waiter comments just a bit too late to save us, adding. "I'm not brave enough to try it." Seared throats are soothed with cooling Mozambican beers as we agree dining in Mouraria is a lot of fun.

Dragon Square (Martim Moniz) is a mix of outdoor art and kiosks serving world foods. On an easy-like-Sunday lunchtime we take time out from working to try El Cartel's Peruvian/ Mexican fusion, ordering *pausa*, *chili con carne* and a couple of beers. Then we spot they also serve *pisco sours*, a cocktail we'd become addicted to in Chile. These arrive in big, solid glasses, are seriously strong, and lead us down the road to a slurry Sunday afternoon.

Tentações de Goa is tucked away on a narrow backstreet just off Martim Moniz square. It's another wardrobe-sized Mouraria

restaurant with only a handful of tables. The food is simple
and authentically delicious Goan fare. Like many of the other
bijou restaurants we've eaten in, it's brimming with Mouraria's
vibrant and warm personality. The rice is so good Andy is
compelled to ask the waitress how they cook it. The secret is in
numerous rinses before cooking. For our money we get a curry
hit and tips for making better rice.

Tasca Kome is located in Baixa, in a side street on the fringes
of Mouraria. It's a Japanese restaurant with a *menu do dia* which
is a steal for a city centre restaurant - €15pp for miso soup, an
elegant plate of sashimi featuring six different fish, a purple
sweet potato dessert, and a glass of wine. Despite being a couple
of streets away from the main tourist drag of *Rua Augusta* most
of the customers are Lisbon office workers.

Although we're lapping up our gastro jaunt around Portugal's
former colonies and trading partners, we *are* still working.
Though we've learnt from years of living abroad that the likes
of eating sushi in downtown Lisbon is no different from tucking
into a madras in Rusholme's curry mile, people arriving in
Portugal for the first time keen to try Portuguese nosh might not
appreciate having recommendations that seem to have nothing to
do with Portuguese food. However, the streets of Mouraria are
home to plenty of very good Portuguese restaurants as well.

By the time our food arrives at Espumantaria do Petisco
we're both already a bit woozy thanks to the following
exchange.

"We make our own sparkling wine, would you like to try a
glass as an aperitif?"

"Oh go on then twist our arms up our backs." We're total
lightweights when it comes to sparkling wines.

Located above Pingo Doce supermarket in Mouraria,
Espumantaria is slightly more upmarket than many of
the cubbyhole restaurants we've eaten in so far, and has a
comfortably contemporary ambiance and menu. They specialise
in *petiscos*, including the likes of a walnut and savoury jam
combo; an okay ceviche, and an exceptional dish consisting of
scrambled eggs with *chouriço*. Like the Spanish, the Portuguese

like their scrambled egg concoctions. Dessert is a crumble (crumbles are also popular in Portugal) which comes with a glass of brandy; an addition which doesn't help alleviate our woozy disposition.

Our favourite, because it's so different, is Chapitô à Mesa, an arty cultural centre on a street leading to Castelo S. Jorge. The centre has a tapas terrace, live music bar, and a restaurant with dreamy sunset views across the Lisbon rooftops. The dining area is reached via a claustrophobically narrow, spiral staircase. Eat too much food and there's a danger of being trapped in the upstairs restaurant until waistlines reduce, which would present another worrying problem as the toilets are downstairs.

Chapitô à Mesa is a winning combination of eclectic surroundings, sparkling views, and food as creative as the decór - peach *gazpacho*; fresh figs in a light sauce; a trio of fish and a melt-in-the-mouth steak. Some staff are a bit on the snooty side, but the pros outnumber this con. Another pro is an artisan shop located in Chapitô's entrance which sells voodoo dolls featuring the faces of unpopular politicians from around the world. Donald Trump is a bestseller.

Whilst exploring Lisbon's foodie scene we take the opportunity to delve into an aspect of Portuguese dining which had surprised us when we encountered it in 490 Taberna STB during our first visit to Setúbal in March - canned gastronomy.

"What does this mean?" I show the waitress the section of the menu, under the heading *conservas*, which has confused me.

"It's canned food." She replies.

"You don't mean it's actually food from tins?" I'm sure there's been a lost in translation moment.

"Exactly, food from tins."

"You have a section on the menu just for food from tins?"

"Yes."

"Tinned food?"

"Yes."

"Seriously?"

"Yes, Portuguese conservas are very good, high quality."

And that's how we were introduced to Portuguese canned gastronomy which, as the waitress assured us, is a cut way above the tinned food we'd been used to elsewhere.

The tins can be mini works of art. In Portugal there's no need to pay to browse an art gallery, just pop into any shop which sells *conservas* and hours can be lost admiring the artwork on tin lids, often colourful depictions of social history. Tins can be witty, historic, abstract, and surreal. The Portuguese passion for preserving fish stretches back to the Iron Age when techniques for preserving fish in sea salt were first introduced to the Iberian Peninsula. These methods were handed down, and improved upon by the Phoenicians, Greeks and Carthaginians before the Romans took it to another level. There are many ruins of Roman fish preserving/garum producing factories found along Portugal's coastline; centres where fish paste was created and 'canned' in specially designed clay pots, ready for exporting to Italy, France, and even North Africa. At Troia, near Setúbal, are the remains of what was the biggest fish preserving centre in the Roman Empire.

Preserving fish in tins in more modern times started when the first commercial canneries in Portugal sprang up in 1853, with factories being opened in Setúbal, the Algarve and around Espinho in the North. All were, unsurprisingly, near areas with a thriving fishing industry, with Setúbal becoming became the main centre for sardine canneries; although canning also involved tuna as well as other fish. The beginning of the 20th century saw new technology, such as can-sealing machines, making the process quicker and more efficient, resulting in an explosion of canneries. Around the same time, the process for preservation of fish changed as well; the traditional practice of frying fish before canning being dumped in favour of boiling it in salt water and sealing it with some of the water it was cooked in, which helped canned fish retain flavour.

By the mid-nineties there were 152 canning factories in Portugal, producing around 34,000 tons each year. The industry declined in the late 80s and throughout the 90s, but in recent years there's been a renaissance. What was once viewed as a cheap source of fish and seafood has become a gourmet industry where quality pieces of fish (some claim Portuguese tinned sardines are tastier than fresh ones) are sealed inside gorgeous, retro-styled tins. As well as tasting surprisingly good (especially to someone who remembers tinned fish as being mushy and often bony) conservas are a healthy option. They are a natural product with no dyes or preservatives; tinned tuna and sardines are a good source of Omega 3; tinned seafood can be high in iron; and canned fish also tends to contain more calcium due to the preserving process. Some doctors in Portugal recommend regular consumption of tinned sardines as being good for the heart.

Even after an increase in demand for Portugal's gourmet canned fish and seafood, there are now only 20 factories in operation. In Setúbal the skeletons of former canneries still line the seafront.

In Lisbon there's been a mini explosion of special *conservas* shops, mostly aimed at visitors. It feels more authentic to pick up pretty little tins in independent supermarkets located up side streets, or anywhere that doesn't exist purely for a tourist market. As well as some restaurants having *conservas* sections on their menus, there are a couple which specialise exclusively in serving customers dishes created with the fish and seafood from tins. We haven't tried Sol e Pesca, featured in Anthony Bourdain's *No Reservations*, but we sample the canned goods at Can the Can on *Praça do Comércio* where arty tins of fish and old magazines fill shelves along one wall, and lampshades and urban chandeliers are made from cans and flat preserve tins. Even the *couvert* of bread and olives arrives served in tins, whereas main courses are presented on slates. We order a cold slate filled with various fish – tuna, anchovies, mackerel – followed by a main course of *polvo com migas Can the Can* which consists of an oven-baked octopus tentacle with spinach and tomato *migas*, and cornbread. It's a tasty enough selection, but ultimately there's only so far you can go gastronomically with canned fish and there's an element of it being a gimmick dinner, especially given the quite hefty price tag for what it is

(€17 for the octopus). In the end, restaurants serving only canned fish and seafood are a culinary curio I was keen to try. But next time I get a yen for ordering tinned fish in a restaurant I'll stick to picking from the *conservas* section of a restaurant with a more rounded menu.

Following our 'late' arrival at the apartment, our relationship with Maria takes a further downturn when the hot water tap in the kitchen sink refuses to provide us with hot water. I pick the short straw and venture downstairs to tell Mrs Tiggy Winkle, sorry I mean Maria, the bad news. I knock the door. There's no answer save for a dog's bark. But I know she's in there, I hear movement. I knock again. Eventually the door opens and Maria's face appears around it. Actually, Maria's white face mask appears around it.

"The hot water in the kitchen isn't working," I blurt out, momentarily taken aback at seeing this ghostly Maria.

"I'm still cleaning my face," - a face which has taken on the same blend of confusion and irritation it had when we rolled up late.

"Well, I *did* wait till ten o'clock before coming to tell you there was a problem," I place an emphasis on the 'ten o'clock' but it flutters past, way above her head.

"It was working yesterday," she says, a bit too accusingly for my liking.

"Well, it definitely isn't working now."

"Hmm," her little brow furrows. "Try this. There's a lever to the left which if you turn should make the water hot."

"Where exactly?" I can't remember seeing any levers near the tap.

"Right beside the spout," she looks at me as though I'm a bit dim. "There's one on the right which makes the water cold when you turn it."

The penny drops with a loud clang, she's telling me how to turn on the hot and cold taps.

"Yeah, I'm familiar with that design, it's quite common," but sarcasm is a waste of breath. I'm desperately trying not to become irritated, insulted that Maria thinks I don't even know how to turn on a tap. "It's not that, something is broken."

"Are you sure?" She obviously doesn't believe I do know how to turn on a tap. "I'll come and have a look when I clean my face."

Half an hour later and my patience is in tatters after an accusing question.

"Are you sure you haven't touched anything? Pressed any buttons on the boiler?"

"The only thing we've touched is the tap."

"Well, it was working yesterday," she just knows we've broken the boiler, even though the hot water in the bathroom next door to the kitchen is working fine. "I'll ask my husband to have a look at it when he gets home from work."

Husband doesn't appear over the next two days and I have to remind Maria about our lack of hot water. It hasn't been an issue as we've eaten out every night, only a slight inconvenience when it comes to washing wine glasses/coffee cups.

When hubby does finally appear he turns on the tap, declares the pressure to be too low (something we'd suggested to Maria) then unscrews something on the spout. It's a filter and it's clogged up with tiny stones. He scrapes it, tapping the stones into the bin, screws it back into place, turns on the tap, and the boiler flares up. Hot water gushes out of the spout. It took him less than a minute. I look at Maria, my turn to be the accuser. Our relationship has never thawed during our stay.

"Didn't that occur to you?"

"Well, it's never happened before," she shrugs.

As her husband was able to diagnose and fix the problem in under 60 seconds I'm not convinced about that.

Us being without hot water in the kitchen could have been avoided if only she'd told her husband when we first told her. However, learning Portuguese taps have filters which can get clogged up is a useful piece of information to have under our belts.

LITTLE THINGS ABOUT SHOW OFF LISBON

Our Lisbon mission is to update and amend walking guides for the city. Having a blueprint which already includes most of the major sights and many lesser known ones makes our job far easier, and also means we can spend more time seeking out the sort of features we like to include in the travel guides we write; the little things and quirks that can often be overlooked. We're also armed with insider tips courtesy of Ken and Carole, who know the city intimately. As we pound *bairro* after *bairro* we reacquaint ourselves with old favourites but also build up new experiences. Often it can be some of the less obvious sights which provoke the strongest emotions, leaving long-lasting impressions.

The Jewish Memorial on *Largo de São Domingos* is a sobering reminder of what intolerance and fanaticism can lead to, in this case the massacre of thousands of Jewish citizens. On Sunday 19 April 1506 a crowd of worshippers were praying for an end to drought and plague devastating the city when one of the congregation claimed he saw the face of Christ in the altar. A *converso* (Jews who had been forced to convert to Roman Catholicism) said it had just been a reflection of a candle. Angered by this, some of the congregation dragged the *converso* outside where he was torn apart by the mob and his body burned in Rossio Square. Now looking for a scapegoat for the drought and pestilence, the mob turned their attention to all the city's *conversos* and, over the next three days, massacred more than 2000 men, women and children.

Near the memorial is a burnt church, the *Igreja de São Domingos*, where the acrid aroma of the fire which gutted it in 1959 still seems to linger. When in the centre of Lisbon we always visit both. To counter the sombreness of these two we then pop into Eduardino's, a hole in the wall *ginjinha* bar, to knock back a sweet and sticky shot of Lisbon's famous cherry liqueur.

We would never have found Casa do Alentejo on *Rua*

99

Portas de Santo Antão if Ken and Carole hadn't told us about it. It is ostensibly a palace fronted by a humble, easy-to-miss doorway which, from the street, gives no clue to the building's palatial interior and Moorish courtyard. Stepping inside is akin to falling down the rabbit hole. There's a tavern on the ground floor whilst the first floor boasts a couple of grand restaurants. It *did* start life as a palace, evolving into a gaming club and a venue for lavish parties in the Roaring Twenties. Now it feels far more demure, in fact there's an air of opulent third age nursing home in some parts, but that may be thanks to the presence of a sextet of snoozing septuagenarians who apparently consider the restaurant's vestibule area as their makeshift bedroom and who shush us as we enthuse (too loudly) about the restaurant's frescoes.

An industrial Aladdin's Cave for foodies, the Time Out Market at *Cais do Sodré*, blew us away the first time we set foot inside it. At 4pm on a Friday in 2014 there were only a handful of people inside the cavernous market. We were able to browse the tasty collection of food kiosks (showcases for up-and-coming chefs) at will, struggling to decide between *francesinhas* and nostril-seducing fried fish tarted up in contemporary fashion, before having our choice of which pale pine stool to perch our bottoms on. Three years later and there's no such luxury from lunchtime onward when it's too frantic to enjoy. However, at 10.30am it's still a relatively calm place to sip a coffee, nibble at a pastry and get nostalgic for the time when we could choose what we wanted to eat and where we wanted to sit without the need to elbow our way through crowds and participate in a mass game of musical chairs. Despite the crowds, it's still a place worth visiting.

On our first visit to Lisbon we were given the heads-up about the sunset scene at *Miradouro de Santa Catarina* by an architect whose apartment we rented in Bairro Alto. The apartment was on the same street as the Bica funicular. It's a fabulously atmospheric location which bursts into life around midnight at weekends; maybe not the best choice of accommodation for anyone who likes to hit the pillow early. The centrepiece of the *miradouro* is a grotesque statue of Adamastor, a mythical creature created by Portugal's most famous poet, Luís de Camões. The statue and *miradouro* is referenced a few times in José Saramago's *The Year of the Death of Ricardo Reis*, but the scene there now bears little resemblance to the one Saramago describes. Neo-hippy locals and visitors in the know congregate to watch sunset to a soundtrack courtesy of whichever musicians turn up for the nightly jam session. As the sky fills with pastel bands and then darkens, both the *Ponte 25 de Abril* suspension bridge and Lisbon's version of Christ the Redeemer, *Cristo Rei*, on the other side of the Tagus, light up and add to the magic of the vista. It is, however, a grungy affair so not everybody's cup of tea, or glass of Superbock (the preferred sunset tipple at Santa Catarina).

Visiting the Jeronimos Monastery, Belém Tower, Discoveries Monument, and eating *pastéis de Belém* from the original *confeitaria* (bakery) next to the Monastery are all Belém musts, even if everyone who visits Lisbon does them. Having ticked off all these on a previous visit, we find Belém's other attractions to be refreshingly crowd-free and equally interesting. The sleek, starship curves of the MAAT (Museum of Art, Architecture and Technology) make for an ultra modern viewing platform whilst the *Museu Coleção Berardo* offers a cool escape from the September sun. Exhibits in the contemporary art museum are fun, funky and occasionally interactive. Walking back to Lisbon along the riverside cycle path/walkway gives a greater insight into the area. However, we walked to Belém that way so choose to return along *Rua das Janelas Verdes*, a street running parallel to the river, where there are elegant town houses, pretty quiet *praças*, and no other tourists. This area is home to the quite bizarre and slightly disturbing Marionette Museum. Inside is the only puppet I've seen which has strings to operate each of its floppy breasts.

Embaixada opposite *Praça Príncipe Real* is an antidote to the homogeneous plague of interchangeable shops which blight many of Europe's main shopping centres. Located in the *Palacete Ribeiro da Cunha*, a 19th century Arabian palace, it offers an old school shopping experience. The interior is interesting enough in its own right for a wander; a maze of nooks and crannies, and shops selling designer fashion and furniture as well as Portuguese crafts. Best of all is the Gin Lovers Bar in the interior courtyard, a classy place to get sloshed on G&Ts. It's emblematic of the Príncipe Real neighbourhood which just about remains off-the-beaten-track and is increasingly one big shrine to trendy shops, cool bars and quirky restaurants (one has an octopus dominating the ceiling). We pop into Embaixada for a 'browse' and leave with a relatively expensive, but unique item of clothing.

For evidence which illustrates how we humans are fundamentally herd animals, simply observe the flow of tourist traffic in any big town or city. The majority of people follow the same few routes, no different from wildebeest migrating across the Serengeti Plains. This pattern causes congestion on some streets, but it also means many others remain crowd-free. Even on the busiest streets there are set 'routes', so that some places become tourist hot spots yet others remain largely ignored. Bustling *Rua Garrett* has two labyrinthine bookshops. Livraria Bertrand do Chiado, the oldest bookshop in the world, has been providing fuel for inquisitive minds for nearly three centuries. It is made up of various rooms, some of which now pay homage to scribes from Portugal's literary past. The Cantinho do Aquilino is where the writer Aquilino Ribeiro once read, wrote and pondered deeply. In the bookshop's cafe is a large mural featuring Fernando Pessoa. The bookshop's popularity hasn't reached that of Porto's Lello & Irmão (not as instagrammable) but there are far more folk browsing its historic shelves than there were a couple of years ago. Livraria Sá da Costa on the opposite side of the street is also made up of a series of interconnecting rooms that seem to go on and on and on into Tardis-like depths. It's a museum of a place where books with nicotine pages are piled high on ancient shelves, and the air is filled with the musty aroma of a million books having been flicked through. They also stock excellent old prints... and yet the crowds outside the door pass by as though it is cloaked by an invisible force field.

One Lisbon street we would never eat in is *Rua Augusta*. Generally speaking, restaurants there exist to feed a tourist market. A random check of a handful of them on Tripadvisor reveals the same results; there are five times as many English language reviews as there are Portuguese reviews. With restaurants just a couple of streets away there's parity between English and Portuguese reviews. However, dining preferences aside, *Rua Augusta* is one of Lisbon's showcase streets and deserves to be strolled, which is what most visitors do. What they don't all do is climb the grand Rua Augusta Arch which separates the street from *Praça do Comércio*. At 10am we have 360 degree views across Lisbon's skyline and the Tagus all to ourselves. We'd linger longer, but even at this relatively early time in August it's too hot to stick around in full sunshine for too long.

Trying to create an easy-to-follow walking route through Alfama, one of the oldest *bairros* in the city, proves a nightmare of a challenge. It is a warren of narrow old streets where interconnecting alleys and covered arched entrances lead off in all directions, some to dead ends. The characters of *Watership Down* would struggle to make any sense out of it. And it's an absolute joy to get lost in. Outside crooked houses, women in housecoats sell *ginjinha* shots at 1€ a glass. Signs beside darkened doorways on narrow alleys identify which are *fado* houses. And there is street art everywhere, from colourful tiles depicting life in the past in the *barrio* to equally evocative examples of contemporary graffiti, breathing new and colourful life onto the peeling surfaces of weary facades. Our favourites are those which feature the prostitute and the count - *fadista* Maria Severa and her guitar strumming lover, Count Vimioso. The scene they depict seems a perfect metaphor for Lisbon itself; a working woman from the lowly back streets confident and comfortable in the company of an aristocrat. Lisbon - a city of princes and paupers.

Finally, a tale which illustrates why you can't always trust what locals tell you. Whilst being shown around the *Castello*

S. Jorge a couple of years ago by Susana Correia, the Press & Communications Manager, we ended in an exhibition hall where sepia photographs showed what the castle looked like just over sixty years ago, before and after the renovation that revealed its true (current) face. Then, it looked more like Colditz, an austere prison with a more modern military façade. When the outer walls of these buildings were torn down between 1938 and 1940, the original fortress was exposed. The exhibition of photos was supposed to be a temporary one. However, Susana asked the exhibitors if they would leave some photos to counter the tales some old people in the city were telling anyone who'd listen.

"They tell people this is a new castle," Susana told us, laughing. "They remember the one that existed before this and know for a fact it looked different. They don't believe the original Castello S. Jorge was concealed behind the walls. I wanted to keep the photos just to prove to them the truth when they wander in muttering 'this is all new you know' ."

QUIETLY STUDIOUS COIMBRA

The *city of students* is the last port of call on our Portugal
cities tour. In August, both Lisbon and Porto are packed to
capacity. Stepping from the train onto the platform at Coimbra
train station feels somewhat like loosening a tight corset (I
imagine) and being able to breathe. As Portugal's popularity
with travellers has risen, visitors *have* swollen the numbers
strolling the streets of Coimbra, but not to the extent it feels
claustrophobic; there are few wandering the narrow alleys
around our accommodation in the folds of the lower town. We
chose it, a split-level affair in the Vintage Lofts Apartments,
because of its retro decor which, despite having a 1970s vibe,
looked all shiny and new on the website. In reality, it's a wee
bit tired; some of the furniture starting to look like much-
used, original pieces. Plus, the toilet doesn't flush. But it's still
fun, funky, and comfortable enough, and a quick phone call
has a member of staff from the nearby Oslo Hotel (the parent
accommodation), armed with wrench and bucket, arriving
pronto. The temperamental loo is soon ready to receive guests
again which, following a longish train journey from Lisbon
where neither of us made use of the 'facilities', we're literally
relieved about.

More big town than sprawling metropolis, Coimbra is an
easy city to explore on foot. Portugal's former capital (1131-
1255) has something of the appearance of a mini-me version
of Porto. The grandest buildings sit atop a hill whilst more
humble abodes tumble, higgledy-piggledy fashion, down to the
Mondego River. Most visitors are drawn to the grand edifices on
Coimbra's crown, the historic buildings which make up Coimbra
University; a UNESCO World Heritage Site. It's been a place
of learning since 13th century, making it the oldest university in
Portugal; something which no doubt led to the 'Coimbra studies'
tag.

The streets around our apartment represent the workaday side
of the city, and are all the more interesting for it. A quick wander

through a confusing artery of alleys reveals small, unfussy restaurants specialising in *leitão* (suckling piglet), haberdashers, off licences, tiny cobbled squares we may never find again, ironmongers, and bakeries with windows full of monster meringues called *suspiros*. These aren't streets which draw many visitors, but they're full of character nonetheless. We often find it can be in back streets like these you gain the greatest insights into what makes a specific location tick.

We only have a couple of days in Coimbra; sufficient time to add more meat to an existing Inntravel city guide. It would be far more difficult to do this without prior knowledge of the destination in large cities like Lisbon or Porto, but we can easily cover Coimbra's old streets more than once, collecting snippets and curios as we go. Favourites are the unusual cupula and arches of the Manga Cloister whose design King João III is said to have sketched on the sleeve (*manga*) of his doublet; the city's market where women in housecoats carry their wares on their heads and stand gossiping beside stalls packed with tubs of olives and *tremoços* (yellow lupin beans - an acquired taste); a glass elevator and a funicular which, for €1.60, transports us from market to university level without the need for scaling steep streets; an elegant cafe where we can enjoy a coffee and views of the Mondego River from a porticoed terrace; and a pastel-coloured, bouncy footbridge named after Pedro e Inês, the city's version of star cross'd lovers whose relationship ends in tragedy.

Coimbra University itself turns out to be a fun place to explore. The collection of Baroque, Renaissance, and Neoclassical buildings house, among other things, an interactive Science Museum and Chemistry Laboratory, where Andy does a Jeff Goldblum and turns into a fly; a Zoological Museum with all manner of other-worldly creatures stuffed into glass bell jars; and the wonderful *Biblioteca Joanine*, Portugal's most famous library where, after dark, an army of bats prevent wood-eating insects from chomping their way through ancient texts. The Joanine is located on the wide square of *Paço das Escolas* whose open southern side looks across the city's orange-tiled rooftops to the river and countryside beyond. Normally, visitors would be wallowing in the panoramic views. Today, everyone's gaze is drawn to dark, bulbous plumes of smoke not far from the city; two forest fires are raging nearby. It's a sobering sight, and one which visibly shocks some people who may not be aware that much of Portugal is burning.

Although Coimbra isn't suffering from the overtourism problems of Lisbon or Porto, a chalked message on steps close to *Paço das Escolas* proclaims "*Dear tourists it's like I live in a zoo.*" I have sympathy for people who live in locations where the balance between resident and visitor has been switched to an extent there's danger of them losing their personality as age-old traditions are eroded. I'm not convinced Coimbra is one of them. As 10% of the university's students are, like us, foreigners, this proclamation smacks more of privileged hypocrisy than a justifiable gripe. I grew up in a place which once burst into life when summer holidaymakers from Glasgow arrived, but which suffered badly when they moved on to pastures new - first Blackpool, and then Spain.

After dark there are even fewer visitors on Coimbra's streets, yet there are no tables free in either of our two first-choice restaurants. That's mainly because Coimbra doesn't have an excess of restaurants, not compared to Porto and Lisbon. Having to opt for third choice Sete, a tiny restaurant beside the *Igreja de Santa Crus*, turns out to be fortuitous. The food - salmon with squid ink couscous and suckling pig pie with pineapple chutney - is delicious. During the day, winding *Rua Quebra Costas* is one of the main tourist drags connecting the lower town with the university. After dark, it transforms into a peach of a place to chill out with a glass of wine; chairs and tables appearing on flatter, cobbled areas between stairs as wine bars and *fado* houses open. We grab a table outside of Quebra and are serenaded by the jazzy sounds from inside the bar as well as melancholic *fado* drifting up from lower down the narrow street. Coimbra is known for *fado*, but not quite in the same way as Lisbon. In the capital, *fado* evolved in taverns frequented by sailors and prostitutes, where both men and women sang haunting songs of longing and loss - *saudade*. Traditionally, *Coimbra Fado* is for men only; university students dressed in cassocks and capes strumming guitars and singing soulful songs of love or ballads with a political slant. As it's August there are no marauding groups of singing students, but there is a folklore concert in front of *Igreja de Santa Crus*. We listen to a group of musicians in traditional costume for a while before navigating the maze of alleys back to our retro apartment. Turning one corner, we emerge in a small, enclosed square which is virtually in darkness. The only flickering light is cast by a sombre political documentary being screened onto a crumbling gable end wall. In the square, human-shaped shadows sit silently on rows of wooden chairs facing the screen, the only movement being when one raises a glass of wine to lips. It could be a scene from a European art house movie. I recognise the square from our earlier meanderings, it's *Largo do Poço*. It stuck in my mind because we bought a bottle of wine from a wine shop there. The owner had told us he let artists stay in the apartment above his shop for a minimal amount (there were paintings strewn about and we'd asked about them). Presumably one of his artist tenants is responsible for the open air, art house movie screening. It's one evocative little scene of life in the studious city which captures the essence of Coimbra in a nutshell.

THINGS START TO GO WRONG

After the first few weeks our daily routine in Galegos settles into a, well, routine. The house dictates some of the pattern. Before eating breakfast we have to sweep the breakfast terrace – a corner where a semicircular stone bench curves around an equally circular table. It's partly shaded by a vine arbour; not enough to keep out the midday sun but perfect for a dreamily dappled *pequeno almoço*. Each morning we sweep clean and each night insects and flora re-decorate the stone paving and benches.

Preparing the area for breakfast takes a while as the view across the golden valley to Marvão distracts. In truth, it's so eye-catching it distracts every time we step outside the house. Breakfast in this setting takes longer than we're used to for a number of reasons. First, the melodic clang of goat bells announces the local flock is heading off to wherever it's going to be grazing that day. The clanging and bleating is invariably accompanied by assertive commands from the permanently shirtless goatherd – "a rum character" according to Ken, although we never discover what makes him rum other than a hinted at shady past – as he tries to control an anarchic herd which has a tendency to attempt to devour the gardens of any house they pass en route. Across the road from Crença is a little 'but and ben' type cottage (never occupied) whose garden is a favourite target. We can't resist watching whatever mischief the goats get up to, whilst also ensuring it's not Crença's plants they're munching enthusiastically. The same scene is played out twice daily as the goats head out in the morning and then return home again at night. The shouts and clanging become comforting markers, a rural version of a factory hooter telling us when the working day starts and ends.

Then there are the birds. Each morning we sit quietly, listening to a Disney-film chorus of chirps, tweets, and squawks. Azure-winged magpies tend to be the loudest, the punk band of this particular bird music festival. Most hypnotic are the bee-eaters, singing their way across the sky, darting and swooping, at times almost coming to a stop on their upward trajectories, wings spread out wide giving them the appearance of feathered crucifixes, the sun adding even more zest to their already vibrant colours. Most exquisite of all are the golden orioles. They rarely venture close enough for me to get a decent photo, and when they do they zip past so fast that all I manage is a bright yellow and black blur. At the same time each day the flock of vultures which live in the cliffs at the border sweep across the sky, moving westward in ominously silent circles. Watching this natural ballet play out on a daily basis swallows time.

Breakfast is followed by swimming pool maintenance, which is a far more complicated business than we could ever have anticipated. The idea of having a swimming pool may seem like everyone's dream but, boy, does it require mollycoddling. In this case it does anyway. First job is to remove/rescue whatever insects/creatures/leaves have fallen into the water during the night. There is always a motley crew – a range of insects to have an etymologist in raptures; from palm weevils to sodden praying mantis. There's often a dead gecko or mouse. On one occasion a drenched, but still alive, mouse flew out of the vacuum pipe when I unscrewed it. The bigger leaves in the pool can act like life-rafts; one was full of ants, looking like minute refugees trying to escape some horror – probably Sheba the mutant pool spider. The pump can't be trusted to work automatically, so has to be manually turned on twice a day and left to gurgle away for a couple of hours. This involves sticking a hand into Sheba's lair, a small concrete pit, at least four times daily. There might also be a mouse in the pool 'pit' in the morning, but I'm less bothered about it than a spider which is able to 'Dyson' over-sized insects. The pool maintenance is so complicated I've had to draw several diagrams to remind me of the various positions levers have to be depending on what programme is required – cleaning, vacuuming, backwashing. The lever labels are in Portuguese, but it wouldn't help even if they were in English; ralo skimmer means absolutely nothing to me. Additionally, to keep it looking all invitingly crystal clear it has to be fed with a cocktail of chemicals – chlorine tablets, pH increaser/decreaser etc. Add in a thorough hoovering of the tiles every couple of days or so and it's virtually a full-time job to keep the pool clean and blue.

Once all this is done, we can start work. In the mornings our 'office' is the shaded outside terrace where we also eat lunch and dinner, but as the day heats up the air temperature becomes too oppressively hot to work and we retreat inside to a darkened room we use as an office. An essential tip from K&C for dealing with the searing Alentejo summer is to have all windows and curtains shut during the day, keeping the heat out and the cool air in, only opening them when the sun isn't blasting against them. We break for an al fresco lunch around 13:30 and then type away again until around 5pm. Then we grab a book and a beer, strip off (the pool area is completely shielded by a natural curtain of trees and bushes, so no threat of frightening the hell out of some unsuspecting passer-by, which would be a rarity anyway, or the goatherd), get prone poolside and treat sickly white bits of flesh to some vitamin D. With frequent forays into the cool pool it is a deliciously decadent way to end the working day.

Apart from frequent forays out and about this becomes the pattern. Given the picture postcard, away-from-it-all, location, you'd think it would be the perfect setting for penning creative pieces. The odd thing is, when I finally sit at my laptop each day I feel totally uninspired and have to grind away at producing travel articles. It's perplexing – all the ingredients seem to be right, but something just isn't clicking when it comes to the writing process. Maybe the fact we're still in transition has something to do with it, maybe the imaginative parts of my brain have been shunted aside by diagrams labelled ralo, skimmer, and pump. Despite an inability to write creatively it's a nirvana-esque existence; a cliché of a travel writing existence even. This paradisaical existence lasts for around four weeks. Then the pool decides it doesn't want to be crystal clear any more, it prefers to be swamp green. No amount of chemicals, hoovering, pumping persuades it to revert to its previously pristine form. We ask for advice from pool experts K&C, they give it, we try it, the pool remains swampy. Not having a perfect pool might sound like a first world problem. But, as well as it not being quite so inviting-looking for slipping into at the end of the day, there's the feeling that despite, as far as we know, following instructions to the letter, the transformation of the pool into something the *Creature from the Black Lagoon* might feel at home in is our fault. We're failing in our mission to look after the property. Things go from bad to worse when we wake to find that half of the water in the pool has evaporated overnight. It has sprung a leak. Again, we feel we're somehow responsible – maybe hoovering with too much gusto. The pool has to be emptied, and is left that way until the local pool expert can fit in time to make repairs.

Whereas the pool being out of bounds is an inconvenience, a luxury item whipped away just as we were getting used to the high-living lifestyle, what happens next completely changes how we feel about living at Crença. The house has three bathrooms. The one upstairs is virtually en suite, and we use it most. Directly below it is a toilet, and at the rear of the kitchen is another large bathroom with a bath/shower. We don't use the last at all, except as pantry/storeroom, as it's dark, and looks like it could be the lair of giant (unseen) spiders. One night whilst Andy is happy lathering away in the shower, the downstairs toilet floods... badly. Head-to-the-lifeboats badly. After an hour of frantic mopping we investigate. The walls are dry, but the water is soapy. It's clearly shower water from above. But as the walls aren't wet, how is that possible?

The following night one of us stands watch as the other showers. No flood. The next night and the one after that is exactly the same and we gain confidence at being able to shower without having to man the pumps downstairs. We decide it was a glitch and there's no need to tell K&C. Complacency sets in until, a few days later, it happens again. We quickly figure out the connection. Both times are when Andy is washing her hair which means a longer time spent in the shower. We deduce there's some problem with water draining away as it seems to be coming upwards; from below the toilet in fact. Our laypersons' diagnosis is there's a cracked pipe below the loo. For a few days we implement a routine where we keep showers short and the person who isn't showering guards the downstairs loo with mop and bucket at the ready. Some days it floods, some days it doesn't. I'm no plumbing expert but in my experience, when things start to go wrong they don't magically repair themselves. We confess to K&C the house has another problem.

Despite us insisting the problem doesn't seem to have anything to do with the toilet's plumbing (the absence of anything disgusting in the floodwater convinces us of that), Ken's first course of action is to open up the cesspit, which unfortunately happens to be beside both the breakfast and lunch/dinner terrace. Ken wants to leave the cesspit open to see if it has any impact on the flooding. It doesn't. But we spend a weekend with the pit open, not enjoying country air which isn't quite so perfumed and pure any more. Neither are our dining spots as appealing as they were. The next course of action by K&C is to seal the base of the toilet where the water rises from. In the very short-term this puts the shower out of bounds until the sealant sets. In theory this isn't a problem, there's still the kitchen bathroom. That evening I turn on the kitchen bathroom shower and get ready to step into the rolltop bath, but my feet are drenched before a foot gets anywhere near the tub. There's water pouring out from beneath the bath; there is not a pipe connected to it. It's not plumbed in; a bit of an oversight. At this point Andy coins a term to describe all the little (and big) things which have blighted our stay in paradise, things that could have been avoided; B-I-Y (botch it yourself). It's a phrase we find we use on a regular basis in Portugal when we discover people don't tend to bring in specialists to solve problems, they 'fix' domestic issues (electrical, plumbing etc.) themselves, or bring in a neighbour or two to help. Thankfully the pool has been fixed, so we are at least able to rinse off our hot, sweaty bodies in clean but chlorinated water. Combined with the pool problems and a few other little niggles, one thing has become clear; Crença is telling us we've outstayed our welcome.

AUTUMN

*There are fruit trees all over the farm – from an orchard
with lemons, oranges, and tangerines to pomegranate,
plum, and loquat trees. The citrus orchard we've
discovered, the location of the other fruit trees remains a
mystery. We know they exist because baskets filled with
various fruits picked on the farm turn up on our doorstep
on a regular basis.*

AN INTRODUCTION TO THE MINHO

With September comes another mission for Inntravel; a new itinerant walking holiday in Portugal's far north, the verdant and very traditional Minho region. In reality, the Minho hasn't technically existed since 1976, but everybody still refers to the twenty-three Portuguese municipalities which hug the border with Galicia, as well as those which sweep south to Guimarães, as being the Minho. This is old Portugal; a land of noble families and ancient traditions which stretch back to the age when great Portuguese explorers set off on their voyages of discoveries, some sailing from Viana do Castelo on Minho's coast. It has a few things in common with the Spain that exists across the border; some words for example. The word for cheese in Castilian is *queso*. Cheese in Portuguese is *queijo*. Cheese in Galician is *queixo*, sounding closer to its neighbour's version than the Castilian pronunciation. In some ways Northern Spain and Minho feel more part of the same entity than Northern Spain and much of rest of Spain which spreads south to the Mediterranean.

"That's not the real Spain," I was told in Oviedo a few years ago by an Asturian who waved a hand dismissively toward the lands on the other side of the Picos de Europa. "This is the true Spain. We were never conquered by the Moors. We don't have siestas, we work hard, and we're punctual."

As the number of niggles at Crença snowball into a critical mass which threatens to consume us, we're especially happy at the opportunity to take time out in another part of Portugal, especially another region we know nothing at all about. We've been aware of the Minho mission for some time, since before we set sail for Portugal. New Slow Travel holidays are months if not years in the planning, involving countless Skype meetings and many hours of desk-based research. Using a mix of online tools and conventional maps we know, up to a point, which potential hiking routes we have to walk and record to connect the dots (i.e. various hotels customers will be staying at); the restaurants

115

and local dishes we fancy sampling; and the quirks/points of interest that pique our interest, and which will add extra value to the guide we produce when the fieldwork is done and dusted. All of those mean we set off on journeys with a comprehensive blueprint. Of course, the best laid plans of mice and all that means what happens on the ground never ever pans out exactly as planned. Life would be boring if it did.

It takes around five hours to drive the 440km from Galegos to our starting point in Durrães. Driving through forests which have been devastated by wild fire around Pedrógão Grande, south east of Coimbra, is sobering and shocking. We've witnessed the after-effects of forest fires before, on La Gomera, Tenerife, and La Palma. But not on this scale. The countryside for tens of kilometres has been ravaged by fire, the air is acrid with the smell of a smouldering black and copper world. It is post-apocalypse scenery, and it's frightening to drive through, especially on a hot summer's day when the temperature remains stubbornly in the thirties and there are still small fires burning all around. For more than thirty minutes we barely speak, partly because there's a sense that to make any sound would be to risk incurring the wrath of the fire gods, but also because the horrific scenes shock us into silence.

In early September, the southern Portuguese countryside is dry and thirsty-looking even without the added impact of wildfires, so the contrast as we travel north and into Minho, where the landscape becomes more verdant, is even more startling. Proclaimed 'the garden of Portugal' by the 19th century writer José Augusto Vieira, Minho is a fertile world of forests, farmlands, and traditional hamlets overlooked by proud manor houses. Our first base, the 16th century Quinta de Malta sits above the Durrães Valley, with views across the impressive Ponte Seca viaduct. Its driveway sets the scene for the stately character of the type of accommodation we'll be staying at on this trip – a long, cobbled road shaded by a vine-covered arbour. On either side of the road, thickets of pale blue hydrangeas allow taster glimpses of a secret garden where wrought iron benches beside dense camellia hedges look out over a rectangular lily pond framed by moss-covered stones. It's a cool spot for escaping from the heat with a meaty novel, something other guests might do. We, on the other hand, have to dump our cases and take to the trail immediately after a quick introductory chat with Catarina 'Kate' who is a font of local knowledge, and basically does everything to keep the *quinta* running smoothly on behalf of its owners.

We hope our first walking route will give us an insight into the personality of the area. It's essential when writing a guide for any location to try to understand what makes it tick; what ingredients make it different from the next place. Sometimes a location reveals itself to us quickly, at other times it can take a few days of exploration before the jigsaw pieces all slot into place. With Durrães it's the former. Even a brief detour into the village's supermarket for snacks provides an insight into life in the area. It's a decent-sized, modern supermarket rather than a quaint, small-town affair, but it appears to have only one member of staff. She has to serve a customer at the meat and cheese counter at the rear of the supermarket before walking the length of the aisles to attend to me at the tills. This is a sleepy town with few shops, but it does have a chocolate factory which is also home to a small confectionery museum.

Our route takes us over a sturdy, stone bridge just above water level, looking more weir than bridge, across a pool in an enchanted glade, and then along cobbled paths lined by stalks of corn, and vines draped across tall trellises; an ingenious way of utilising the land. Nurturing vines on trellises leaves the ground below free for growing a second crop. It's intelligent farming as well as being aesthetically pleasing. We weave in and out of the forest, passing through a hamlet consisting of a handful of agricultural cottages and an old church, before we stop for a rest at the *Ponte das Tabuas*, a bridge dating from 1135; although, the ancient stones we perch our bums on are from the 16th century. At this point our route crosses the Portuguese Way, the *Caminho de Santiago* leading to Santiago de Compostela in Galicia. Here we meet our first pilgrims, who wave a cheery "*bom caminho*" as they stride past. From the old bridge we return toward Durrães, following confusing paths through the forest, criss-crossing streams via stone slab bridges laid by the Romans, before we're dwarfed by the towering arches of Ponte Seca viaduct near the outskirts of the village. The walk is finished off with a couple of icy beers overlooking the valley from the wide terrace at the Quinta de Malta.

Dinner is served in the *quinta's* dining/living room; a large hall with a grand fireplace around which are plush, antique leather sofas. The dining table is relatively small given the size of the room and is set for only four people – us and a Portuguese couple who, we learn, aren't guests. They're villagers who have been roped in to keep us company; such is the hospitality shown to guests. The woman is heavily pregnant and speaks some English, the man is a walking guide who doesn't. He offers, or rather his wife does on his behalf, to walk with us in order to tell us more about the area. It would be exceedingly useful... if we were able to communicate without the help of his wife and, as she looks ready to give birth at any second, I'm pretty sure she wouldn't be joining us. We politely decline the offer. The food is homely, cooked by the owner, and served by Catarina who also fills in awkward gaps in the stilted conversation by recounting local anecdotes and tales. A starter of *ovos verdes* (green eggs) is followed by clay bowls filled with chicken, rice, and vegetables. It's simple and filling, and dinner is done and dusted before the clock strikes nine. There's still a significant part of the night to pass, and research/preparation for tomorrow to be carried out before we place heads on pillows, so we ask Catarina if we can buy a bottle of red wine to take back to the room.

"Of course," she replies with her customary smile, after looking slightly shocked for a heartbeat. Her casual follow up comment possibly explains why. "Normally we only drink wine with food."

We get the feeling that this part of Portugal could be slightly conservative as we slink back to our room feeling like a pair of alkies.

LAZARUS ROOSTERS AND PIG'S BLOOD

We begin to work our way north starting from the *Santuário Nossa Senhora da Aparecida* in nearby Balugães in the municipality of Barcelos. Barcelos may not be a name which is familiar to anyone who isn't Portuguese, but everyone who's visited Portugal should have spotted the multi-coloured bird found in every home in Portugal whose origins lie in the Minho municipality - the Barcelos rooster.

A Galician pilgrim passing through Barcelos on his way to Santiago de Compostela was accused of stealing silver, a crime he insisted he didn't commit, and sentenced to death. Before being left to swing at the end of a rope he pleaded to be allowed to speak to the judge who'd passed sentence. The Galician's request was granted and he was taken to the magistrate who was dining with friends. The Galician, again insisting he was innocent, pointed to a roasted rooster on a plate in the centre of the table and proclaimed, "to prove my innocence, that rooster will crow when they hang me."

The judge and friends guffawed at such a ridiculous claim, but nobody touched the rooster after the Galician was led away to the gallows and his fate. Then the impossible happened. As the noose was placed around the Galician's neck, the rooster rose from the platter and crowed (sounds like that old joke about food being so undercooked a good vet could have it back on its feet). The miracle left nobody in doubt regarding the Galician's innocence. The judge abandoned his meal and sprinted to the gallows just in time, and thanks to a poorly placed slipknot, to stop the hanging. He pardoned the Galician and sent him on his way, exonerated. Thereafter the *Galo de Barcelos* came to represent honesty, integrity, trust and honour, and every Portuguese home has one for luck.

From Balugães, we join the Portuguese Way for a while; distinctive yellow scallop shells pointing our route forward. It's not busy, positively quiet compared to its Spanish counterparts, but there are more people on the route than we're used to seeing on the hiking trails we normally traipse. It doesn't detract, in fact it adds a smile-inducing sense of camaraderie. Smile-inducing because just about everyone we meet beams a *"bom caminho"* and it's impossible not to smile back. It's interesting to note many of the pilgrims we pass are single women. The *Caminho* is mainly on country lanes, the only traffic being a handful of pilgrims and the occasional tractor pulling trailers filled with corn cobs. Every so often we see *espigueiros*, stone granaries with sides of slatted wood. These are raised from the ground on stone plinths to deter vermin and are also common across the border in Spain. Although we pass a number of impromptu pilgrims' rests – tables and chairs set up beside the path outside cottages and farms - we choose the benches at the *Igreja Matriz de Vitorinho dos Piães* to eat a picnic lunch consisting of dried banana chips, crisps, and pear-shaped, coconut-flavoured cakes. Beggars can't be choosers when you pick up lunch at wherever is open and sells food along the trail. Sharing the church's picnic zone are a couple of *Caminho* pilgrims. Yet again they are single, young females. One sings away happily as she rinses and squeezes faded tee-shirts in a fountain's stone bowl. They are an exceedingly cheery lot these Portuguese pilgrims. Eventually our path parts from the *Caminho* as we veer off to our next overnight base, in the *Freguesia de Facha* (*freguesias* are like parishes). Where we arrived at the Quinta de Malta by its delightful, vine-covered drive, we enter Quinta do Casal do Contado by the back door. However, being another stately mansion, the back door is a rather spectacular way to arrive – skirting the banks of an olive lake before strolling through a sun-dappled chestnut grove to arrive at the main house where we find manager Vitor. The plan was to have dinner at the house, but as there are no other guests Vitor has other ideas; he'll take us to dinner at one of his favourite restaurants in Ponte de Lima to introduce us to a classic Minho speciality.

Restaurant Rotunda da Feitosa, located beside a roundabout on the outskirts of Ponte de Lima, is unlikely to be stumbled across by visitors to the town. It has 'locals' restaurant' written all over it. It's also renowned for producing excellent *sarrabulho* which is why we're here. *Sarrabulho* is basically pigs' blood rice. I can imagine the outlines of people's backs as they run screaming from the very idea of eating something which involves pig's blood, but it's an incredibly popular dish in these parts; locals seek out restaurants which specialise in making it. Vitor, as a member of a *sarrabuhlo confraria* (a brotherhood), knows all the best places, so is an ideal companion for helping us negotiate our first meal of pig's blood rice.

We plonk ourselves beneath a TV where Sporting Lisbon are beating Basel in the Champions League, much to the disappointment of the locals (all Porto supporters), and let Vitor do the ordering. When he orders *sarrabulho* the waiter's eyes flick towards us and back to Vitor again before he asks in Portuguese, "Are you sure?" He's a man who has had previous experience of Brits being 'surprised' by the region's speciality dish.

Sarrabuhlo's origins date back to the Middle Ages just after the Black Death. Food was so scarce that the poorest people, unable to afford meat itself, used animal blood mixed with bread to lend food a hint of meatiness. The result was considered so tasty it has endured as the signature dish of the Minho. It is served in two parts. The first is *arroz de sarrabulho*, which is rice cooked in pig's blood with cubes of blood sausage (a bit like black pudding), seasoning, spices, and various cuts of meat. Once cooked, most of the meat is removed and the dish is served in a bowl, almost like a risotto. The second part, *papas de sarrabulho*, consists of the chunks of the cooked meat (pork, chicken, beef, sausage, blood sausage) served with potatoes. This duo makes for a seriously hearty twosome; an intimidating amount of food is placed on the table in front of us. Helping ease progress down the throat is a red *vinho verde* served in a porcelain cup without a handle; the traditional vessel used for drinking red *vinho verde*.

We attack the mountain of meat and bloody rice (it doesn't really look bloody, more like refried kidney beans in tone) whilst Vitor reveals a surprisingly comprehensive knowledge about British football. Where *papas de sarrabulho*, being a tasty meat and spuds combination, doesn't surprise the taste-buds, *arroz de sarrabulho* is a revelation. It is rich, creamy, full of flavour and delicious with a capital D. A couple of spoonfuls and it becomes crystal clear why it was elevated from a pauper's plate to a regional speciality; this is a proud prince of a dish. The slightly fizzy *vinho verde* works well as an accompaniment, its lightness a welcome contrast to the heaviness of the food. We're quick to sign up as *sarrabulho* converts, but there's no way we can finish it, there's enough food on the table for double our number.

THE BRIDGE OF FORGETFULNESS

From Quinta do Casal do Contado we walk along dusty tracks beside olive groves and vineyards, and then narrow cobbled lanes banked by high stone walls until we arrive at the River Lima in the hamlet of Passagem where, once upon a time, a ferry transported people, goods, and livestock across the river. There is no ferry now, just a carpet of golden corn cobs drying in the sun. The only sign of life is a tabby who walks gingerly across the cob carpet, treating it as if it were a minefield. Beyond the corn, the jade river is a wondrous sight to us. After 14 years of living on an island where there are no rivers we still get overly excited whenever we encounter bodies of fresh water. From this point we follow the course of the river all the way to Ponte de Lima.

Founded in 1125, Ponte de Lima takes its name from a bridge which has spanned the River Lima for over 2000 years. Up until the late Middle Ages this bridge was the only safe place to cross the water. Subsequently, it became an integral part of the main Roman road (the Via XIX) linking Braga with Astorga in Spain. Later it became part of the *Caminho de Santiago*.

The approach to Portugal's oldest town is lovely, an avenue of plane trees called *Avenida dos Plátanos* acts like nature's guard of honour. Ahead we can see the old bridge, whilst on our left the river sparkles in the sunlight. Here in the north, as opposed to the oppressive heat still being experienced further south, the temperature is perfect. We exit Plane Tree Avenue to find a surprise – a funfair runs the length of the town; a garish barrier of flashing lights and squawking klaxons which separates the pretty features of the old town from the River Lima. It's not a welcome sight. Part of our remit is to compile photographs of 'the journey' to be used in travel articles, brochures and on Inntravel's website. Ponte de Lima's historic, riverside façade was top of my list of potential standout shots – the image which might capture the overall essence of the holiday. Not with added funfair it won't. We knew the town's big celebration, *Feiras*

Novas, took place in September; the trip had been planned to avoid it. It's not that we don't like big, brash, and bouncy *fiestas* (*festas* in Portugal), we love them. But finding accommodation would have been problematic, and getting any work done during the *Feiras Novas* would be virtually impossible. We know from past experience of carnival on Tenerife that traditional celebrations of this magnitude consume everything. What we didn't know about the *Feiras Novas* was the funfair stayed in town for another week after the *festa* was over, taking up a huge part of the main car park. Another thing we'd failed to realise was the *Feiras Novas* celebrations merged seamlessly into the ones for the *Vindima* – the wine harvest. The *Feiras Novas* are in honour of *Nossa Senhora das Dores* (Our Lady of the Sorrows) but I'm not sure the image we see everywhere of a wide-eyed woman with too much mascara, scarlet lipstick, beauty spot and wearing heart-shaped earrings is *Nosso Senhora*; it could, however, be a *Simpsons* version of *Pulp Fiction's* Maria de Medeiros.

On the up side, there's a vibrancy to Ponte de Lima that contrasts nicely with the reserved nature of the places we've stayed in so far. There are also many inviting looking restaurants, and we're hungry for gastro experiences offering something different from the ones in Alentejo.

Our introduction to Ponte de Lima's culinary scene is courtesy of Maria do Céu, Director of Marketing for Solares de Portugal, an organisation based in Ponte de Lima which promotes quality and unusual accommodation in Portugal's manor houses, country estates, and farmhouses. She has a whirlwind of a personality, and is passionate about helping maintain Portugal's heritage by promoting those manor houses which have opened themselves up to hosting tourists as guests. She's also bags of fun and tells great stories, as we discover when she takes us for dinner at Taberna Cadeira Velha. When the waiter approaches with a menu Maria waves it away, and negotiates what she wants to order – a range of *petiscos*. Whether the dishes she asks for are actually on the menu, who knows? But the waiter agrees to them all anyway. Maria speaks

English like she was born in Britain, she studied in Brighton. At one point she recounts a story about how the Portuguese were responsible for tea being called tea – the name coming from the T scrawled on tea boxes. This T had been written by Portuguese dockers and was short for '*transito*' (in transit). Whenever she says "cup of tea" there's no hint of a Portuguese accent, in fact she sounds as though she could be a Londoner ordering in a cafe in an episode of Eastenders. The throaty laugh which accompanies tales is infectious; she's great company. Like Vitor the previous night, Maria orders a feast. This time it includes puffy *pataniscas* (salted cod patties); *alheira* sausage (traditional pork-less sausage created by Portuguese Jews during the inquisition); beef carpaccio; *pulpo a la gallega* (a nod to the influences from the nearby neighbours); and a bowl of unidentifiable bits sprinkled with fresh cilantro.

"Do you know what those are?" Maria asks as I chew on a grisly morsel, almost positive I spotted a hair attached as I popped it into my mouth. I haven't eaten them before but I've got a damn good idea.

"Chopped pig ears?"

Cue Maria's throaty laugh.

Over the next two days we explore Ponte de Lima and surrounding area, putting together a town route which takes in the highlights of the Garden Festival that runs from May till October. Although there is a main festival site on the opposite side of the river which features an eclectic selection of specially created small gardens around a central theme, there are also 20 other exhibits in and around the town's existing parks and gardens. From Ponte do Barca, another picturesque northern Portuguese town which was the alleged birthplace of Ferdinand Magellan (you can buy boat-shaped pastries called *Magalhães* there), we map out a walking route which follows the River Lima back to Ponte de Lima. The section immediately after leaving Ponte do Barca is our favourite stretch of river so far as it has a wilder, more carefree personality than the one on the opposite approach to Ponte de Lima, Outside Ponte do Barca trees grow so close to the bank the forest almost dips its roots in the water; there are old mills; ruins of stone bridges; ornate fountains half devoured by the undergrowth; vine-covered arbour walkways; and birds. Herons are common, but we also spot a brace of electric blue *guarda-rios* (kingfishers) flashing by at the speed of light.

Our onward journey to our final Minho destination takes us over the river on the old bridge, and back onto the *Caminho de Santiago*. That we're on the *Caminho* is unmistakeable; apart from a couple of restaurants on the northern side of the bridge offering special pilgrims' menus, there are a row of hiking boots lined up neatly outside a hostel named Albergue de Peregrinos. It's a *Caminho* tradition. The route is a pleasant rerun of the sort of scenery we've been enjoying all week, but accompanying us is a soundtrack with a distinctly Latino beat. Sometimes it feels as though the source of the music is just around the next corner, sometimes it fades into the distance. There's a lively party somewhere. Our destination might only be a house, but it's such a grand house we can see it from many points along the way. Located amid 13 acres of vineyards and orchards, set high above the valley with views over Ponte de Lima, Paço de Calheiros is considered one of the most beautiful examples of 17th century manor houses in Portugal. It's the family seat of Francisco, Count of Calheiros and has been the family home for more than six centuries. As well as extensive vineyards surrounding the house, there are gardens, a tennis court, orchards, chestnut woods with a small herd of red deer, and a large swimming pool with views across the valley.

As we wind our way upward through vineyards and cornfields, the music grows louder and louder until its source becomes clear, it's coming from the Count's church. Well, maybe not his church, but the one in Calheiros just outside the gates to his manor. This is *vinho verde* country and harvest time means parties. In Ponte de Lima there were convoys of tractors with trailers overflowing with plump grapes, waiting to deposit their loads in the town's cooperative *adega*. Up to 2000 local producers bring their grapes to this central point. There are so many tractors some have to queue overnight. Once that 'load' is off their minds, the party can begin. In Calheiros this means a procession with religious figures carried aloft and a lot of accordion playing (accordions being the instrument of choice in this area). After dark, the accordions get dumped and the rhythm is sexed up by sexy salsa and reggaeton. It's just like being at a *fiesta* back in the Canary Islands.

DINNER WITH THE COUNT

"Shite," I look at the pool of liquid spreading outward from our feet. "Shite. Shite. Shite."

It had been a good day till this point. It had been a very good day. Now it's in danger of going completely tits up.

It's 18:00. We're standing impotently at a taxi rank where, thanks to the *Feiras Novas* funfair which has completely taken over the riverside, there are no taxis. Our car is in the middle of wetlands 10km away, and we're due to meet Francisco, the Count of Calheiros, for pre-dinner drinkies at his mansion (12km from where our car is parked) in an hour. The pool at our feet is *vinho verde*, the contents of a bottle we've just purchased which, a few seconds earlier, was inside Andy's rucksack which itself was perched far too precariously on the bench it just toppled off. Not only are we going to be late, we're going to roll up smelling like a couple of winos.

"What the hell happened there?" I load my metaphoric pistol with recriminations as we draw up the battle lines. When things go wrong 'in the field' and we find the situation on the ground isn't what it was supposed to be, frustrations are often turned inward toward each other purely because there's nobody else to shout at. The usual drill is we verbally punch each other for a few minutes and then, when the frustration has been vented, turn our attention to coming up with solutions to whatever problem we happen to be facing.

Why a town the size of Ponte de Lima has no taxis is a mystery. Google Maps show a number of taxi offices, none of them are actually where Google suggests they are. The fact there are no taxis has scuppered us. There is a number on the post beside the big yellow, deceitful letters on the tarmac. However, I detest using the phone when my grasp of the language is such that any chance of being understood is only because of the frantic sign language which accompanies my bad pronunciation and bastardised (i.e. guessed at) sentences. But it has to be done. I at least know how to say "*voce fala ingles?*" - do you speak

English. The answer I get to that question is "*nao*". I muddle on valiantly, throwing what relevant words and phrases I know at him:

"*Precisamos um taxi agora... Ponte Romana... Ponte de Lima... parada de taxi,*" I don't know if the last is Portuguese or Spanish, but we're not far from Spain and the general rule of communication is to try to get it over the net if nothing else.

"*Sim,*" he replies, understanding something. Whether it's the right something is the big question. He throws a number at me which sounds like he'll be with us in either fifteen minutes or fifty minutes.

"Do we have a taxi?" Andy asks.

"Honestly," I shrug. "I really don't know."

I might have made our meanderings sound all cosy and easy; wandering without a care in the world along leafy lanes etc. the path ahead clear and problem-free. A friend remarked a couple of years ago that when out walking with one of her friends she told them. "I know people who get paid to do this." The 'this' is the bit that's above the water, the photos people see on Facebook, Twitter, or Instagram. That's the fun and easy part. What they don't see, the frantic paddling below the surface, is us standing at a crossroads where unmarked tracks converge in the middle of a forest and where the correct route looks exactly like the three incorrect routes. What they don't see is us walking happily along a track for 5km just to find the trail has been fenced off by a new landowner who's decided to turn their property into a fortress. What they don't see is us sheltering under pines in monsoon rain and howling wind wondering how we're going to record accurate directions when it's far too wet to use the Dictaphone, and any paper we have is a sodden mess. And what they don't see is us having to figure out the logistics of getting to the start of walking routes we've pieced together ourselves when there's no public transport available, or then having to find a way to get back to our car after hiking for 18km. These aren't moans; we love what we do and feel extremely privileged to be able to do it and get paid. But we know just how hard we've worked to reach this point; it's not a stroll in the park. Logistics of travel is often the biggest problem when creating Slow Travel holidays. Where transport, bus and train times, friendly taxi drivers etc. are all arranged for customers when they go on an Inntravel holiday, none of it exists when we roll into town or, more usually, some off-the-beaten-track place in the middle of nowhere. We're the guinea pigs, finding ways to make walking routes work so that car-less customers know exactly how to get to and from the best locations as easily and conveniently as possible.

In this particular case we've been researching a walking route to/from the *Lagoas de Bertiandos*. The plan was to dump the car at the Lagoon's Interpretation Centre and walk back to Ponte de Lima where, having checked first, we 'knew' there were taxis. It had been a lovely little walk; the route taking us past long-horned *barossa* cattle and along wooden walkways through leafy Minho swamplands, a haven for birds outside summer months, to the northern bank of the River Lima. Riverside walks are generally winners anyway, and our view is that if we like something a lot so will other people who enjoy slow travel. But the Lima has a few little add-ons to boost the enjoyability factor even more. The northern bank is more rural than the southern side where the town is located. Walking along it is a tranquil affair, and there's the Karl Pilkington factor - "I'd rather live in a cave with a view of a palace than live in a palace with a view of a cave." From the Lima's northern bank there are views of one of Portugal's most picturesque riverside towns, even if at the moment its best features are masked by the existence of the funfair. All in all it's an excellent walking route and we were pleased as punch with ourselves, until we crossed the Roman Bridge into Ponte de Lima and discovered it was a taxi-less town.

A taxi drives up after only ten minutes and creates a moral dilemma. It's not the driver I phoned, but this taxi is available. Do we jump in on the basis I'm not 100% sure the other taxi will even turn up, or do we wait? With the gnawing feeling we might be shooting ourselves in the foot, our principles regarding doing the right thing dictate we have to wait.

Five minutes later João, a knight in a green and black steed (Portuguese taxi colours), rolls up to save the day. We arrive back at Paço de Calheiros with ten minutes to spare, just enough time to swap sweaty, wine-sodden clothes for fresh ones.

The Count had arranged to meet us for an aperitif in the shade of a vine-covered arbour in the grounds of his palatial mansion. Francisco inherited the estate in 1980 and spent years renovating the place before opening its doors to guests in 1987. As it will soon be part of Inntravel's *Manor Houses of the Minho* walking holiday, we're paving the way for what future customers will experience and need to chat with Francisco about 'how everything will work'. Whilst most guests should stay in the elegant manor house, we're housed in the former stables which we don't mind at all, in fact we prefer the more casual, modern stables to the rich, and very traditional decor of rooms in the main house.

When we descend the old stone steps from the driveway to the arbour, Francisco isn't there. There is, however, a group of around twenty Americans, all with glasses of *vinho verde* in hands. Conversation stops as we gatecrash what we rapidly realise is an exclusive gathering arranged solely for a party of American hikers. We stand in the wings, awkwardly, waiting for Francisco to appear and inform everybody we're not just a pair of Brit freeloaders. "Why are you here?" one of the Americans asks to which Andy rolls out some spiel about "new Slow Travel holiday... blah, blah. Researching and writing... blah, blah. Travel writers... blah, blah. Meeting the Count here... blah, blah" before the penny drops what they are really asking is "why have you muscled into our private party?"

Francisco finally appears, late (maybe he struggled to catch a taxi as well), looking exactly what we hoped a Portuguese Count would look like. He's tanned and roguishly handsome with an unruly shock of silver hair; his eyes sparkle as he speaks; his hands flamboyantly accentuate every word; a smile permanently plays across his lips as though everything amuses him; and he's wearing a green, collarless jacket which gives him the appearance of Christopher Plummer's Captain Von Trapp.

He launches into a series of anecdotes starting with a statement about the *vinho verde* wine we're drinking, produced on the estate.

"It is so light you can drink lots of it and not get drunk."

The stories flow as he shows us all around his family home, pointing out glossy magazines featuring his family beside various other members of the European nobility. One photograph shows one of his sons with Prince William. The resemblance is uncanny, they could be brothers. Francisco is a born raconteur, his stories are sprawling and funny; far more amusing than a laconic Texan who wisecracks his way around the manor house. As we walk, various individuals break off from the group and approach us. Every one of them asks the same question."How did you find this place?" When we answer we're including it as part of a walking holiday each looks a tad crestfallen, as if they were the only people who knew of its existence. Maybe that's what they've been told. All in all though, they're an interesting and nice enough group. People who explore destinations on foot and choose to stay in unusual places like this usually are. As the other guests peruse the books and magazines in Francisco's living room, a surprisingly modest affair, he finds a moment to talk to us.

"Is it okay if we meet up tomorrow afternoon?" he asks."You see, I have to go to a party in Galicia after dinner and it will be very late before I get back."

Not only is he going to a party after he's hosted a dinner with his guests, so that will be somewhere between 10 and midnight, that party happens to be in another country. The border might only be a thirty-minute drive away, but nevertheless it sounds impressively decadent.

Francisco is such an affable chap, chatting away constantly, the tour of the house overruns and we enter the stately dining room, more Medieval banqueting hall, fifteen minutes later than planned. Francisco had already mentioned his cook had been with the family a long time, so long she clearly feels the kitchen and dining room are her domain to be ruled how she deems fit. Subsequently, cook served the soup when dinner was due to start rather than waiting until guests were seated. Cold bowls of *caldo verde* decorate the long table, waiting for us wayward diners. Francisco smiles sheepishly, looking more like a small boy, and then completely ignores the fact the soup is stone cold.

Seating arrangements are on the strange side. The group of American hikers occupy the main table, with Francisco seated at the head. We, on the other hand, are like the poor relations as our table sits on its own in a corner. At least we're not alone. We share the table with a fascinating Norwegian couple; he is a revered, possibly even Nobel award-winning, scientist who specialises in genetics. They become our European allies as we mumble and grumble about being stuck in a corner whilst the Americans are being treated like VIPs. Over the course of the meal, the scientist shares some interesting facts about genetics (I can't remember any, science was never a strong point) whilst I tell them about Francisco heading off to the prestigious Spanish party once dinner is over. Midway through the meal Francisco stands, clinks his glass with a spoon, and launches into a speech which begins with him thanking everyone for coming to his house before it rapidly veers off into a diatribe about the state of the world today, the importance of tradition, and the need for people to work together rather than create divisions. His topic meanders down a winding road before it becomes apparent where its heading; into increasingly dodgy waters, given who makes up the majority of his audience.

"Take your president..." he starts. I sit up, wondering what on earth is coming next and how the Americans will react. But Francisco is no stranger to mixed company or political discourse. Without mentioning the American President's name or being directly critical or disapproving, he manages to sound both disapproving and critical. Some of the group quietly apologise for the voting habits of their fellow Americans, others clap their agreement. In the end he successfully navigates the waters without incident. I guess you're unlikely to find many MAGAs travelling around a relatively unknown part of Portugal.

As his guests sip dessert wine, Francisco excuses himself from the table and comes across to ours.

133

"Was dinner okay?" He asks. But before Andy or I reply with the noncommittal "yes, it was fine" we use when the food in any restaurant is only, well, fine. The Norwegian scientist's wife leans forward and says, rather coldly and accusingly.

"I believe you are abandoning us, you are going to another party... in Spain."

Francisco's eyes flash briefly in my direction, for an instant I'm sure I see 'you are a betrayer of confidences' written in them.

"Ah, yes," Francisco replies. "There's an important party in Galicia I really have to attend."

He returns to the head of the main table and addresses his American guests again.

"I'm afraid I will have to leave you soon," he clearly feels the need to confess to everyone that we are not his only date this night. "I have to go to a party in Spain immediately after dinner is over."

The response from the Americans is unanimous. There are favourable laughs accompanied by comments which show unmitigated approval. They relish this glimpse into the glamorous lifestyle of Europe's aristocracy. They probably can't wait to get home to tell family and friends about their experience with Portugal's nobility. The Count picks up on this and embellishes further, mentioning there will be 500 other rich and famous guests, it will be a lavish affair and so on. The Americans lap it up. I reckon I'm forgiven for my indiscretion.

"But before I depart," Francisco continues. "There is something rather special I want you to see." He indicates we follow him outside.

On the expansive gravel driveway are a troupe of dancers and musicians in traditional costume; the women in peasant skirts and puffy blouses, the men wearing waistcoats and with red sashes around the waists. They swirl in circles, hands in the air, to jaunty tunes from musicians playing drums and accordions. As the dancers end their performance, fireworks light up the sky above us.

"You see," Francisco beams, holding his hands in the air. "I arranged all of this this just for you."

Whether the Americans know there's a *festa* taking place in the churchyard across from the manor house I don't know, but they lap up every theatrical minute of it. And so do we.

The circular route we follow from Paço de Calheiros takes us high into the hills behind the estate, into a land where chestnut-coloured wild horses roam free. By the time we return to the house it is well after lunchtime, the Count should have recovered enough from his partying for us to have our meeting with him before we have to move on. But we're struggling to track him down. The Americans are out all day hiking and there's nobody to be seen around the estate. Everybody else must be sleeping off a Saturday night of partying. We check the office in the main house; nobody, not a soul to ask where our missing count might be. I scour the grounds. One vine-covered arbour leads to the forest with the herd of roe deer, another leads to outbuildings where I discover a barn filled with a fortune's worth of dusty, gorgeous classic cars. But there's still no sign of Francisco. The place is like a stately house version of the Marie Celeste. Finally, I climb to the swimming pool built into the hillside above the house. As I clear the last step I spot a lone sun-lounger on the far side of the pool. On it, fast asleep, is a man in a rumpled suit. I quietly retreat and make my way back to the stable, bumping into Andy as she emerges from the main house.

"I've found the Count," I tell her.

An hour later and it looks as though we're going to have to leave Calheiros without ever having had our meeting with the Count. But just as we finish packing there's a knock on the stable door.

"Ah, this is where you are," Francisco beams. "I've been looking for you everywhere."

We say nothing.

24 HOURS TO CAPTURE THE AVEIRO LAGOON

Occasionally when we're helping put together a Slow Travel holiday we end up with additional impromptu 'missions'. Sometimes these can be quirky little affairs. When we were creating the city walking routes in Lisbon we were asked to pick up a series of *Cartas Militar de Portugal* (Portuguese Military Maps) at the *Instituto Geográfico do Exército*. Taking a metro to the outskirts of Lisbon we expected to find a specialist map shop, instead we found ourselves handing over passports and being escorted through a military base by soldiers. It was a bit surreal for all concerned. It wasn't every day they had a pair of British tourists turning up at the guardhouse looking for hiking maps. To be fair, the personnel *did* sort us out with the maps we wanted, even though they seemed to find it as amusing as we did unsettling.

Just as we're planning on heading back to Alentejo, James from Inntravel adds on a little mission - to take photographs for a new cycling holiday which capture the feel of the Aveiro Lagoon and surrounding area for use in a travel brochure and on the website. The timescale, less than 24 hours, doesn't allow any scope if anything goes wrong - i.e. weather conditions deteriorate - and not knowing anything at all about Aveiro means we are going in blind. But the 45km long Aveiro Lagoon runs alongside a strip of land so thin that at one point it's less than 300m wide; a decent wave could swallow all of it. This means we can cover a substantial amount of the lagoon area in the short window of opportunity we have. Knowing some of the key features of the area, we concoct a plan based around a wish list of photographs.

First there's the 'must' shot. Costa Nova looks more like a movie set than a town, and photos of its famous striped houses are top of the wish list. When we arrive the sky is devoid of clouds; perfect. But, as it's already 1pm, the sun is dropping west and deep shadows have spread across the striped facades of the row of perky houses which face inland and east toward the Aveiro Lagoon. They are still a sight to see. Built initially in the 19th century as warehouses for fishing equipment, the rising popularity of people taking beach holidays in the 20th century led to them being bought by well to do families who spruced them up, adding striking stripes, to be used as summer homes.

The Aveiro Lagoon itself is an essential aspect of any photo spread about the area. Although the picturesque houses of Costa Nova are a tourist magnet (even though there aren't many other tourists at all on this warm and sunny mid-September day), there's a richness of working local life to be found on the lagoon. The shallowness of the water and narrow channels leading from the main body of water meant special boats had to be designed for fishing in various areas and for transporting the likes of seaweed (used to fertilise fields) and salt. A small harbour at one end of Costa Nova provides plenty of shooting material as it's home to a number of vibrantly-coloured lagoon vessels.

As the holiday is specifically a cycling one, getting shots of cyclists on specially created bike and walking paths which link Costa Nova and Vagueira would be useful. But that requires cyclists to appear just at the right time. Some actually do, and on an attractive section of wooden walkway, but the woman is wearing so-loud-they-hurt-my-ears scarlet pants with matching stripy jumper and the man sports a lemon Pringle jersey and yellow chinos. They look as though they're dressed more for sipping cocktails in a golf course clubhouse than enjoying a outdoor activity. However, to compensate, shortly after they pass a man leisurely stand-up paddling glides by on the lagoon's mirror-calm waters.

Although the lagoon continues beyond Vagueira to the south of Costa Nova, we decide, given the shackles of time, to make it the point we turn back. The town itself is not photogenic, but the area around the elegantly long Praia da Vagueira has loads of potential material - brightly painted, giant wooden sardines decorate grassy mounds; there are messy mountains of mangles of faded fishing nets; bronzed surfers ride the waves; traditional boats lie beached on white dunes; and a long, wooden walkway snakes into the distance along the back of the beach behind the dunes.

Until Aveiro port was built in the 19th century the narrow strip of land facing the Atlantic on the western side of the lagoon was just one long beach. Getting a beach photo under a cloudless sky was never going to be much of a problem here, except as the afternoon stretches toward early evening a soft haziness enters the fray, blurring the scene.

At the northern end of the strip lies Barra, another town which doesn't rate highly in the good looks department. However, it is the home of the red and white striped *Faro da Barra*, at 62m high it's the tallest lighthouse in Portugal. Barra lies right at the entrance to the port whose construction transformed the area. The comings and goings of ships provide an opportunity for some bonus shots - a battalion of seagulls launching an assault on a large fishing boat; an army of fishermen and women casting their lines from the sea defences. Shots such as these help illustrate the real life of a place. I snap as many as I can as the afternoon turns, in gentle pastel shades, to dusk.

The manager of our hotel in Costa Nova recommends a relatively new restaurant, Bronze. It's a modern affair right on the beach and has floor-to-ceiling glass windows, so we can enjoy the views without finding our food flavoured by sand particles. As the restaurant's windows face west and out to sea it would be a great place to dine and drink at sunset. We are just a wee bit too late for that experience. The waitress talks me into their signature salt cod dish. Andy suggests I only take her advice because I can't say no to a smiling, pretty face; her evidence being she knows I'm not a great fan of salt cod, except as *bacalhau à brás*. In my defence, I'm always open to suggestions about the dishes restaurants do best, irrespective of what the waiting staff look like. Bronze's *bacalhau* is as good as the waitress had promised, and highly photogenic into the bargain.

Daybreak dawns, except it doesn't... not really. We wake

to find the world outside our hotel window in Costa Nova still looks like it could be a film set, but this time one from a Stephen King adaptation. A dense sea mist hangs heavily across the land and lagoon. Everything is obscured by a thick fog which looks in no hurry to burn off. As far as photography is concerned, this is a bust. Although there's virtually no chance of being able to take any decent photos, we still want to see what the town of Aveiro looks like. Lounging beside a lagoon on Portugal's north west coast, Aveiro is often referred to as the Venice of Portugal. The gloomy grey fog doesn't show it at its best by any means, but it doesn't take a lot of imagination to see that under a sunny gaze Aveiro would be rather splendid. It *does* have canals lined by historic edifices, but not grandiose Gothic, Byzantine and Renaissance ones like the Venetian beauty. Saying that, the jaunty Art Deco buildings which decorate Aveiro's watery avenues are far more suited to its coquettish personality.

It also has canal boats – a flamboyant fleet of gondolas ready to whisk romantic dreamers, or selfie-obsessed snappers, on a silkily smooth cruise along liquid streets. Except, despite 'gondolas' being the word that dances into the head when the sleek vessels are first seen, these are not gondolas, they are *barcos moliceiros*; a quite different beast. For a start, these long, flat-bottomed craft were originally used for harvesting and transporting *moliço*, a collective name for sea grasses including eelgrass, widgeonweed, and pondweed, all of which were used as agricultural fertilizer.

As well as having a distinctive design, each *barco moliceiro* is customised during construction; the hull decorated with unique art work. Different sections of the *moliceiro* are painted to reflect themes ranging from historical and religious to work-related and scenes from everyday life. However, the theme which gets prime position and which is most likely to have people doing a cartoon double-take is one described as 'erotic' or 'burlesque'. Personally, I'd call it Portugal's version of saucy seaside postcards, circa 1960s Britain, painted on a boat. One I spot depicts a priest looking at a girl whose skirt has been lifted by the breeze, exposing her backside, and has him exclaiming, "*á ventinho abençoado*" (the blessed wind). Another shows a generously-bosomed girl in a low cut dress holding out a plate of a local speciality sweet, *ovos moles*, to a man who remarks, "q*ue rico par de ovos moles*" - what a rich pair of soft eggs. Those are two of the tamer ones. I scamper about the canals, a voyeuristic photographer seeking provocative prows to notch up. There's a lot of material of the sort that will amuse some, bring scowls to the faces of others. I'm pretty sure none will end up in an Inntravel brochure. The saucy scenes belong to another time, no question about that, and some will view them as being undeserving of a place in modern society. But the fact they belong to another time is the point. They are a tradition, an integral part of the area's past. In a way they are no different from scenes of yore on a faded tapestry, hieroglyphics on an ancient tomb, or primitive drawings on the wall of a cave. Like them or loathe them, they're a part of history. I'm a great believer in not sweeping the past under a carpet, even when it relates to something once seen as frivolous but now considered dodgy. Anyway, their continued existence helps keep the art of *moliceiro*-making alive.

We haven't seen it at its best but we've seen enough to know Aveiro is somewhere we want to return to, hopefully when it's not auditioning for a role in a horror movie.

Our trip to the Minho has been an illuminating and enjoyable diversion from the worries about our longer term situation in Portugal. It has shown us how diverse Portugal is in terms of scenery, tradition, and even the character of the people. Now we realise just how much we don't know about this fascinating country. The trip has made us yearn to be more settled, so we can have a solid base from which to explore, and learn more. As the car eats up the kilometres, visions of problematic swimming pools, open drains, and flooded bathrooms begin to dominate our thoughts, forcing memories of sparkling wines, hearty meals, and larger than life characters out. Neither of us feel any joy at the prospect of returning to the ongoing domestic problems at Galegos. We agree that as soon as we get back we will intensify our efforts to find a new home.

DESPERATELY SEEKING SUSANNA

The plan had only ever been to stay a few weeks at Crença, but the house and location has seduced us into staying nearly four months. At one point we even pondered putting in an offer for the place as it *is* paradisaical. Some fortunate person will love it the way it deserves to be cherished. We know we're not suited to remote living in the long-term, and there are things we're missing – the amenities of a nearby decent-sized town for a start. A diverse choice of dining out options is another. The sequence of niggling problems with the house has eaten up not only our time, but that of K&C's as well. I think we're all feeling our time in Galegos has stretched beyond its sell-by date. A trip to Setúbal to view a potential property rams home just how much we crave a hit of urban sophistication every now and again.

Out of all the estate agents we'd registered with only one kept in touch after our initial emails, visits to offices etc. Susanna Fonte from Optimhome. Susanna has been a shining beacon of hope in an otherwise depressing long-term rental market; coming up with suggestions even though none have matched what we're after. Our repeated "nope, not quite right" responses haven't dampened her enthusiasm or efforts to track down the right place for us. Summer has been a problem time in the rental market in our first-choice area. Setúbal isn't well known to the British tourism market, but its exceptional beaches are magnets to the Portuguese. In summer the area is flooded by visitors from across the country, with any spare accommodation for miles around being snapped up by Portuguese beach-lovers. The timing of our move from Tenerife couldn't have been worse as there's nothing of charm on the market between June and September – the Portuguese summer holidays. Susanna had warned us about this at the time but had filled us with optimism about a change in this situation as soon as the summer holidays were over.

Sure enough, as September dawns she comes up with a potentially perfect property in Arrábida Natural Park, a short drive from both Setúbal and Azeitão. The drive over to Setúbal seems endless, the 35C heat not helping with what has become a bland and boring journey of necessity, the gloss of driving through endless wheat-coloured plains to get anywhere has long since worn off to the point the urban ugliness on the outskirts of Setúbal is a welcome sight, a sign of civilisation. Before meeting Susanna we pass an hour in the Alegro Centre, one of those homogeneous European shopping malls, marvelling that the Jumbo supermarket there stocks ten types of feta cheese, and salivating over junk food (the Portuguese version at least) on display at the centre's food hall; where a humble *bifana* lunch tastes like a Michelin offering.

Our meeting point with Susanna is in Azeitão. Seeing the town again serves as a reminder how much we'd loved being there, and how desperate we are to return. This area is where we wanted to be from the start.

Susanna in person is a reflection of her email persona, bubbly and optimistic; the sort of person who makes you smile even though you're worrying about the dark clouds gathering above. She's attractive, stylish, petite, laughs constantly, and she speaks excellent English, as does an equally amiable Azeitão estate agent she has in tow. The property they show us is inside the Natural Park. A short drive down a country lane contrasts with the thirsty landscape we drove across to get here. Whereas it was parched and scraggly after a long hot summer (still going on), Arrábida remains verdant and lush. The house is detached and one of only three in an otherwise rural setting. It should be perfect, but it isn't. It has a large, covered outside terrace with stone barbecue (good), a too-immaculate garden (not good as it looks too neat to use and has 'this is the domain of the hired gardener' about it), dated décor and furnishings, and claustrophobic characterless rooms (bad). The phrase 'like an Eastbourne bungalow' pops into my mind even though, as far as I know, I've never actually seen an Eastbourne bungalow. I Google it and bingo, bang on the nose. In theory, the road leading past the house is a quiet country lane; however, it leads to the park's beaches which we now know draw hordes of people in the summer. It also leads to a town-sized cement factory. Even in the short time we're there a number of trucks covered in cement dust come roaring past. We make the appropriate 'we'll think about it' noises to Susanna and her colleague, but we all know we aren't going to bite with this one.

"Living here would depress the hell out of me," Andy whispers when Susanna's out of earshot. I don't feel quite that way about it, I'd consider taking it. But I'm heavily influenced by the draw of the area and the desire to leave Galegos. Deep down I know she's right. As we're leaving, the local estate agent asks if we'd like to join him for a drink at a bar in the town. It's another reminder of just how friendly people are in these parts. We'd love to, but decline as we have the long drive to the back of beyond to tackle.

Somewhere just west of Estremoz we get a blow out. It takes us hours to limp our way home on the spare tyre. By the time we crawl up the drive to Crença we're like the shredded tyre in the boot of the car, totally deflated.

A couple of weeks later and we're back in the outskirts of Setúbal, parked outside a restaurant in the small, and not particularly attractive, workaday village of Brejos do Assa. It's another sizzler of a day and when Susanna and her husband João roll up they look as though they're dressed for having fun in the sun rather than showing us around a house. Relaxing on a summer day is exactly what they are dressed for. It turns out they have a holiday home on a nearby golf course and are taking time from chilling-out with the family to show us the property. It occurs to me Brejos do Assa doesn't look like the sort of place which would have a plush golf course nearby.

We jump into their car and quickly leave tarmac to head down a series of dirt tracks. I reckon I have good navigational skills, but after a couple of turns I've no idea where we are in relation to the village we've just left. After a few minutes driving João pulls up outside some large gates leading to a *quinta* at what is literally the end of the road.

"We're here," Susanna beams before jumping from the car to pull at a piece of rope dangling at the side of the gates. An old bell clangs and, after a few moments, a dimunutive woman of indeterminate age wearing a fedora appears and opens the metal gates.

"This is Dona Caterina," Susanna introduces us to the owner of the property. Dona Catarina doesn't speak English but does speak German; she's Portuguese but her late husband was German. Dona Catarina is 5ft nothing and has the deeply tanned face of someone who spends a lot of time working outdoors. Her greying hair is short, almost boyish, and she has a mothering aura about her which combined with a perpetually smiling face makes her look like a kind person.

She leads us up a wide, dirt path through a shaded tunnel created by palm trees and pines to a low, wooden gate where she says something and smiles.

"These are to keep the sheep out," Susanna translates. "To stop them eating the flowers in the garden."

We step through the gates into a compound where a neat, square lawn is bordered by low, white cottages (former farm outbuildings) with tiled roofs. Where the world outside the low gate is wild and carefree in an organised sort of way, inside is more landscaped, but not in Mary, Mary quite contrary fashion. There are hydrangeas, orchids, roses, strelitzias, palms, laurels and camellia.

There are five houses on the farm. One is used by Dona Catarina when she stays over (her main home is in Seixal on the other side of the Setúbal Peninsula), one is rented long-term by Senhor Luís and his wife Teresa. Senhor Luís lives in Porto and only uses the house on some weekends (this happens to be one of them). At one point Teresa appears and hugs Dona Catarina. There's a wonderfully relaxed, welcoming feel to the *quinta*. The other three cottages, until this point, have been rented out during summers. But summer rental involves a lot of work and Dona Catarina would prefer having people rent on a long-term basis. There are two cottages up for grabs. One has a single bedroom, the other, the one we're interested in, Casa Camelia (they're all named after flowers), has two. It's a long, narrow cottage consisting of two decent-sized bedrooms, an open kitchen with support beams made from railway sleepers, a smallish bathroom, and a generous living room with a high, sloped ceiling. In size it's not dissimilar to the house we owned on Tenerife. Where that one was formerly an animal shed, this was used for pressing wine. Half the kitchen is taken up by large, stone wine vats which now act as a place to put knick-knacks. Dona Catarina's husband had never removed the vats as "you never know when they might become useful again." The kitchen would be a perfect size without the vats, but Dona Catarina leaves them in place because they now hold sentimental value. The house has a small back terrace overlooking a field where the sheep rest overnight, and a small pine forest. There's also a larger, covered terrace to the front which is shared with the cottage next door; although, Susanna insists that, apart from during the summer months, we'll virtually have the whole farm to ourselves most of the time. From the cottages, Dona Catarina leads us along a plant-lined path - we smell rosemary and curry as we brush past - to an orange and lemon orchard next to a small swimming pool overlooking the surrounding farmlands. As we lean on the gate leading to the orchard we listen to the sound of birdsong, some chirps and melodies have become familiar during our time in Crença. It is utterly charming, and rural even though it's close to two towns.

Via Susanna we talk about how we love to listen to the birds, how beautiful the gardens are, and whether wine from Douro is better than wine from Alentejo. Despite the language barrier, which Susanna has told us is a concern for Dona Catarina, we seem to hit it off. It's obvious she's chuffed by our sincere praise of her little oasis.

We have many reservations about the cottage. The fact that although this a farm it's also basically a holiday compound is a major one. We're not used to sharing space with other people. It's also €800 a month which is a lot of dosh for a small house with little privacy and some shared amenities, including a washing machine. But that amount does include gas and electricity. More importantly, it's delightful with bags of quirky charm, and we're at the point where we're ready to take anything that isn't a dump in order to be based in this area. We tell Susanna and Dona Catarina we'll think about the cottage and let them know in a couple of days. As we walk down the shaded, subtropical driveway ahead of Dona Catarina and Susanna who are busy chatting away, Andy turns to me and says, "why wait a couple of days? We know we're going to take it, if she'll have us. Why not just say so right now?"

I take a deep breath and ponder for a second before replying, "you're right, it's daft to delay for no reason."

We interrupt Susanna and tell her we'd like to rent the cottage. She passes this news on to Dona Catarina whose eyes instantly well up with tears. She steps forward and hugs Andy, before doing the same with me. She's clearly a soft wee soul. For our part, we're relieved she's happy to have us. We agree conditions and set the date.

This time there are no mishaps on our drive back to Galegos. When we arrive back at Crença K&C are there, Ken up to his waste in the open cesspit.

"The house was fab," Andy tells them. "We've said we'll take it. We move at the end of the month."

"WOOHOO," Ken raises both his hands to the heavens and cries joyfully.

I guess he feels it's time we moved on as well.

No Longer in Transit

A feeling of being unsettled that's lingered in the shadows ever since we arrived in Portugal has suddenly evaporated like the morning mists. Now the road ahead has become clear(er) we realise just how much not knowing what lay in store, in terms of long-term accommodation, had left us jittery and jumpy at times. Up until this point there's been a sense of being in limbo, of having lost control over being able to choose where we want to be. The rental market, or lack of, in the Setúbal area caught us out. That's partly because we have specific (some may call fussy) requirements. If we wanted to live in an apartment block maybe life wouldn't have been quite so difficult. But we don't. Holding out for a home we actually want to live in, and in the area we desire, has taken a toll on stress levels. Galegos was only ever a short-term solution, even though it was one we've stretched to snapping point. Nevertheless, we'll be sorry to leave Crença. It is an idyllic and extra special location, and we've had the luxury of living in a small mansion for four months. We'll be eternally grateful to Ken and Carole for throwing us that lifeline. Now we're swapping this palatial old house for a wine vat. We must be mad, but in truth we're flying high as the vultures above at the idea of being able to live so close to our first choice location.

We hardly spent any of September in Galegos. Gadding about other parts of Portugal combined with house-hunting in Setúbal ate up the month. We did manage to notch up a Medieval fair in Castelo de Vide at the start of September. It was the second themed fair we'd been to in the area. The first was the *Ammaia Festum* held each May/June at the ruins of the Roman Town of Ammaia just outside Portagem. That one involved many toga-clad women, scowling Roman centurions, a chariot, and mock battles against heathens who were curiously dressed in Highlander-type belted plaids. Even the refreshments and snacks on offer reflected the Romanesque setting – *cafum* (coffee), *cervejum* (beer), *sumum* (fruit juice), *agum* (water), *batatum fritum* (French fries); non-Portuguese speakers having to work out two translations to figure out what each was. Unfortunately the day we went was one of the only two days we had rain in all the time we were in Galegos.

Castelo do Vide's annual Medieval *festa* was on a much grander scale, the area around *Praça dom Pedro V* completely time-warped back to Medieval times. It's described as a 'living history' festival, meaning many townsfolk get into the spirit of things by dressing in appropriate garb. Women tend to come out best when it comes to Middle Ages fashion, the Maid Marion look being a flattering one, whereas most of the men came across as down-on-their-luck peasants wearing belted sacks. Given the period it reflects, there's an appropriate mix of Christian and Moor influences. On one side of the *praça*, Knights Templars prepared for a jousting competition. On the other, belly dancers sashayed their way along the cobbles. In between were jesters, fire-eaters, musicians, and artisans selling wares from stalls with Ye Olde Worlde names such as *A Chave do Destino* (the key of destiny – a jewellers) or the *Viking Pharmacia*, which specialised in different flavoured sangrias (honey, melon, red fruit, black). Food and drink featured heavily, and there still weren't enough stalls to sate the appetites of roaming revellers. Long wooden tables outside mock taverns overflowed with people on hay bale benches tucking into suckling pig, bowls of spicy offal (*sarapatel*) and drinking from tin flagons brimming with frothy mead. It was a good venue for wandering and grazing. The *sarapatel* and mead got a thumbs up from us whereas our first try of *pão com chouriço* (chorizo encased in *fogaça* bread) was probably our last. (Note: I've since had *pão com chouriço* in Óbidos which has made me re-evaluate this position. It was bloody marvellous.)

On the early evening before we're due to depart Crença, we crack a Bohemian beer to toast the sun-kissed view we'll be leaving. But before we can take a sip the tranquillity is smashed by the sound of a right old commotion in the garden at the front of the house – a *cabra* attack. For four months we've watched the goats jingle-bell their way along the lane, occasionally

148

launching assaults on the garden of the unoccupied cottage across the road but never straying from the cobbled path which separates Crença from the garage and driveway... until now. There's no shirtless goatherd in sight, the goats have gone rogue and swamp the place, masticating mouths frantically grabbing at the flowers, fruits, and plants we've watered religiously each day for a quartet of months. We run at them with arms spread wide shouting, and laughing, herding them back onto their righteous path. At least they're relatively obedient, even if some take out a few extra floral casualties as they nimbly skip back across the dry-stone wall to rejoin their route homeward. A few sweeps clear out reluctant stragglers, and we return to our even more welcome *cervejas*. We'll miss these little idiosyncrasies of rural Alentejo living.

Despite the prospect of heading to pastures new, we're crotchety with each other as we pack Cindy with the essentials we'll need to tide us over until we return for the mostly unopened boxes in the pool house. Travelling with us are mainly clothes, IT equipment, and kitchen utensils. Crença was decently equipped with kitchenware, but we still had to stock up those which we tend to use in our cooking. No doubt the kitchen at Casa Camelia will be no different, especially as it's likely to be stocked for a holidaying market.

As we squeeze boxes into the back of our Punto we snap at each other like narky Jack Russels over stupid, pointless things which we'll forget in a few hours. I don't know why, maybe it's just the stress of moving combined with concerns that Cindy isn't up to these long, hot journeys. She's an island girl, used to zipping around Tenerife where it rarely gets too hot and never gets too cold. She's also a fair old age and has been prone to overheating if we get stuck in traffic on hot days, and that was on Tenerife where summer temperatures aren't usually as excessive as here. Our 'go to' mechanics there fixed this problem a couple of times, but it keeps recurring. The upshot is, by the time we're ready to leave we're hardly exchanging any words at all. We should be happy, smiling people. But we're really not.

As Andy takes a last look around the house, I check out the pool house to make sure there's nothing we want from any of the boxes stored there. I open one to see a yellow face smiling up at me. It's Flat Eric. We're not cuddly toy people by any stretch of the imagination, but we own two which accompanied us to Tenerife from Stockport that we don't consider to be cuddly toys at all, Flat Eric and Ted. Flat Eric is a renegade. Anyone who saw Levi adverts in the late 1990s will know why. Eric is a legend. His compadre Ted is a little more difficult to explain. He came with a bottle of perfume and would be a conventional teddy bear if he wasn't wearing a red Giorgio jumper, which he's never seemed too happy about. Ted and Eric are a compatible, odd couple who, at some point, became an integral part of the family. Our twenty-five-year-old niece, Emily, told us recently she'd spotted a Flat Eric at an antiques fair in Leeds and was so excited she was desperate to have him even though she didn't have the money. The folk selling him, noticing how thrilled Emily was at finding Flat Eric, gave him to her as a present, happy he was going to a home where he'd be loved. Flat Eric invokes those sort of reactions.

Flat Eric and Ted have been living in the spider-infested pool house since our furniture arrived from the Canaries, so they deserve a change of scene. I sit them in a space just behind and between the driver and passenger seats so they can see out of the window. I know it's my imagination but Eric's smile looks even wider than normal, and Ted doesn't have quite as grumpy an expression as he usually does.

Andy completes her last check of the house. We're ready to leave. No words pass between us as we get into the car and buckle up. The atmosphere is decidedly moody. Andy starts the engine, turns her head to make sure she can still see through the rear mirror… and spots the two faces looking up at her. She bursts out laughing, and tears well in her eyes. The dark clouds which have been resting heavily on our shoulders explode into sunshine. After a few moments Andy reaches across and gives me a hug.

"I don't know why, but seeing those two daft faces looking

out of the window as though they're thrilled to be going on an adventure has just made my day. Finally I feel as excited as they look."

Now we're all in the right frame of mind, ready and eager for the next chapter to unravel.

Getting into the Rhythm of Farm Life

I sit on the whitewashed ledge outside our front door, turn my face to the sun, and breathe a huge satisfied sigh. This feels different. The burden of uncertainty has flown off into the blue sky. For the first time since we drove onto the ferry in Santa Cruz de Tenerife we feel settled. Now we can make plans.

There was one final task which had to be undertaken before we reached this quasi Zen-like state, moving the rest of our furniture/belongings from beyond the back of beyond to Setúbal or, more accurately, Palmela as that's the municipality where the *quinta* is located. Even that task gave an insight into the character of the people who live in this area. Whilst filling out the paperwork required to hire a 15m van from a car rental office in Setúbal, the woman dealing with us spotted our address was in the same village she lived in. As she checked the van for damage, she annotated the documents in her hands to show the van already had small scratches all over it.

"That way you shouldn't have a problem if there are any minor mishaps," she smiled as she ticked away at her sheaf of papers.

It was just as well she did. The drive from Sétubal to Alentejo and back was easy as Portuguese roads tend to be sparsely populated with other vehicles. In fact I'd go as far as to say it was enjoyable, the sense of power at sitting in an elevated position in a biggish vehicle unlocked the white van man demon inside. The only squeaky bum moments came at either end of the drive, due to a brace of narrow driveways lined by trees with low-hanging branches which screeched their way across the van's paintwork. At those times I gave silent thanks to the generous foresight of the woman in the rental office.

It doesn't take us long to organise living and working arrangements. The house has two bedrooms, which are unworkable as bedrooms as you have to walk through the main bedroom to get anywhere from the spare room. That ain't going to happen, so it becomes our office with views over the central garden area and lawn. Everything else remains the same, albeit with our personal stamp added – a picture here, a few photos there, a wine island/desk we'd brought from Tenerife etc. The office leads into our bedroom which leads into the kitchen (where the front door is) which leads into a small hall (with access to bathroom and a back door which opens onto a rear terrace) which leads into the living/dining room. The bedroom and office are bathed in sunlight in the morning, the living room gets the rays in the afternoon and evening. It's an easy, and comfortable little space to inhabit.

With a full stop placed at the end of our time in Alentejo, we turn our attention to becoming acquainted with our new surroundings. First we learn the farm isn't really a farm in the way we think. Dona Catarina owns thirteen sheep, but they don't seem to have any purpose. She has ducks, but again for no real reason other than to waddle about the duck pond. There are also a lot of cats around the place. We haven't quite figured out how many as new feline faces keep turning up at various parts of the land. However, there are at least ten. Having a window into the the world of the *quinta's* cats is akin to watching a soap opera. There are laughs, tears, drama, high drama, love affairs, incestuous behaviour, shocking revelations, favourite characters, new faces introduced regularly, and dastardly villains. Not everybody is who they at first seem.

The Cast of Cats of the Quinta - There are some whose real names we know (Ricky, Lily, Princesa, Johnny, Bob, Felix); others whose names we've made up ourselves (Batman) or who remain nameless; and one with mental health problems whose name we can never remember - Poombaloo may or may not be correct.

Felix is the old man of the group at nearly 20 years old. He's a scrawny, half-blind tortoiseshell who staggers about the place making pitiful, brain-piercing demands for food. Felix is permanently hungry, eats constantly, and remains skeletal; not a good sign. It's obvious he's going to be one of the first to be written out of 'the show.' Dona Catarina tends to carry him everywhere and keep him indoors most of the time, lessening the impact of his noisy demands. Being allowed to spend time in a house is a luxury not afforded to the other cats who live the outside life of farm cats.

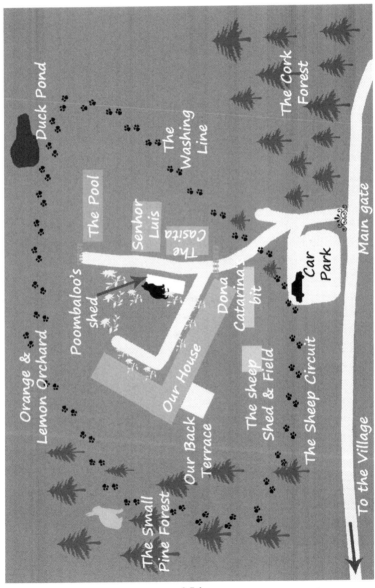

Ricky appears to be the bad boy of the bunch, a black panther of a cat who swaggers around the place insolently, perpetually seeking one of the female cats so he can have his wicked way with her. We don't think Ricky likes us much as he has developed an unpleasant habit. Whenever we eat outside on our back terrace, he ambles over to a spot near us, digs a hole, and takes a crap. I don't know what that cat eats but whatever it is, it stinks to the high heavens. We often hear Dona Catarina shouting, "NO, RICKY, NO!" - a sign he's in the process of leaving his mark somewhere inappropriate.

Lily is Ricky's sister, also black but with different coloured eyes from her sibling. We can never remember which one has chestnut eyes and which has green ones, but Lily has a chunk out of the tip of her right ear which helps immensely with identification. She's one of the sweetest of the moggie crew, and courts our friendship from day one by offering her soft and silky belly for a rub.

Poombaloo is the third jet-black cat, but there's no mistaking him as he never leaves his house, which is a white outbuilding at one side of the lawn. On one side there's a small wooden door with a cat-sized hole cut into it. Poombaloo often sits at this entrance, scuttling back inside his house if human, sheep, or another cat comes near. On the lawn side of his house, a narrow window leads onto the terracotta-tiled roof of a mini *butano* shed. This is where Poombaloo spends most of his time, watching out for danger. If he ventures further he ends up being chased by one of the other cats. Poombaloo, sadly, is bullied relentlessly.

Princesa is the prettiest cat on the farm with big green eyes, a white underbelly, and soft orange and faded black back, sides and face. She lives in the car park and is a bit of a tart. Whenever anyone approaches she throws herself to the ground in front of them and squirms around in the dust. On two feet it can be difficult enough to get past but she behaves the same when we're in the car, forcing us to stop, get out, and physically remove her.

Johnny and Bob are virtually identical in looks and personality. Their markings are the same except one has mostly grey markings whereas the other has a pale amber hue. The only way we can remember which is which is by renaming the grey one Lord Greyjohn. They are deeply, deeply suspicious of us and leg it to a safe distance when we appear, from which they observe us with half-closed eyes and expressions which say, "we know you will beat us badly if we stray too close". Johnny and Bob are Princesa's offspring and, although, fully grown adult males, follow their mother about everywhere.

Batman's a portly white and black cat with a Batman mask who lives in the sheep shed. Batman's another cat who maintains a safe distance from us. We see him a lot as our back terrace looks over the field with the shed where the sheep sleep overnight. Batman provides regular lunchtime entertainment as he constantly tries to creep up on wood pigeons, Eurasian jays, and hoopoes searching the grass for grubs and insects. Sadly for him, his 'cuddly' frame means he isn't the quickest cat on the farm, and the birds know it. They virtually ignore their white and black stalker, knowing he's never going to get close before they take to the air.

We haven't quite figured the rest out yet. There's another Batman-like feline who hangs around the swimming pool area. I got close once, or rather he got close to me. I was talking to Dona Catarina and the cat strolled around the edge of the pool to nuzzle her hands, then he ambled over to me and I made the mistake of thinking he wanted the same. When I reached out to pet him, he bit my finger, and that was the end of that friendship.

There are fruit trees all over the farm, ranging from a large orchard with lemons, oranges, and tangerines to hidden pockets of pomegranate, plum, and loquat trees. The citrus orchard we've discovered, the location of the other fruit trees remains a mystery. We know they exist only because baskets filled with various fruits turn up on our doorstep on a regular basis, courtesy of either Dona Catarina or Senhor Fernando. This is an area with many small-scale farms whose inhabitants produce fruit and vegetables mostly for their own use, or to swap with neighbours. There are so many orange trees in Brejos do Assa we could shed tears at the number of wasted windfall fruits we pass every time we leave the house. Hundreds litter the ground, uncollected.

Our route from farm to the main road leading to Sétubal is an interesting little journey in itself. First we pass a field with the cutest dwarf goats ever seen, their cuteness only outdone when they produce ridiculously tiny kids. Rows of vines lead to a stretch bordered by olive trees on one side and a duck farm on the other. There's no fence around this duck farm so the ducks, and hens, wander wherever they wish. We regularly have to stop the car in order to gently shoo Jemima Puddle-Duck and friends from their dust baths in potholes in the road so we can continue on our way. From the duck farm there are two ways to the main road. One leads past allotments and a couple of pot-bellied pigs to the centre of the village. The other runs beside a field which is home to the most eclectic mix of animals I've seen outside a zoo. Each time we pass this field one of us will gasp, "was that a... ?" So far we've spotted mules, horses, long-horned *Barrosã* cattle (each with an egret companion), two reindeer, and three camels. When we ask Dona Catarina and Senhor Fernando why there's a Noah's Ark of animals in the field, Dona Catarina just shrugs a "*nao sei*" and tells us there also used to be an ostrich who'd eat the buttons off the jackets of anyone who wandered too close, whilst Fernando corrects us by pointing out the camels aren't camels, they're one-humped dromedaries.

Senhor Fernando is the farm's gardener/handyman. He's a lithe, laid-back, laconic man in his mid-thirties who is a font of local knowledge. Or he would be if we could understand half the nuggets he shares with us. Fernando's accent is thick as maple syrup and almost impenetrable to our untrained ears. His words are hypnotically melodic, but run sing-song fashion into each other without pause, all joined together like the processional caterpillars he informs us will march down from the pine trees in January/February. Our Portuguese is nowhere near good enough to be able to understand more than a fraction of what he utters. Fernando reminds me of some of the people I grew up with in the West of Scotland. People who'd never get near a university but who knew all sorts of fascinating and useful things about the world; their education gleaned from experience and books read for enjoyment rather than as part of a course. Fernando shows us what berries we can eat from the trees around the farm; tells us about speciality foods and wines to try in various villages and towns around the area; and where the best *festas* are. At least he tries to tell us. Even though we look baffled half the time, he still perseveres. We fare slightly better with Dona Catarina. She was married to a German and subsequently her Portuguese, adjusted for foreign ears, is clearer. There aren't the same amount of words ending in 'shzz' sounds. She's also extremely patient, seemingly able to understand our Span-uguese (our sentences often include a combination of Spanish and Portuguese words) or, as we're in Portugal, Portu-nish. The problem with this is it leads to a false sense of security. Every time we think we've made progress (i.e. held a half-decent conversation with Dona Catarina) we stray from the farm and encounter someone who isn't Dona Catarina. These encounters invariably end with blank looks all round, and any confidence in being able to communicate in Portuguese at even the most basic level is completely smashed against the rocks of incomprehension.

Notice that when I refer to Dona Catarina it's always as Dona, whereas when I mention Senhor Fernando the 'senhor' is sometimes there, and sometimes not. This reflects our uncertainty at how to address him. The Portuguese seem quite formal people, we noticed this especially in northern parts, so it feels important we mirror the way people address each other. Dona Catarina insists on calling me Senhor Jack, and Andy is always Dona Andrea. At first we think this is due to unfamiliarity, but she refers to everyone as '*senhor*' or '*dona*'. Even when she talks about Fernando it's always Senhor Fernando. There's a respect shown to everyone irrespective of social/occupational standing. Actually talking to Fernando (if that's what I can call confused attempts at conversations) feels a more casual affair so I sometimes drop the '*senhor*'. I'd take my lead from Senhor Fernando himself, but he never, ever refers to us by name so I'm left in the dark... in all sorts of ways.

Dona Catarina has another some-time helper called Marcelo.

Marcelo is a lovely Brazilian guy who has a wide smile permanently fixed to his face. He's a calming influence on Dona Catarina whenever the '*natureza*' creates problems (which it does regularly), or something goes wrong with the farm's electrics/water. Marcelo has at least one 'proper' job, installing heating systems, but still spends a lot of his free time assisting Dona Catarina on the farm. DC (our shorthand version of her name, used only when talking to each other) and her husband helped Marcelo with paperwork and various other things when he first moved to Portugal. Now he repays that friendship by assisting DC when she needs it, including teaching her to drive after her husband passed away. It's fascinating to listen to the contrasts when Marcelo and Fernando speak. Marcelo's Brazilian Portuguese is far clearer, those Eastern European sounding pronunciations are absent. If anything, there's a slight American twang to his dialect. We still can't understand most of what Marcelo says, but at least we can make out the words and then Google translate them later.

It only takes a few days to get to know the daily rhythm of the farm. Senhor Fernando arrives early morning to let the sheep out of the field where they overnight. Thereafter the flock begins a relentless circuit which involves pulling at trees in the car park, eating grass in the lower fields, trying to grab oranges from the orchard (sheep get very excited at the prospect of a juicy orange – who knew?), snuffling around in the sandy dust of the small pine forest beside our house, and back to their field to begin the circuit again. At various times of the day we hear Dona Catarina shouting "*andar, andar*" to call them to meals, or when they've breached the inner defences and are devastating the out-of-bounds garden area where the houses are located. Occasionally we'll see a sheep run past the window with camellia flower in gob closely following by DC. As DC doesn't arrive till mid-morning when she's not staying over at the farm, occasionally we'll spot an incursion into the garden and have to coax the guilty sheep back to their part of the farm without scaring them. '*Andar*' is a useful word to know when this happens. DC treats these dim animals as pets rather than farm animals, so gentle coaxing accompanied by a lot of '*andar*' is the preferred way of persuading them to vacate the premises; something I discovered after employing a 'rush at them shouting with arms wide open' approach which caused utter havoc in the ranks and earned a look of consternation from DC. Apart from that nothing much happens. There are various farm-work noises as Fernando tends to the land, and occasional murderous screams as cats stray into another's territory. But mostly it's a blissful oasis in which to work.

We rise at 07:30; eat breakfast, strolling to the orchard to collect supplies for fresh orange juice when required; sit down to write at 08:30; break for lunch at 13:30 (taken on the suntrap of a back terrace under shade as it's too hot to sit in full sunshine); move our laptops to the covered front terrace for the afternoon (by that time it's too hot to work inside the house); finish working at 17:30; grab a beer, or make a *Porto tonico*, and decamp to a wooden table and chairs beside a small pond on the far side of the lawn (this gets the last of the sun) where we round off the working day relaxing to the sound of birdsong. All in all it feels like a perfect fit.

ANOTHER PERFECT DAY IN THE CITY BY THE BAY

Two snippets about Setúbal, the biggest town near us. The very first scene of season two of the Netflix series *The Crown* is in Setúbal harbour, where the Royal Yacht Britannia was moored during the Queen's visit to Lisbon in 1957. The second is it's José Mourinho's home town. In fact, as we arrive the town has just named an avenue after the precocious football manager. One of the first things I tick off from my Setúbal 'to do' list is to have a photo taken with the sign for Avenida José Mourinho. José's manager of the team I support, Manchester United, and I like him anyway. The world needs flamboyant, outspoken, and some might say annoying, characters like José Mourinho.

Senhor Zé, as José is known in his own town (along with countless other Josés), is back in Setúbal for the inauguration of the avenue. Local newspapers feature stories about the homecoming of the 'special one'. He enjoys being back in Setúbal apparently. Here he's not the manager of Real Madrid/Chelsea/Man Utd, he's just Senhor Zé. It's that sort of place, a friendly, down-to-earth working class town. Dona Catarina tells us his father, also Senhor Zé, managed the town's football club, Vitória F.C.

The Atlantic Ocean and Sado Estuary, which on most days sparkles invitingly in a bay which curves around to almost meet the sandy tip of the Troia Peninsula, are partly responsible for this working class persona, drawing workers to the area since Roman times when salted fish and *garum* (a sought-after fermented fish sauce) factories were located there. The protective arm of the Troia Peninsula made the bay a perfect port location, especially as new territories to the south, east, and west were being discovered by adventurous Portuguese explorers (aka opportunistic, ruthless entrepreneurs). Those same qualities also attracted Moorish invaders, subsequently the area is home to a series of fortifications; rock solid constructions standing watchful on a trio of hilltops in Arrábida National Park.

Fishing and port trade have been the cornerstone of the town's activity over the centuries; in the late 19th century it became one of the main centres in Portugal for the canning of fish. In its heyday there were well over 100 factories lining the seafront, attracting workers from Portugal's colonies as well as from its hinterland; continuing a tradition of conserving which had started in the 1st century.

We'd been told that Setúbal was a town which was down on its luck. But we were hooked from our first visit as what we saw was an honest, friendly, fascinating, multicultural Portuguese town with a rich history. It was a town which felt as though it was about to rise from the ashes and emerge from the obscuring shadow cast by preening Lisbon across the Tagus.

It's a 15 minute drive from our house to the centre of Setúbal. Most people seek free parking, which is severely limited. We're happy to use the main car park near the town's market as it's cheap - €5 for a whole day. The first thing we notice when we park up just off Avenida José Mourinho is the aroma of freshly fried fish. One of the things we loved about living in Puerto de la Cruz on Tenerife was early morning strolls around the harbour where the smell of freshly fried fish drove us insane with hunger. Setúbal is the same, but on a far bigger scale. In Setúbal the aroma more often than not comes from a local obsession, *choco frito* (fried cuttlefish).

There are a lot of men with wiry physiques, stained clothes and weather-beaten faces hanging around. I'm initially suspicious, just because I'm always suspicious when I see folk lingering about car park areas when they don't actually have cars. I try not to automatically judge folk, but fail a lot, as I do again now. The shifty-looking men are fisherman, weary and grimy following their efforts at sea. The car park is beside one of Setúbal's crowning glories, the *Mercado do Livramento* - one of the great markets of the world. The back street leading to the market is bustling with 'off-duty' fisherman who sit on the kerb in front of plastic basins filled with clams or *caracóis* (snails). The smell of uncooked inhabitants of the sea is pretty overpowering along this street. Where the street is bustling, early morning the market is a hive of Setúbalenses shouting their orders for the freshest of fresh products. The first thing which catches the eye is a huge rear wall of *azulejos* depicting the life of the town at the beginning of the 20th century. There are around 5700 blue tiles in all. Each entrance at the front of the market is worthy of a visit as they all feature various local scenes constructed from these hand-painted ceramic tiles. The market itself, built in 1876, consists of long aisles lined by stalls. There are various themed areas for fruit and veg, breads and pastries, flowers and spices, cheeses and jams, fresh and cured meats, and fish and seafood. Each section has a larger than life sculpture illustrating what's on sale in the market. One of a butcher is particularly eye-catching as he wears an apron splattered with blood. The Portuguese, like the Spanish, don't shy away from the fact that meat comes from a living thing rather than something anonymous which has been neatly cut and packaged so supermarket customers don't have to think about where their fillets actually came from. Around the edge of the market are butchers, wine shops, and cafes. However, it is the fish and seafood section which sets it apart from other markets, it's a marine treasure chest featuring as wide a selection of fish and seafood as I've seen anywhere. There are familiar characters (bream, mackerel, sea bass, ugly monkfish etc.) and unfamiliar ones (scabbard fish). And then there are the monstrous-sized ones. At one counter, a fishmonger hacks at the whale-sized body of a tuna. Nearby is the enormous head of a swordfish. Markets like this are not the sort of places vegetarians want to stray into. We would love to order a fillet of this a fillet of that, but listening to the rapid-fire transactions taking place using words which zip fast our ears at such speed we can't separate one from another, we bottle it. We are simply not at the stage where we can give instructions in Portuguese about what part of a fish we want. We need to plan a strategy, and research key phrases before we can buy anything from this market that doesn't just involve pointing and saying "*uma, por favor.*"

The *Mercado do Livramento* leads onto the town's main artery, *Avenida Luisa Todi*, which dissects the harbour-side from the old quarter. Named after a famous Portuguese opera singer born in the town in the 18th century, it's an attractive, wide, tree-lined thoroughfare with cafes and fountains dotted along its length. On the opposite side of the avenue from the market lies the old quarter, a warren of narrow cobbled streets lined by cottages. Some are dilapidated, some pristine. Directly opposite the market is the main square, *Praça do Bocage*, named after the dapper poet on the Corinthian plinth centrepiece of the square. Flanking the *praça* are pretty, pastel town houses, including the porticoed, royal purple town hall, and the *Igreja de São Julião* which started life in the 13th century as a humble place for fishermen to worship. Now it's rather more grand, especially its wonderfully elaborate Manueline side entrance, a masterpiece of ropey, twisted columns. There are a number of *pastelarias* and cafes dotted around the square, one with a menu whose drinks and food are themed around Moscatel, another of Setúbal's specialities. Best people-watching spot is from the shade of the modernistic upside down umbrellas at Delice Garden. From *Praça do Bocage*, cobbled spokes spread in all directions. We systematically explore each.

Due east takes us along shopping streets which are just about wide enough to swing an alley cat. It's refreshing to see independent shop names which are completely unfamiliar; no homogeneous city centre outlets here. Songs from the 80s blasting out from speakers hung above the street accompany us on our meanderings whilst the street itself is brightened up by ornate decorations made from recycled plastic. The street widens at *Largo da Misericórdia* where a pavement water fountain splashes the generous calves of a bronze sculpture being admired by a trio of Spanish women (we regularly latch on to Spanish voices we hear purely because we can recognise words for a change).

"It's by Fernando Botero," one tells us as we join them to admire the voluptuous figure.

I'm no art aficionado by a long shot, but I can recognise certain artists' works and the Colombian artist's style is instantly recognisable, a bit like the South America version of Beryl

Cook. I've seen his sculptures and paintings in various locations around Spain. It turns out the sculpture isn't by Botero at all, but by a student who studied under him.

Another 'spoke' takes us north to *Parque do Bonfim*, the green heart of the city next to Vitória F.C.'s stadium. It's a tranquil spot for a coffee and a *pastel de nata* overlooking a pond with ducks and swans. Pleasant though it is, it would be a run of the mill park if it weren't for one curious feature, a series of colourful sculptures with bulbous bodies, rectangular heads, and pointy noses. Created by local artist Maria Pó, each represents Setúbal in one way or another – the poet Bocage is there, as is a friar from Arrábida, a fish seller, wine producer, and a supporter of Vitória F.C. We begin to realise that, for all its working class ambiance, Setúbal has a strong artistic side. It makes the place even more appealing.

West from *Praça do Bocage* takes us through old streets which are badly run down, but which aren't without charm or interest. A sculpture of a blindfolded woman honours Mariana Torres, a canning factory worker murdered by officials during a strike in 1911 in protest at exploitative wages. Working class heroes as well as art, the place gets even better. There are loads of little restaurants tucked away in these streets, many with metal barbecues outside from which nose-grabbing smoke emanates from charred fish; this is a place for further exploration.

Eventually we emerge at the harbour where there's an impressive fleet of cobalt blue fishing boats of various sizes, a flotilla of bobbing seagulls, and a handful of cormorants perched on wooden stanchions. Backing the harbour is a walkway brightened up by the '*Golfinho Parade*' – a selection of 20 colourfully painted dolphins chosen from over 300 participants in a contest designed to honour the 'stars' of the Sado Estuary. The dolphins on show reflect either something connected with Setúbal or the people who designed it (e.g. piano keys on a dolphin designed by a musical college). Behind the dolphins lie a row of fish and seafood restaurants. The town is full of fish and seafood restaurants, but these are in prime spot as they're a fish throw away from the boats which provide the main ingredients for their menus.

It's not quite lunch time so we wander further, passing the town's small white sand beach which isn't a beach. I learn, after reading a discussion on Tripadvisor about Setúbal not having any beaches, that what we'd think of as being a decent beach isn't even considered a beach by the Portuguese (this has been confirmed by more than one resident of Lisbon). The rational is that any strips of sand not facing the sea, e.g. on a river or an estuary, aren't considered beaches irrespective of whether they're sandy or not. I have a theory that the reason why many non-Portuguese aren't aware of the number of nice beaches there are close to Lisbon is that, because locals have dismissed them as not being beaches, they're told 'nope, no beaches here' when they ask the question on the likes of Tripadvisor. It's all down to cultural interpretation. People in this part of Portugal have so many exceptional beaches they can afford to be selective in what they class as a beach. For anyone who isn't applying Portuguese standards, take it from me beach-less Setúbal has a couple of very nice beaches.

The long thin strip beyond the harbour is a delightful spot for a stroll. The forest sweeps down to the coast with the *Forte de São Filipe* standing protectively above the tree line; there are neat lawns where people laze in the shade under sail-shaped canvas shelters and in over-sized wooden crates; a guitarist strums lightly, adding his *saudade* soundtrack to the chilled-out vibe; sailing dinghies scythe quietly through the turquoise water just offshore; fisherman cast their lines from the promenade; and, in the sizzling October sunshine, sunbathers turn a deep shade of bronze on the soft, white sands on beaches which aren't beaches. At one point we pass a notice which proclaims "*Just another perfect day in the city by the bay*" which pretty much captures how we're feeling.

We reach the end of the promenade at a large rock which blocks off further progress and retrace our steps back to the harbour for lunch. By this time the restaurants are brimming with locals. Friday lunch by the harbour looks like it's *the* thing to do. Restaurants with covered terraces and floor-to-ceiling windows seem the most popular and subsequently fill up first. We're frazzled anyway, it's still too hot to be out in the sun for any length of time, so make a decision about which restaurant to try after a scientific application of an 'eeny, meeny, miny, moe' formula. O Ramila doesn't have a terrace, just a door leading into a darkened room which looks invitingly cool. It's a Tardis of a restaurant; inside is cavernous, like a food hall. We hesitate for a second, big means bad when it comes to food doesn't it? But before we can backtrack, a waiter directs us to a table below a fish tank with residents who observe us with accusing eyes. There are only a few other diners when we enter, but by the time we've made our choices the restaurant has filled to capacity. Big here doesn't mean bad at all, big can be essential to cope with demand. When we try to order we have to shout to be heard above the boisterous jamboree of locals. We ask for salad, sardines, and *choco frito* accompanied by a bottle from one of the big local vineyards, José Maria da Fonseca's BSE. It's not the most appealing name for a crisp, fresh white wine, but it's a tonic on a hot autumn day. When the *choco frito* arrives it doesn't look anything like the cuttlefish we tried in other countries, the battered strips look more like they could have come out of a British chippy. It's chunky, succulent, and bursting with flavour... and one portion is enough for two. The sardines, delicious though they might be, are a dish too much. The lot comes to around €30.

We leave O Ramila feeling slightly woozy thanks to the combination of wine and being too long in the sunshine, and also feeling uncomfortably overfull. All in all, it's a great start to a Friday tradition.

The Friday Tradition, Gastronomy and Setúbal

One of the factors which attracted us to the Setúbal area was the promise of what appeared to be a thriving culinary scene. It didn't take us long to figure out that, like the north of Tenerife, there's a strong culture of dining out, which means plenty of restaurants aimed first and foremost at the local population. It's not an affluent area, as a result eating out seems incredible value - generous lunches for two always come in at around €30. The cuisine on offer is more diverse than in some other parts of Portugal. Fish and seafood is abundant, but there are also multicultural influences in the dining scene, and a scattering of restaurants whose chefs serve intriguing, contemporary reboots of traditional dishes.

We choose which restaurant to eat at in a similar way we choose which movies to watch. On a given day we might have a yen for pure escapism (junk food), though-provoking fare (contemporary creative cuisine), old classics (traditional), art-house (avant-garde) or a perennial favourite (familiar comfort food). What we rarely want are remakes featuring the same tired plot and 'stars' over and over again... except for when it comes to choco frito which has quickly become an addiction; one which most of the population of Setúbal suffers from.

Saying all that, if we were to compile a top ten of favourite types of menus, the top three would include those which featured creative cuisine, fish and seafood, and tapas-type dishes. Bottom of the list would be menus dominated by hearty meat offerings. When it comes to traditional fare involving chunks of meat, what arrives on the table doesn't tend to vary much from country to country around Europe; which is partly why the food inland in Alentejo didn't thrill us over the long haul. Having, or not having, diverse gastronomic choice is a deal-breaker as far as we're concerned. Setúbal's culinary scene looks promising, but there's only one way to find out for sure.

O Ramila behind the harbour was the launchpad for an ongoing and leisurely exploration of the restaurant scene which helps us become better acquainted with the area and its gastronomy. It also kick-starts a Friday tradition; finding somewhere different in which to sample the area's culinary offerings over long lunches, accompanied by local *vinhos* to toast the start of the weekend.

Pestiscos - As long-time fans of tapas and mezes, we were thrilled to discover Portugal also had a culture of sharing small plates of food, in this case called petiscos. Setúbal has a decent selection of petisqueiras and it doesn't take us long to decide on our favourites.

Loja de Machada is a friendly Bohemian bar/restaurant located on a pretty *praça* just off *Avenida Luísa Todi*. We'd eaten in the small square during our recce visit and had been charmed by it; partly due to its character, and partly thanks to a trio of student bands, all wearing the sort of uniforms which inspired Harry Potter, who descended on the *praça* to hold a mini battle of the bands. There's nothing fancy about the menu which includes the likes of *chouriço* with scrambled egg, sweet red pepper with *ventresca* (tuna), stuffed mushrooms etc. But it's all tasty and it's the sort of bar where you could easily hang out drinking wine and discussing cult movies.

After our recce visit, we were already hooked by 490 Taberna STB on *Avenida Luísa Todi*. It's one of those restaurants which occupies a middle ground between traditional Portuguese and the contemporary new breed which serves reinvented local favourites. Quail eggs and *presunto* (cured ham) on mini toasts is brunch in one bite; neat little dishes of octopus salad refresh the mouth; and salt cod cakes (*pataniscas*), spicy chicken wings, and crispy potato skins served in a wire basket are all addictively moreish. Portions aren't overpowering, which tends to leave space for their neat trio of desserts which include the ubiquitous Portuguese version of crème Catalan.

Attractively quaint In Sado is more of a traditional *petisqueira*. It sits at the rear of the main square, looking more like an old-fashioned antique shop full of curios such as Singer sewing machines, box TVs, and record players. The portions are generous for petiscos and include pots of home-made crisps (sometimes confusingly served as 'chips' in Portugal), melted cheese with walnuts, *choco frito*, salt cod patties, gratinated scallops, and scrambled eggs with ham and mushrooms. We generally order too much food, but leave just enough space for their salted caramel cheesecake, layered in a jam jar, which is beyond divine.

Fish & Seafood - It's difficult to choose badly when it comes to fish and seafood restaurants in Setúbal. There are three areas which each offer a different dining experience. Prime position is opposite the harbour, with the smell of the ozone and the cry of gulls adding appropriate accompaniments to platters of freshly fried fish. Lining *Avenida Luísa Todi* are some cavernous, glass-fronted restaurants which exude a more sophisticated air. Finally, there's the fishermen's quarter in the backstreets of the old town, an area which deters people who don't know Setúbal as its narrow alleys appear run down to the point of dilapidation. Here are some the most atmospheric fish restaurants, and the aroma of fish being grilled on industrial-sized barbecues is enough to drive nostrils insane.

On a sizzling October afternoon we take refuge under an umbrella on the wood-deck terrace at Martroia opposite the town beach that isn't a beach. Despite shade-hugging we're still too hot. Summer temperatures are lingering well past their sell-by date. I make the mistake of wearing socks and my feet quickly feel like they're bloating like a cornered blowfish, so I remove them; probably not something other diners want to witness when they're tucking into an Azeitão cheese starter. Located beyond the end of the harbour-strip of fish restaurants and connected to a fish and seafood cash & carry, Martroia's menu offers more inventive seafood than the others. Alongside octopus salad, and gratinated scallops are spicy seafood *chamuças* (samosas), and seafood wraps. All of which prove an ideal selection for a hot day, especially combined with a light and zingy *vinho verde*, which has become our preferred choice for lunchtime dining.

Their puddings also stand out from the crowd; moist cakes paired with ice cream and crumble served on a rough wood slabs.

A perfect time for a first dipping of the toes into the fishermen's district is the *Semana da Ostra* (oyster week) which takes place late October, early November. We celebrate it at Tasca do Xico do Cana, an unfussy and unsophisticated fish restaurant located on the corner of a small alley and *praça* on the western side of the town. The oysters arrive on a bed of ice on a tin tray. Seven grilled sardines, a mixed selection of boiled potatoes/*migas*/boiled sweet potatoes, french fries, and *espada preto* (black scabbard fish) are all served on tin trays as well. The presentation is basic, but what these places are all about is dishing up good fish and seafood. We chose the *espada preto* on Fernando's advice. He'd told us it was the tastiest fish in town. But it has to be *espada preto* not the inferior *espada branca*. His advice is sound as a pound, *espada preto* is a seriously tasty fish as promised. As he brings dishes to our table, the waiter regales us with tales about past life in Setúbal, how sardines used to be the food of the poor but now they're expensive (although they don't seem so to us), and why Moscatel from anywhere other than Setúbal isn't proper Moscatel.

Not all the best seafood restaurants in the area are on the coast. Located in an agricultural hamlet near the *Moinho de Maré da Mourisca*, Pérola da Mourisca is one of those restaurants you have to know about to know about. It's packed with locals when we roll up; thankfully I'd made a stuttering reservation over the phone or lunch would be a bust. The menu isn't quite what I'd expect from a traditional restaurant in an out of the way rural area; it's more sophisticated, featuring many attractive sounding dishes. Despite thinking one of the areas we're on safe ground when it comes to understanding Portuguese is what's on menus, we find some of the items on this one difficult to decipher, so we let the waiter decide our meal for us. We don't have a problem doing this, the rationale being restaurants with a good reputation tend to like to show off what they do best. Our trust is rewarded with a parade of dishes, some of which are minor surprises, like an opening salvo of sheep's butter with chunky bread. The bitter is snow-white with a distinctive but addictive flavour. In truth I could happily get through a whole loaf of bread spread with this butter. Red peppers filled with moist crab; quail eggs on mini toasts; goat's cheese on *morcela* (blood sausage); clams in white wine; and *choco frito* (of course) all combine to show why getting a table at Pérola da Mourisca isn't easy.

Creative and contemporary - The choice of restaurants serving avant-garde or re-booted traditional cuisine isn't as prevalent as it was on Tenerife, but there are positive signs it's a burgeoning trend in the area. We've learned that people's dining habits just about everywhere we've been veer toward the conservative; locals of any land generally favouring what they're familiar with and being wary of the new and different. Where the traditional restaurants are packed at weekends, the new flavours on the block in Setúbal seem to only be at the beginning of their mission to convert local palates. For us, it could be perfect timing for a couple of reasons. From a travel writing point of view, it's immensely gratifying to be in at the start, discovering exciting restaurants that are virtual unknowns. It's also satisfying from a taste-bud point of view. The more new different dining experiences there are in any location, the happier our buds are.

We discover one of these restaurants by total accident. Looking for somewhere with a view fit for a celebration, we stumble across Decor e Salteado, a recently-opened, contemporary restaurant overlooking the estuary. It's located in a residential area on *Avenida Belo Horizonte*, a part of town visitors wouldn't be in unless they a) knew about the restaurant or b) were lost. The design is elegantly modern meets tastefully artistic with tables being set over two floors, the upper overlooking the lower. The restaurant is run by a couple of tall, lithe, and amiable male dancers who have put together one of the more creative menus we've seen in Setúbal. Sweet red peppers filled with crab meat are followed by Mexican *bombas* (spicy mince in a potato ball), *puntilhitas* (fried baby squid in a spicy pepper sauce), and the most taste-bud-wowing dish I've eaten in some time - scallops with goat cheese ice cream. It's a marvel of dish, and has us planning a return visit before we've finished devouring it.

Meat – It should be obvious by now that we don't seek out restaurants specialising in meat. However, there's something inviting and intriguing about De Pedra e Sal on Largo do Dr. Francisco even though it specialises in grilled meat. Every time we wander by, we pause to look through glass windows framed by powder blue and sunshine yellow azulejos, and decorated with huge bell jars filled with colourful substances. Inside are flashes of flames that briefly illuminate cosy couples tucking into dishes which do not look like the usual mountains of meat on a plate we've experienced so far. It isn't the sort of restaurant we'd normally frequent, but we're compelled to give it a try. The interior is the epitome of urban chic without being pretentious. Ropey lighting features (not in the dodgy sense), fresh pine shelving units and tables, and funky tiled counters all combine to make it stylish whilst maintaining an intimate ambiance. We're seated at a table right beside the open kitchen. The heat, as slabs of meat are flame-grilled, makes the whole restaurant toasty… too toasty. Even on a cool autumn evening I feel like someone who's been accused of being a witch during the Inquisition. The open kitchen provides fascinating entertainment thanks to a fiery performance from chefs as they cook and plate the food; the presentation proving a talking point in itself. A lip-licking trio of oysters served on a wooden board get the juices flowing. Then comes flame-grilled duck for me, steak for Andy. Both are served on chunky salt bricks, which are stunning looking and ingenious. There's no need to salt your meat here, just drag it across its 'plate.' We might not be the biggest fans of slabs of meat, but if it was cooked and served like this more often we might have to review this stance.

Junk - Sometimes we get a yen for burgers; but they have to be proper burgers rather than something which has come off a franchise production line. During hot months we also enjoy the occasional G&T, so Burguesa Burger & Gin sounds as though it might tick a couple of boxes. Located in the maze of backstreets in the old town, it's stylishly studenty; the sort of place where you wouldn't look out of place tucking into a book as well as an artisan burger. Although a burger joint, it's still one with a distinctive Portuguese personality. You're unlikely to find its gamey *alheira* croquettes with rocket and nuts as a starter in a Portuguese branch of Maccie D's. Burgers also reflect local preferences; my wild boar burger and Andy's salmon and hake combo both come served in Madeiran *bolo do caco* rolls and are accompanied by chunky, herby chips whose name translates as 'camp potatoes.' It's an ideal choice for whenever we fancy the culinary equivalent of slobbing out on the sofa, wearing comfy clothes and watching something trashy on TV.

The menus might vary, but what all these restaurants have in common is their patrons are almost exclusively Portuguese. It might be different during summer months, but even then the great majority of beach-seeking tourists that boost Setúbal's population are from other parts of the country. This is an area where the locals most definitely enjoy dining out. Becoming jaded with the food scene doesn't look as though it's something which is likely to pose us a problem in this tasty slice of Portugal.

CATCH VINTE E DOIS, BUREAUCRACY AND STUFF

It's dull, time-consuming, and can be hellishly frustrating, but sorting out bureaucratic tasks is an essential part of laying the foundations for living in another country. Having been through it before on Tenerife we know it can be a complicated business. Patience is key and you never, ever get uppity with *funcionários*, the equivalent of end-of-level bosses who can either make progress to the 'next level' easier or an awful lot more difficult. We weren't aware of this when we first set foot on Tenerife and, subsequently, locked horns more than we should with power-mad officials. The worst was possibly the woman who, even though we were already paying tax by this point, refused to register us with the Tenerife Health Service. She declared us to not be officially married and dismissed our marriage certificate as being invalid. She'd never seen a UK registry office marriage certificate before, therefore it couldn't possibly be an official document. I hit the roof with that one.

I'm not going to go into great detail in relation to the steps involved, so don't read anything as a blueprint. Something we learnt aeons ago when working for the British Civil Service is far too many people lose out, or get things wrong because of what friends/family who've been through similar procedures tell them. Everybody's circumstances are different, and that fact alone can impact hugely on which route through the administrative maze any of us end up having to follow.

Registering for a Fiscal Number - To undertake any official process in Portugal you need a fiscal number (*Número de Identificação Fiscal – NIF*). It's more commonly known as the *Número de Contribuinte*. We hear people being asked for this all the time in shops and at supermarket checkouts, which completely baffled us at first. Why would a shop want to know our NIF? Eventually we discovered that a percentage of what people fork out in shops/travel costs etc. can be offset against various tax categories. It's not a particularly high amount, but every little bit counts. I've read that around €80 a year can be saved on rail travel to and from work just by providing the NIF. It's a system which was introduced in 2013 to encourage more people to do things by the book and reduce the size of the country's black market. The likes of Spain and Greece should take note of this initiative.

Getting a NIF proves surprisingly easy. We roll up at the tax office in Setúbal with every official document of identification we own (another thing we learnt to do on Tenerife where some *funcionários* tried to outwit us by asking for the most obscure document irrespective of whether it was listed on their website as an essential document to be presented). We take a ticket and wait our turn. We don't have to wait long before our number pings up. We hand over passports and rental agreements and that's it. A non-officious official registers us on the system and prints out documents with our NIF on it, bingo. Within 30 minutes of entering the tax office we leave with NIFs in hand, our key to unlocking the next steps.

Registering as an EU citizen resident in Portugal - The issue registering as an EU citizen resident isn't so much documentation as finding the appropriate place to register. We start at Setúbal Town Hall, located in a purple colonial building on *Praça de Bocage*; a pleasant setting for carrying out admin work. Get the bureaucratic business out of the way and then chill-out with a coffee on the cobbled square. Except, as the farm is in Brejos do Assa, it's not our administrative centre. Another friendly *funcionário* points us in the direction of Palmela Town Hall. The *quinta* is located almost equidistant between Setúbal and Palmela and we're still at the stage of not knowing who belongs to where or where you do what.

Palmela's Town Hall is nearly as aesthetically pleasing as Setúbal's, and also located on a small *praça*. But it's not the building we need to register at either. That's at a place called the *Junta de Freguesia* beside the town's market. Yet another helpful *funcionário* makes us an appointment to see someone there. This is how time slowly slips away.

A few days later we turn up at the *Junta de Freguesia*, fill out the required forms, and find out that, although it will take a week before our documentation is ready, we don't have to return to this office (no big deal as it's only 15 minutes away). There's a satellite office, a *freguesia*, in the village near the *quinta* and we can collect our documents there. Apparently there's a hierarchy of council offices in Portugal, *freguesias* are at the bottom of the pyramid, like a parish office dealing with very localised issues.

Seven days later we drive two kilometres to where the *freguesia* should be and can't spot anything looking remotely like a government building. There's a lone bar, a creche, and a flock of sheep, but that's it. We drive up and down the road a couple of times, passing vines, hens, and more sheep. But no office. Eventually we park at the bar and pop inside where a couple of farmers in flat caps nurse glasses of *vinho tinto*.

"*Onde fica a fregusia, por favor?*" I keep the question concise, hoping any answer that comes my way will be the same.

One of the men points to an area outside the back of the bar.

I say "*obrigado*" and step outside to tell Andy the unlikely location of the office. We traipse to the rear of the bar where there's a closed door protected by an iron grill. There's a notice on the grill listing opening hours which show it should be open now - 12.45. It isn't. As it's Friday we decide whoever was manning the office has knocked off early. They're possibly even in the bar.

The following Monday we return to the *freguesia* at a more 'sensible' hour. This time it's open. The office is tiny; the only person inside is a woman wearing a floral housecoat, who I assume is the cleaner. Except she isn't the cleaner at all, she's the official we need to speak to. I make a note to myself to stop judging people on their appearance and we attempt to tell the woman why we're there. She struggles to understand us and we struggle to understand her.

"*Estamos aqui recolher documentos,*" I try. She looks at us blankly and says something we don't understand, her words muffled in an invisible fog. I try again, adjusting slightly.

"*Eshtamosh aqui recolher documentosh.*" Again another blank look. We both throw random words and phrases at her - "*documentos*", "*moradores*", "*a mulher em Palmela disse*", until something eventually clicks and she turns to a tray with two sets of papers on it. I can see the names on both. The first is for someone called Rodriguez, the other for someone with the surname Montgomery. Andy points to the second set of papers.

"*Somos nos,*" she says. That's us.

"Ah," the woman replies, finally understanding, as she hands us our proof of registration. Step two completed.

Here's the thing that astounds me. It's a tiny office, there were no other people waiting to be seen and she had only two sets of papers on her desk, one of which was clearly not for people with a Portuguese surname. This is a small village where we haven't bumped into anyone who wasn't Portuguese or Brazilian. When two foreigners walked into her office to collect documents why didn't it occur that we might just be the same people whose clearly non-Portuguese name was on one of the only two sets of documents she has to deal with? Maybe she really was the cleaner after all.

Postal deliveries Part 1- Why oh why do we insist on making life difficult for ourselves? On Tenerife our house was *sin numero* (without a number) because it wasn't on a road. We did have a post box at the entrance to the pitch and putt golf course we lived inside. But it wasn't reliable for important documents, so we used an *apartado* - a postal box in the local post office. It made receiving anything by courier service a tricky business. The *quinta* has a name, in fact it has two names. Neither are recognised by official bureaucratic or postal systems. Once again we live in a house out of sight of a road. There is a bank of post boxes 500m away, where the tarmac begins, but Dona Catarina doesn't use hers and the front has been missing for some time. Until the post office replace it we are, ostensibly, address-less. This clearly makes dealing with any arm of officialdom a tricky business until we have a post box number we can give them. This is an irritant. More worrying is that our passports run out in November. Not only do we need ones for officialdom, we have a work trip out of the country planned, and we won't be able to go if we don't have passports. The process itself is far easier than it was the last time we had to renew a decade ago. We've been able to do the renewal online, taking and uploading our own photos. I'm sure the system has a warped sense of humour. All the 'decent' photos I uploaded were rejected for bizarre reasons (no face detected, no head outline visible) but the worst image, in both quality and how I actually looked (demented and down and out) passed. We started the process whilst we were in Crença and it's all been a breeze. Now all we need is to have our new passports delivered by courier service. This is when we discover how poor courier services are in this part of Portugal. The first time we learn courier delivery is going to be a problem is when we receive notification the passports can't be delivered. In Tenerife we'd give courier services our phone number and then 'talk them in' to a point we could meet them and pick up our goods. In Portugal there's no option of 'talking them in'. We need to provide an alternative address, "a neighbour perhaps?" As the neighbours are also farms on dirt tracks, that's not a viable option. We get on a not so merry-go-round of attempted deliveries followed by notifications of failure. Dona Catarina says we can use her main home address in Seixal, and she'll stay home when she knows the passports are due to be delivered. But it transpires we can't change the delivery address online. It's Catch 22 and we can't see any way around it. As the day we're due to catch a plane draws ever closer our passports are so close and yet so far away. Finally, common sense and human intervention save the day. An assistant working for the courier service takes pity on us and phones the delivery driver as he attempts to make another doomed-to-fail delivery and diverts him to Dona Catarina's house in Seixal. A few hours later there's a knock on our door. We open it to find Dona Catarina standing there with a big smile on her face and two buff-coloured envelopes in her hand. We will be able to go to the ball.

Thankfully there's a more relaxed approach to who can sign for documents here than in some locations and the driver had no problem with Dona Catarina signing for packages which didn't actually have her name or address on them.

Opening a bank account - Although it's been a bit of a winding road to get the documentation we need, everyone we've met along it has been incredibly helpful. The people are as amiable as the Canarians on Tenerife, an island whose slogan is *Tenerife Amable*. This is vitally important to us. There are other parts of Europe we considered moving to because the countryside is beautiful, the towns historic and picturesque, and the food deliciously diverse. But, generally speaking, if we haven't found the people to be particularly friendly, then it's a non starter as far as we're concerned.

The first crotchety person we encounter on the Setúbal Peninsula is a bank clerk in the Santander Bank in *Praça Bocage* in the centre of Setúbal. Ironically, we thought once we had our official documents, opening a bank account would be a straightforward process. It turns out to be the most complicated of the lot. We chose Santander because the website had an English option and made the process of opening an account seem easy. But, under the misapprehension that banks would welcome potential new customers with open arms, we're taken aback when a peevish bank clerk builds barrier after barrier, virtually throwing documents back in our faces because we don't have something called a '*Recibo Verde*'. It seems bizarre she's obstructing us from putting business her way. In Tenerife when we asked what we needed to open an account, a bank clerk in Puerto de la Cruz smiled and answered simply "*dinero*" - money. Anyone opening an account there might even get a free set of pans for their troubles. We hadn't banked on a new set of pans, but what we didn't expect was animosity. However, she is no *funcionário* we are required to deal with for documentation. She's just another worker in a bank, and there are plenty of alternative banks around. We tell her, with some satisfaction, we'll be putting our dosh elsewhere. A microscopic insect biting an elephant's skin that might be, but it makes us feel better to metaphorically say, "stuff you."

Part of the issue is because of measures introduced to tighten banking up since the Portuguese banking crisis between 2010 and 2014. Rules might be there to protect the public and tighten banking practices, but they can make it more difficult for foreigners to open an account.

Thankfully, we find ourselves back to dealing with friendly Portuguese at our second choice of bank, where bank staff go out of their way to steer us through the process of opening an account… as well as offering advice on the best places to go wild camping on the Troia Peninsula. It's something we frequently find in dealings with Portuguese across a wide range of activities, both business and leisure based. People often ask us how much we like living in Setúbal before, after hearing our positive responses, coming up with tips about places which will help us enjoy living here even more. People are clearly proud of their town. Their collective attitude prompts comparison with other places we've recently spent time in. Ask for a craft beer in a small town in Provence and the response is likely to be a definitive "*Non!*" Ask for a craft beer in the Canaries and the response might be a no, but then bar staff will suggest an alternative they have which has a stronger flavour than the average lager. Ask for a craft beer in this part of Portugal and they'll suggest an alternative they have which has a stronger flavour than the average lager; tell you where you *can* get craft beer, and then give a history lesson about the area in general.

The process of setting up an account takes forever, but that's partly because the clerk is so chatty. Our address is a potential problem, the *quinta's* address just doesn't seem to officially exist. However, we now have a post box - part of a tenement block of post boxes on the last bit of tarmac before our dirt roads begin. These blocks of post boxes are common around Portugal as there is a whole network of dirt track roads. The question we ask ourselves is this. In a country where dirt track roads and houses whose post boxes are hundreds of metres away are the norm, why does it continually come as a surprise and a potential problem when we tell folk we live on a road with no name. Surely, this must be a common state of affairs?

Still, our friendly bank teller presses a button here, changes some wording there, ticks a few boxes and finally hits send. Hey presto, we have a bank account. Now we can get properly connected to the internet.

Phones, television and the internet - To finalise the setting up of our Portuguese bank account we need to respond to an SMS message from the bank on a Portuguese phone. To get a Portuguese phone we need a Portuguese bank account. Impasse. Okay, we could have bought a pay-as-you-go, but we already have two Spanish phones and it seemed like too much faffing about. With new, provisional, bank account details to hand we immediately decamp to the Alegro Shopping Centre where a number of providers offer ADSL/phone/TV packages that make us realise even more that we were paying a lot for not a lot in the Canaries. ADSL speeds of 40mbs sound like warp-drive fast in comparison to the 1-6 mbs we were supposed to be getting on Tenerife, not that we ever saw ADSL speeds of anything close to that.

Until now we've been using a Vodafone mobile hotspot which has given us far faster internet and sharper TV streaming images than we ever had. But it costs us €30 every 15 days or so. However, despite being less than 50km from Lisbon, only one provider operates ADSL packages for the area we're in; our fault for picking semi-rural I guess. And that's NOS, the dominant operator in Portugal. Still, it all sounds like a good deal and we sign up for the full package. For €10 less a month than we paid for fixed phone line and broadband in the Canaries we can have satellite TV, home phone, mobile phone and ADSL. Now, all systems really are go. Well, nearly all.

Postal deliveries Part 2 - When the new door is fixed to our postbox life becomes a lot easier as far as normal postal deliveries are concerned. It's not something we ever thought about before, but not having a recognised postal address creates so many barriers to modern living. It's incredible the freedom a small plastic door can bring. Anything involving couriers remains problematic; however, Portugal's Post Office (*Correios*) seems to be efficient and reliable. Letters posted in Britain turn up in our post box within a few days. How items which can't be posted through the letterbox are dealt with is completely unexpected and provides another insight into life in this area.

One day we open our postbox to find a white and red slip with the *Correios* logo on it informing us we have a parcel to be collected. Palmela Post Office is a 15 minute drive away. In Puerto de la Cruz on Tenerife we could write off an afternoon whenever we had to post or collect anything from the main *Correos* (the Spanish version). In Palmela it's an in and out again affair. There aren't queues. We hand over the slip and the clerk disappears into a room at the back. He's gone for some time before he emerges, parcel-less and rubbing his head. Then he rummages about in drawers behind the counter, again with no success. He stares at the slip for a few moments and then I see a light bulb go off in his head.

"It's not here," he exclaims. "It's at the post office in Brejos do Assa."

"Where is the post office in Brejos do Assa?" A post office in our village? This is news to us.

"Opposite the restaurant,"

Still blank faces from us. There's definitely no post office opposite the restaurant.

"In the supermarket."

"Ah," the penny drops. It's not a post office, it's a sub-post office inside the village's mini-market.

It's a wasted journey, but we've learnt something which could save us loads of time if all we have to do to pick up parcels is to pop to the local shop.

The mini-market is an odd little affair, run by a sweet, elderly couple who also own a bar next door; they pop between the two to serve customers. The shop has a small meat and bread counter, and is okay for picking up basic supplies as well as miscellaneous things. It's also a social centre, everyone takes forever to be served as they come to chat as much as to stock up on groceries. The sub-post office part is a small glass counter which sells clocks and ornaments. The area behind it is littered with empty cardboard boxes. Only the woman owner, Dona Natalia, deals with the post. We hand over our slip, she toddles behind the counter and starts flinging empty boxes about until she finds what she's looking for. We sign the slip, she hands our parcel over, we both say "*bom dia*" and off we toddle. It's a quirky system but it works a hell of a lot better than courier services.

Poor Cindy - Apart from a couple of glitches, our Fiat Punto Cindy has been a reliable companion over the last 14 years; she's part of the family. When we relocated to Tenerife we chose a small car after experiencing the relatively narrow streets and limited parking spaces in the island's traditional northern towns. Zipping (I'm being generous here, she is a Punto when all is said and done) around an island and covering hundreds of kilometres in a day on the European mainland are two very different scenarios, especially in temperatures which exceed 30C day after day. On long-distance drives we're slightly anxious the demands will be too much for her. Portugal's legislation hammers in the final nails on her fate. After three months we have to complete paperwork to register Cindy in Portugal so we can continue to legally drive her. It's one of the many situations where moving between EU countries isn't as seamless and easy as it should be. It's also expensive. It riles me to think that someone is making money out of what should be a straightforward affair; we're all supposed to be part of the same club, isn't ease of movement partly the point? But there are obstacles strewn around all over the place. Even with online payment systems such as PayPal. Move to another country and open a bank account and you can't simply change your account details on PayPal. You have to close your account and open another. There are lots of little niggles like this when it comes to switching countries. Registering the car initially seems like a relatively straightforward business. We turn up at the appropriate office in Setúbal with the relevant paperwork, find out we have to have a MOT and happily toddle off to finish the process. Happily, until we discover the whole process will cost us over €1000. Forking out that amount of money for a 14 year-old car doesn't make it a viable option. We reach the conclusion we have to buy another car, one which is more suited to covering long distances. Then we discover cars in Portugal are 40% more expensive than they are in the UK or Germany (source: Dona Catarina). Andy's brother John is in the car business and compares prices when we phone him for advice whenever we see a model we like the look of. However, buying a new (to us) car only solves part of our problem. The bigger issue is what to do with Cindy in the longer term. We try to give her away, but nobody here wants her for the same reason we're buying a new car; it'll cost. If we wanted to sell her we'd have to drive her to Spain, but that would involve a lot of organising, and we don't want to risk any long drives. Dona Catarina comes up with a solution we don't particularly like the idea of, but realise it's the only sensible option available; scrap her. It seems a criminal thing to do, especially as she's still in decent shape and perfectly adequate for pottering around the place. It turns out there's a scrap yard a few kilometres away which is also an officially designated site for dealing with 'end of life' cars. It's quite a sweet way of putting it, but it doesn't help with the notion we're having the family pet put down when there's nothing wrong with it. But it is a relief to discover they'll deal with Spanish cars, meaning we don't have to risk driving to an equivalent site across the border. It's also a relief to know we can resolve the problem of what to do with Cindy easily and at no expense; the scrap yard will actually pay us a nominal amount - thankfully not 30 pieces of silver. Even though we now know what steps we have to take we don't have the guts to go through with it, not yet at least. And we don't have to. The farm's rough car park covers a large area; Cindy being left there for a few more months won't be in anyone's way. We replace her with a sexy, electric blue Nissan Juke called Suzy Q (even doing that rouses guilty feelings) and put Cindy out to pasture under a palm tree where she can enjoy a few months of 'retirement' in a nice little spot whilst serving as a sun deck for the farm's cats. One day we'll have to do the inevitable, just not yet.

FLAMINGOS ON THE DOORSTEP

There's a scene in the Coens brothers' film *O Brother, Where Art Thou?* where George Clooney's character Everett McGill proclaims "Well, ain't this place a geographical oddity. Two weeks from everywhere!"

Quinta Novesium is a similar geographical oddity. It's a 15 minute drive from everywhere. 15 minutes in one direction is Setúbal on the coast. 15 minutes in another is the hill town of Palmela with its Moorish castle. And 15 minutes in yet another direction is the *Reserva Natural do Estuário do Sado*, basically the wetlands of the Sado Estuary.

Once it flows inland beyond Setúbal's port area, the Sado spreads its watery roots in all directions. Snake-like slivers of water wind through flatlands, creating a confusing maze of inlets that are home to numerous migratory birds, including spoonbills and flamingos, as well as the only pods of bottlenose dolphins in Portugal. The flatlands are also home to foxes, badgers, wildcats, gennets, and Cabrera's vole. With ingredients like these it's high on our list of places to visit. We waste no time in jumping in the car and heading to the *Moinho de Maré da Mourisca*, a renovated 17th century tidal mill that is a good base for exploring the wetlands and which just happens to be, obviously, a 15 minute drive from the house.

Heading south east from the *quinta* we're immediately into a typically Alentejano world of cork forests, free-roaming cattle and flocks of sheep, and small farmsteads. The *Moinho* lies at the end of a dirt track, more cork oaks obscuring the mill itself until we break free from the woods and a completely different landscape fills the car's windscreen. Stretching ahead and to either side is a sprawling expanse of wetlands where unruly rectangles of former salt pans and current oyster beds lie bordered by grassy dykes. The blinding white *Moinho de Maré da Mourisca* acts like a beacon on the edge of this beguiling landscape. We park the car in a rough, dusty car park and follow a cobbled path walkway which leads between muddy inlets. The tide is currently out so flat-bottomed estuary boats lie impotent, marooned in the mire below rickety, wooden jetties. Lining the path to the *Moinho* are funky, bronze sculptures of the birds we may or may not see – flamingos, heron, spoonbills. The *Moinho* itself is partly small museum, consisting of a few photos of local birdlife, a mock mill depicting the building's former working life, and an ostrich in fancy dress. The woman at the information desk informs us this is one of the best times in the year for bird-spotting, before the flamingos head south for the winter. The mill is also part cultural centre; concerts are held here. In addition, there's a cafe whose exterior terrace is peppered with the sort of canvas director chairs and rattan sofas that wouldn't look out of place in a beachside chill-out bar. Exotic birdlife aside, it looks like a cool little spot to just hang out. There's probably a great sunset scene here. As it's lunchtime, we order a couple of *tosta mixtas* with fresh orange juice whilst we soak up the enchanting vibe and watch waders break the surface of the glassy pools below us.

In theory there are a series of walking routes from the *Moinho*. I say 'in theory' because we've discovered that official municipality websites in this area have a tendency to 'big up' the opportunities for hiking in their municipalities but, when we dig a little deeper to find out what these actually are, there doesn't seem to be any official routes at all, not waymarked/ signposted ones anyway. Information boards often show little hiker icons dotted around the place, but finding evidence of the existence of specific routes is something which has proved beyond our capabilities so far. The *Moinho* has one such map and, to be fair, a signpost which shows the start of a walking route. But after a couple of hundred metres, where dykes split in multiple directions, the signage just gives up the ghost, as though someone simply couldn't be bothered marking the whole route. It doesn't really matter, it's a delight of an area to wander, lapping up sedate surroundings and the exquisite light – sharp and vibrant. One track leads to a hide; a cooling shelter from the hot October sun. From its shady interior we spot a couple of heron, a handful of egrets, and a spoonbill. The last is especially thrilling to see. In the opposite direction, tentatively following the official (mystery) route, we explore paths linking old salt pans. Some connect with other paths; some take us to watery dead-ends. No wonder they gave up trying to mark a walking route, it's a bewildering maze of paths atop dykes around countless rectangular pools, and alongside narrow channels which lead into more open stretches of water and the wider Sado beyond. Apart from the Mediterranean climate, it could be *Great Expectation's* Kentish marshes. It's a calming landscape, save for when high-stepping *pernilongos* (black-winged stilts) panic at our approach and take to the air, screaming at us in shrill tones for disturbing their peaceful paddling. One dyke path leads past a fisherman's hut to a wider channel where there is a row of ramshackle wooden jetties, oyster beds, and the sound of a rush of running water from an open sluice gate. It's the furthest point we can walk from the *Moinho*; the channel ahead, now filling with water, blocks our onward passage. On the other side of this channel are what we've been hoping to see; a flamboyance of flamingos. The ungainly, yet elegant pink birds are close enough the be able to recognise, but too far away to get a decent photograph of any, even with a 200mm lens. They're canny creatures as well. When we try to reach the closest point to where the flock is located, they calmly start to strut in the opposite direction. There's no rushing involved, they just quietly move a little bit further away. However, the thrill of being able to see flamingos in the wild not far from where we live outweighs any disappointment at not being able to get as close as we'd like. And, as it's only that magical 15 minute drive from the house, we can pop down and explore further any time we want.

ADJUSTING TO LONG TERM RENTAL

After the honeymoon period is over at Casa Camelia one thing becomes crystal clear, none of us are used to dealing with long-term renting. Not Andy nor I, not Dona Catarina, and definitely not the house itself.

Both Andy and I bought houses at an early age. In my case, as a sodden rather than wet-behind-the-ears twenty-three year old, for no other reason than it was the done thing during the Thatcher years. Despite having a decent job I couldn't afford the investment and put myself into debt from the moment I signed on the dotted line. For the following year or so after buying an apartment, I had to survive on thinly-spread, meat paste sandwiches for lunch, a small jar lasting two to three days. My lack of dosh did motivate me to learn to cook, using a sparse selection of cheap ingredients to create enough dishes to feed me for a week, sparking an ongoing interesting in gastronomy. My choice of where to buy, a flat in Levenshulme, was also a serious error of judgement; inner city Manchester in 1985 not being the most desirable of areas. But Levenshulme did have its merits. The multiculturalism lent it a richness and diversity I'd never experienced growing up on a small Scottish island. However, it wasn't a smart place to buy property. When I met and then moved in with Andy, who lived in a charming, 19th century mill cottage tucked away in a hidden oasis in Great Moor in Stockport, I sold at a loss. At a time when many people were raking in huge profits from house sales, I had to pay to sell mine. In theory I'm no stranger to rental, having grown up in a council apartment. In fact, sailing dangerously close to Monty Python *We Were So Poor* waters, in the 1970s when we moved to a newly-built council block from a three-roomed flat with no bathroom and an outside toilet, it was a huge step upwards. With its inside toilet, bathroom, and central heating it seemed to us like living in the lap of luxury .

But all that was many, many years ago. For over 30 of them we've been used to owning our own home. Not only that, the two homes we've lived in together were tucked away; hidden from view. In Britain it was Andy's mill cottage in Stockport, so concealed even local taxi drivers didn't know it existed. On Tenerife, it was a former livestock shed surrounded by trees and banana plantations. In both, when we closed our gate at the end of the working day the rest of the world ceased to exist. From having almost hermit-like privacy all our married life, we've now got virtually no privacy at all. Step outside our front door and Fernando is watering the grass, or Dona Catarina is pruning flowers. Step outside our back door and Dona Catarina is feeding the sheep in the adjacent field, or Fernando is chainsawing trees. It's not unpleasant, especially as we like both of them, it's just strange to be in such close proximity to other people all day long. One sultry night in early October we sat on the back terrace drinking wine, playing music quietly, and watching the sun cast a dreamy, pastel band across the sky. The next morning when we saw Dona Catarina she remarked, "you had a little party last night." It wasn't meant in any disapproving way, but it made us feel less comfortable about behaving the way we normally would behave in and around our own house.

The irony is that until us, all Dona Catarina's tenants have been Portuguese on their holidays. People being in party mode around the farm isn't uncommon. Not that the working class Portuguese who tend to rent the cottages are wild party animals. Although the Portuguese summer holidays (June-September) were over when we moved in, there were a handful of families who rented out cottages during weekends in early October. Some arrived with far more family members than there were bedrooms. The cottage which adjoins ours, and which we share a large terrace with, only has one bedroom. One weekend we became obsessed, the weird folk lurking behind twitching curtains, trying to figure out exactly how many adults were staying in the house. We settled on six - an older couple who we assumed to be mother and father, three girls in their late teens/early 20s, and a boy, also late teens. The mind boggled at what the sleeping arrangements might be, and marvelled at how six adults could manage sharing one small bathroom without resorting to violence. It was even more bewildering watching the number of folk who poured in and out of the one other cottage Dona Catarina rents out short-term. It's larger than the one next to us, but is also a one-bedroom cottage (we found out later there's also a loft area with two single mattresses) and yet it accommodated two large, extended families over one weekend. It's quite interesting to note the holiday patterns of another culture. When these families arrive they go nowhere else for the duration of their stay. Everyone strips down to swimming costumes, barbecues are set up, and the children take up residence in the small swimming pool. When the other cottages are rented out it feels as though the farm has suddenly become a beach resort, which makes the experience of living here surreal. Initially we felt like the interlopers and, in a way, we are as most of the holidaymakers are return visitors; Dona Catarina knows them all by name. They're more like old friends; she joins them for barbecue lunches, sitting chatting away happily for hours, whereas communication with us is limited and stilted. It's clear she enjoys company, she's perkier when there are 'weekenders' about. We're the ones in danger of upsetting the apple cart by changing the way things are; taking next year's cheap holiday accommodation out of the game. Typing away in our makeshift office, it's disconcerting to see bronzed, thong-wearing bottoms pass the window at regular intervals. The families are all polite, friendly, quiet (the Portuguese seem far more demure than the Spanish) and respectful, but long-term rental and holiday rentals don't mix purely because we're working and they're all in holiday mode. They must wonder about the odd foreigners who rarely leave the house. When they're lapping up life in the hot sun outside, we're recluses, huddling over laptops behind half-closed curtains - an attempt to keep the heat out and the cool in.

Susanna had warned us about this situation when we agreed to rent the house, but sharing the farm with holidaying Portuguese for a part of the year seemed a small price to pay for having it virtually to ourselves outside of summer and the occasional holiday weekend.

It's not just Dona Catarina who rents out her cottages, every farm around us takes in holidaymakers during summer. Setúbal has sensational beaches and Portuguese holidaymakers descend in their droves in summer, flooding the rental market, which is why we struggled so much to find long-term accommodation in May. People rake in the money; renting rooms, flats, cottages, whatever they have, over a three-month period.

By late October the families stopped coming and a more conventional existence ensued; one which didn't feel like we were living in a holiday resort, albeit one in an unlikely agricultural setting.

However, unsurprisingly, Dona Catarina has developed a short-term rental mentality over the years. She treats us exactly the way she would her holidaymakers in that she doesn't think we should have to do anything for ourselves. This doesn't apply when we're inside the house. From the moment we moved in she behaved as if it were our house, to a ridiculous level sometimes. She is so reluctant to intrude when she wants to ask us about something we have to nearly physically drag her through the front door. It's more in relation to the outside spaces which highlights how she hasn't adjusted to the difference between us and her other renters. Dona Catarina still wants to do absolutely everything for us, as she would summer rentals. This means we can't lift a finger to do anything for ourselves. When she sees Andy sweeping the outside terrace she comes scampering across the lawn, shouting, "*Nao, Dona Andrea, eu vou fazer isso.*" (no, Dona Andrea, I'll do that). We suspect her rationale is 'If Dona Andrea feels she has to sweep, the terrace must be dirty and I've been neglecting my duties'. When we buy basil and oregano to plant in the border around the back terrace, a couple of days later we discover Dona Catarina has planted other herbs and flowers around them. If we've had to go to the trouble of adding plants to the border, obviously it wasn't being cared for enough. It's very sweet and her intentions are good, but it all contributes to a lack of ownership which, in turn, means we don't feel like it's our home to do with what we want. On our part, we don't occupy our space as much as we should. Whenever anyone stayed in the cottage next door, we steered clear of our terrace.

It's not that we are antisocial as such, just struggling to come to terms with sharing space. After all, we are British and don't handle it well when others impact on our self-imposed boundaries.

It takes time to adjust, for both us and Don Catarina. Little by little the signs are there we're learning to live with each other on a longer-term basis. Instead of feeling a lack of privacy as Dona Catarina passes our 'office' window every morning with a "*bom dia, tudo bem?*" we grow to enjoy it, opening the window to have a chat (as much of one as we can manage in Portuguese). Sometimes Fernando ambles over and joins in, casting his usual 'hard to understand' pearls of local wisdom. It's an invaluable Portuguese lesson for the day. We begin to appreciate more their presence and also patience with us; not only is our Portuguese improving as a result of regular interaction, we pick up all sorts of snippets about life in in this area and Portugal in general that we never would otherwise. The feeling of living under a microscope dissipates and we begin to appreciate the benefits of life in what is ostensibly a small community.

The house particularly poses its own short-term rental issues; it isn't designed or ready for long-term living. There isn't even a washing machine (but there is a dishwasher). On our terrace there is a utility room with washing machine and dryer which we share with Dona Catarina. Again, it's initially odd not to be able to wash clothes whenever we want to. We have to work around each other, Dona Catarina automatically deferring if she spots Andy with a basket of washing at the same time as she's heading to the utility room. The washing line is also shared (a throwback to council tenement living), which isn't a problem as it's located in a small field behind the woodshed and there's loads of space. What is strange is being mobbed by a flock of sheep when trying to hang the washing out - it's one of their grazing spots. Although it takes time to adjust to sharing the machine, fundamentally we approve of doing so as it's more ecologically sound.

There *is* a cooker, but only two of the four jets on the hob work properly. We can live with that. Our friend Jo, on her hillside on La Gomera, had a cooker like that for years; two of its jets having annoyingly feeble and pointless flickers of flames. Our fridge is a small, holiday-home affair which might suffice for a weekend but doesn't have enough space to store the food we buy in an average week, especially not in such a hot climate when we need to keep more items in the fridge than we would in Britain. One of the first things we do is buy another small fridge which Marcelo installs on a plinth over a concrete basin (originally for draining grape juice or something) in the hall. We name this overspill fridge *the frivolous fridge* after noticing we've subconsciously stocked it with 'goodies' rather than essentials. It's home to white wine, beer, tonic water, chocolate, hummus and other dips, maple syrup, bacon and so on. It quickly becomes apparent that it's not just in the refrigeration side of things the house is lacking, it's simply not geared up for living. Clothing storage in the house amounts to a Queen Anne wardrobe and dresser, neither of which hold much at all. We don't know how long we'll end up staying in Portugal but it will be a year at least. There's no way we can happily exist in the house for that time without some additions, so we decide to invest €500 to transform it to suit our needs. Top of the list are a couple of sets of drawers, a cloth cupboard, and a trio of storage boxes which fit under the bed. There's an Espaço Casa and a De Borla nearby (15 minutes away). Both are excellent for good value and aesthetically pleasing household items and implements; the sort of shops which stock all sorts of knick-knacks you don't know you want until you spot them. We pick up lots of goodies from these two without having to cough up much money - snazzy pasta/rice/flour storage tins; a multi-levelled, space-saving spice rack etc. Bit by bit, we transform the cottage from one which feels like a holiday home to a comfortable abode which has our mark stamped all over it. We replace pictures of gloomy Bavarian castles and a Martini mirror with a batik picked up in Sri Lanka, and a Singapore Sling poster from Raffles Hotel. We use the wood-covered wine vats in the kitchen as wide shelving for recipe books, framed photos, and assorted bottles of booze. We pick up a funky set of garden furniture (mocha-coloured wicker chairs, stools and table with orange cushions) at a sale. These completely transform the appearance of the back terrace, giving it more of a chill-out bar vibe, especially after we add solar garden lighting to the herb border and place a few exterior mock candles around the place. The new-look back terrace is what puts the brakes on Dona Catarina treating us the same as her short-term tenants. We're unsure of how she'll react when she notices its modern makeover, but when she sees the new chairs with their vibrant orange cushions she comes running over.

"*Que bonito,*" she coos approvingly. "*tão elegante.*" - How lovely, so elegant.

From that moment there's a noticeable change on both our parts. For Dona Catarina the *centimo* finally drops we aren't the same as her other renters up to this point. She responds positively to the fact we've taken more ownership, and almost visibly relaxes when she sees we've invested in our immediate surroundings. Maybe it shows her we're not going to just disappear one night. For us, the addition of the garden furniture has proved an unexpected catalyst. They might only be pieces of furniture, but from the moment we arrange them on the terrace, and settle into the chairs with a glass of *Porto tónico* as the end of the day, everything does feel different. It's like a missing jigsaw piece. For the first time Casa Camellia doesn't feel like a place we're renting on a farm. It feels like home.

WHITE GRASS & WINDMILLS

"What the hell is that?"

I pull back the curtains to see the sheep field is covered in a white carpet; the grass is frosty. Overnight, summer has packed its bags and fled south with the flamingos. Being shocked at seeing white grass might sound overly melodramatic to anyone in northern Europe, but to us the sight of white grass outside our house is not so much a rarity as a first since we left Britain. You don't get frost at coastal level in the Canary Islands, so for years we've lived without white grass. We did wake to a snow-covered Mount Teide at various times of the year, but it was still sunbathing weather at the coast. Apart from when we travelled elsewhere, the closest we got to freezing mornings was when we stayed at the Parador de Cañadas del Teide in Teide National Park during winter and woke up to find the pond outside the hotel covered with a sheet of ice. But that was at over 2000m. On another occasion at the Hotel Villalba in Vilaflor we had to scrape ice off the windscreen of the car first thing in the morning. However, the hotel is located 1600m above sea level. And that's it.

Gazing over the glistening field as though watching a weather phenomenon reminds me of our first spring on Tenerife when, after a particularly dry winter, we stood on our terrace entranced by the soft pitter-patter of April showers, the first rain we'd seen in three months. The white grass prompts a similar reaction, especially as a couple of days ago the temperatures were still mid 30s. At 08:30 it's now 5C, and for the first time in months we're actually cold. The contrast is quite remarkable. It might sound bizarre, but there's a slight thrill at having to dig through boxes to find warming hiking clothes which were bought for walking in cooler climes. People who don't know the north of Tenerife very well would talk about the weather being cool and cloudy compared to the south. Most of what is written in English about Tenerife's weather is balderdash. In reality, I'd wear a jacket a few times at night in the winter, and even then it would be a light jacket. When it got 'cold' between January and March I'd switch to long sleeves. Some would point to Canarios in the north wearing woolly tights, thick jumpers, and heavy coats whilst tourists in the south were in tee-shirts and shorts. What they don't realise is the winter wear in traditional parts of the Canaries is purely a fashion statement rather than sensibly dressing for actual weather conditions; the locals using the slightest decrease in temperatures to throw on something different after months and months of summer clothing. We did the exact same thing ourselves. Year one we dressed like tourists, thinking the locals were odd to be wandering around in winter clothing when temps were 22C. By year two, whilst we didn't go fully native, we changed to jeans, socks and long sleeves at the same time the Canarios went into Inuit mode. We *did* light a fire at night in January and February, but that's because Canarian houses don't have central heating. Whilst 15/17C at night is pleasant enough walking around in, sitting inside an old house with thick walls, which kept the place cool in summer and kept out the sun's warmth in winter, it would get decidedly parky.

As we've planned our first proper hike for today, it takes a quick rethink of what to wear; we change to base-layers, light fleeces, and lightweight waterproof jackets instead of just tee-shirts. Even watching my breath 'smoke' as we walk to the car is a novelty. Whereas we can throw on extra clothes, Cindy, our Fiat Punto, is a subtropical island girl and not at all used to having to wake up in such low temperatures. She coughs and splutters a few times before her engine reluctantly turns over. This isn't something we anticipated. We make a mental note to research how to add anti-freeze.

Despite official websites being flowery and poetic about the walking possibilities in the municipalities around us, we haven't been able to track down many existing official routes. Most information is ambiguous at best. From our initial exploration, our impressions are that there isn't much evidence of marked walking trails in these parts. I don't understand why some tourist boards try to lure prospective visitors to a destination with promises of a plethora of outdoor activities, such as hiking, when in reality there's little or no infrastructure to back it up. What do they think is going to happen when Joe and Josephine Walker turn up in their hiking gear, enthused and ready to take to the countryside, asking "right, where are these wonderful hiking routes?" Subsequently the *Rota das Moinhos* (Route of the Windmills) in Palmela is a rarity as it is, more or less, an existing, official walking trail.

We park our car at Palmela Castle (a 15 minute drive away, naturally), an impressively robust Moorish fortress which can be spotted from miles away. It's perched on a hill at only 240m above sea level. 240m in many locations might be a mere pimple on the land, in flat Portugal it affords views to other castles in Lisbon, Sesimbra and Setúbal, as well as south across the endless Alentejo plains. The castle has watched over the Tagus and Sado estuaries since the 8th and 9th centuries when it was built by the occupying Moors. In the 12th-century, the Christian army re-took Palmela and it was then ceded to the military Order of Santiago. In 1423 King D João I ordered the enlargement and reinforcement of the castle, including the construction of a church and a convent which has been operating as a *pousada* (similar to Spanish *paradors*) since 1970.

Although the weather is cold by southern European standards, it's a typically sunny day without a cloud to break the expanse of blue. The air temperature is chilly, but the sun's rays are warming when we set off, descending a Roman road that takes us into the Vale de Barris, a concealed valley of vineyards and silver olive groves. As soon as we reach the valley floor we immediately start to climb again, following a dirt track through stone pines and then an overgrown path where thirsty-looking, brittle scrub scratches at our clothes. By the time we're halfway up the hill we've switched from being slightly cool to feeling hot and sweaty; the light fleeces come off. We must have lasted all of 30 minutes before stripping down to tee-shirts. The air temperature might be cool, but the sun is still fierce. After a huff and puff ascent, we level out at a ridge where there are views across Setúbal to the Sado Estuary and the finger-thin Troia Peninsula beyond. Setúbal isn't an attractive city from a distance, but the Sado is a hypnotic, sparkling jewel. A strip of pale gold sand starting at Troia curves along the coast for such a distance it disappears into the horizon. It is a Siren of a coastline whose song has us craving to discover what the world across the Sado Estuary on that spindly sliver of land is like. From this point the walking becomes easy, a stroll along a gently undulating ridge which alternately has views across the Sado or into the Vale de Barris, on the opposite side of which we can see our return route; another ridge with a row of squat, white windmills with sail-less spokes.

Every so often, on trees, we see square green signs showing an arrow and a human form running. We'd noticed similar at Setúbal's beaches that aren't beaches. There, however, the human form was running on top of a wave so we figured they were pointing toward tsunami evacuation points, or there was a Jesus wannabee in the vicinity. In the forest it can mean only one of two things. Which way to sprint if you've got a wild boar on your tail, or which way to leg it if there's a forest fire. We decide the latter is the more likely explanation. Eventually we reach a sign which is slightly different; it illustrates a family squeezed together in a building; the place where the running humans converge. The building itself is an open wooden hut surrounded by trees. I can't say I'd feel particularly happy or, more importantly, safe standing in an open log cabin waiting to be rescued whilst fire raged all around.

Our route takes us back across the valley floor. It's a pretty valley peppered with olive groves and neat cypress trees even though the ground cover is a scruffy mess of dry shrubs after months of being starved of water. A rocky path climbs to the windmill ridge and our first proper views into Arrábida Natural Park, a verdant wilderness which stretches for 35km west from Palmela Castle. The windmill ridge acts as a natural barrier between Arrábida and the Lisbon commuter belt which spreads from the northern side of the ridge to the Tagus. A 45 degree swing in one direction and we can see Lisbon. Spin the other way and the panorama changes to a rural vista of ridges, valleys and hills. Once in Arrábida's embrace Lisbon simply ceases to exist.

The return route to Palmela is a cracker. We enjoy ridge walks at the best of times but this one is especially good. The valley itself is a treat for the eyes; there are glimpses of the Sado at various points; directly ahead Palmela Castle sits proudly on its hilltop; and there are windmills every couple of hundred metres. Some are dilapidated and abandoned, others immaculately restored and being used as homes. There's even an archaeological dig taking place at a site a noticeboard in Portuguese tell us is called Chibanes; a Bronze Age settlement which became an Iron Age settlement which became a Roman village. As we near the end of the ridge, and the start of the town of Palmela, we notice a trio of waymarks; a reminder that although this is an official walking route we haven't passed one signpost, or seen evidence of any other route markings. They're faded and intriguing. One is a standard red and white stripe. One is of a wine goblet. The third is the cross of Santiago.

The ridge culminates at a cluster of windmills, the final one being next to a small building from which a nostalgia-inducing aroma emanates. A sign on the wall informs us it's a *Moinhos Vivos* - a working windmill which still produces flour for bread baked in the adjacent building. Unfortunately said bread is still being baked and won't be ready till later in the day. The smell has made us ravenous, and the hour is getting on, so we head to the first place in Palmela we can grab some food; a cafe called Wine Love directly opposite the bus station, right where the ridge descends to the town. It's a glass cube of a place with views across to Lisbon, and is popular with students from a nearby college. The menu has sandwiches, crepes, some tapas, and *tostas* (toasties). I order, or think I order, two *tostas mistas* (ham and cheese toasties), a couple of coffees, and two cans of *Sumo laranja* (the Portuguese version of Fanta Orange but nowhere near as sweet). It comes to €7 which doesn't seem anything like enough. I suspect some of my order was lost in translation; the waitress doesn't speak English and I ordered in bad Portuguese. The coffee and orange juice arrives quickly, the toastie doesn't, confirming my fears about mis-ordering.

Just as I'm about to have another attempt, the waitress appears with a long plate on which there are four generous slices of ham and cheese toastie sprinkled with herbs. Like other Portuguese toasties we've tried, it's chunky, rich, and filling. Despite feeling hungry we only just manage to chomp our way through it. As I manage to squeeze in the last piece the waitress appears with another long plate.

"*E a outra tosta mista,*" she smiles as she places the second toastie in front of us. We'd forgotten Portuguese toasties are so huge they're virtually double portions. There's no way we can attempt it, especially as I'm starting to feel slightly queasy. I tell Andy I don't feel great and she confirms she feels the same. It's not the food, we both immediately know the cause; we've had it before a long time ago. It's mild sunstroke. Fooled by the cooler air temperature when we set off, we walked too far in full sunshine before we put on the hats we always carry; a rookie error. Dona Catarina has already told us she always wears a hat if she's in the sun for even a short period. We've learnt three things today. Listen more carefully to Dona Catarina's advice. In future only order one *tosta mista* between the two of us. And there might just be some cracking walking routes in this part of Portugal after all.

WARM DAYS, COLD NIGHTS

Summer ends in maybe not dramatic fashion, but with a pronounced full stop. Daytime temperatures virtually drop ten degrees overnight. In reality, as that's from 32C to 22C, it's not as though it suddenly goes cold. Sunshine which is warm but which doesn't fry the skin is a relief.

One of the joys of living in a warm climate is being able to eat al fresco for much of the year. It was something we enjoyed in the Canaries, and it hasn't been any different in Portugal where nearly every morning feels like we're filming an advert for a cereal commercial. As the farm has a citrus orchard, the experience is enhanced by grabbing a wicker basket and heading down to the orange grove to pick fresh fruit before the sheep nab them. It transpires sheep love oranges. They crowd Dona Catarina like irate footballers ganging up on a referee to dispute a decision, hoping their 'bullying' will cause her to spill a few when she's filling her basket (baskets have to be placed above ground to deter the woolly thieves). She's such a soft touch she slips them a few anyway, encouraging more thuggish behaviour whenever anyone enters the orchard. It can be quite disconcerting to suddenly be surrounded by a gang of orange-craving junkies trying to mug us. Fresh November morns means breakfast is moved inside, as is dinner. Only lunch remains an outdoor activity; hardly a sympathy-deserving situation I know. The greatest change comes with after dark temperatures; these plummet. Where days are still warm enough for tee-shirts (sunbathing weather as far as Northern Europeans are concerned), at night the temperatures match those of my home island, Bute. This is something we're unprepared for, and something the house is also unprepared for.

Obviously, cool nights aren't new to us. On Tenerife we would have to light a fire at night between January and 20 February. The date *was* that specific. Every year, regular as clockwork, we'd set the fire on the night of February 20th and that would be it, ready for lighting the following Christmas Day night when it was only lit to ramp up the festive atmosphere. In December temperatures, a fire made the house sweltering rather than cosy. Friends and family scoffed at reports of our house being cold, regularly remarking. "Fourteen degrees is nothing, it's minus five here." To which I'd point out "not inside your house it isn't." What people generally don't appreciate is in southern parts of Europe many houses don't enjoy the luxury of central heating systems. In Britain when it's 14C outside it can be 24C inside. In the Canaries when it's 14C outside it's 14C inside as well. Ironically, people who live in warm climates are generally better at dealing with cooler interior temperatures than many Brits. On Tenerife we regularly witnessed visitors caught out when they found themselves in unheated restaurants/bars without appropriate clothing, especially at altitude where temperatures can seriously drop. I regularly see restaurant reviews on UGC (user generated content) travel sites moaning about eating in uncomfortably cold restaurants in the Canaries in winter. To be fair, sometimes local practices would drive us mad. The staff in the Canarian restaurant at the top of our road were guilty of leaving the doors open because they were too warm, meaning diners had to keep their coats on whilst they ate to counter the chilly breeze whipping round them and their *conejo en salmorejo* (rabbit in savoury sauce). The worst case was in a bar restaurant in a hill town on El Hierro during a nippy February night. The owner had plonked himself on a bar stool right at the door, his body inside the restaurant his right arm outside. The reason? He was chain-smoking and by keeping the hand holding the cigarette outside the bar felt he couldn't be found guilty of breaking any smoking laws if the local *policía* turned up. Cooler inside living is something you adjust to, and once you do, it feels a far healthier way of life. We now feel claustrophobic whenever we return to Britain and enter shops which are uncomfortably hot and airless thanks to synthetic central heating.

However, it never reached 5C where we lived on Tenerife. The structure of our Portuguese cottage is not dissimilar to the one we had on Tenerife, but there we had a huge cast iron wood-burning stove which would send its warming embrace throughout the house. Here we have a smallish, antiquated stove with a letterbox door which can't accommodate any decent-sized pieces of wood. It has a voracious appetite for wood. It also has a hot plate. "Good for heating soup," Fernando tells us. But as we have gas hobs in the kitchen, I don't envisage we're going to be doing much of that. It's effective enough at warming our living room when it gets going, but it takes around two hours to reach that stage. Part of the problem involves the ceiling. In both kitchen and living room, wooden planks which aren't snuggly together are the only barrier between us and terracotta roof tiles. When the wind blows we can feel draughts through these tiles. Similarly, windows don't fit their frames perfectly. All the frames in the house have small gaps between them and the walls; something we didn't spot, or care about, during hot days and nights. The back door is flimsy to say the least. Thankfully it doesn't last long as just as it begins to get cold something starts to eat it from the inside. We bring Dona Catarina in to the house to listen the to audible chomping.

"Oh!" she cries when she hears the loud munch, munch, munch before covering her mouth and giggling.

Within a few days we have a brand new, breeze-resistant UPVC door courtesy of Senhor Zé, a neighbour in his 70s who has a large allotment to maintain, hunts wild boar, and still finds time to help Dona Catarina out with some of the bigger tasks, like replacing doors. Senhor Zé is deaf which means he shouts everything. This means he always sounds angry even though his eyes twinkle mischievously when he barks orders. We have no idea what Senhor Zé says when he speaks to us and he has no idea what we say when we reply. Senhor Zé sometimes brings items from his allotment. One time he turned up with an enormous courgette. It supplemented four meals and we still only managed to get through half of it.

The trouble is the farm's cottages were never designed for long-term living, they were converted from outbuildings into accommodation for summer rentals. Nobody until us has actually lived in them outside summer months. Our first plan of defence against winter is to buy rolls of self-adhesive foam insulation strips for the windows. These have an immediate, if limited, impact. Then we buy a portable oil heater. We owned one on Tenerife and it proved invaluable for quickly taking the chill out of rooms. We use it to warm the bedroom before we get out of bed in the morning, as well as before and after showering. It also keeps our makeshift office relatively cosy during the day. Throws are purchased to a) hide the ghastly, garish green stripes of the sofa and b) act as leg warmers until the stove warms the room. Faux fur rugs are bought for the bedroom to create a feet-friendly barrier between the soles of our feet and the chilly tiles. In this fashion we begin to adjust to living in temperatures we're not used to dealing with. Some things remain outside of our control. On our covered terrace is a huge wicker basket which regularly, and magically, fills with neatly chopped firewood, courtesy of wood fairy Fernando. Sometimes, when Fernando is busy with other chores around the farm, the wood fairy doesn't visit. No problem, I simply toddle off to the woodshed to fill the basket myself. But I have to time it so Dona Catarina isn't in the vicinity. I know if she spots me she'll look crestfallen, as though she's been guilty of neglecting her duties as a landlady, and there'll be an apologetic, "sorry Senhor Jack, I'll ask Senhor Fernando to bring you more wood immediately." On Tenerife I had to chop my own wood. For someone with an occupation which can involve long periods sitting on my backside, regular wood management was like a visit to an outdoor gym.

The biggest domestic issue we face surrounds a Russian roulette game of *butano* bottles. We're old hands at using butane gas to heat the water and for cooking. On Tenerife, one large bottle fuelled both, lasting approximately three weeks. We always had a spare so when one ran out we could immediately switch to the other, and then replace the empty bottle. Here there are two bottles to make life comfortable; one is connected to the cooker, the other to the water boiler. How long each lasts we have no idea as Fernando has responsibility for keeping us in fuel. This wouldn't be a problem if a full bottle was attached to each pipe and we were able to gauge how long each lasted, giving us a rough 'heads up' about when either was due to run out. This was the system we practiced on Tenerife and we knew almost to the day when the bottle was about to 'go'; forewarned being forearmed and all that jazz. However, there's a rotation system for many things around the farm. When anything breaks/ stops working it isn't replaced by something new, it's replaced by a similar item from another part of the farm; something which isn't currently being used elsewhere. Subsequently, door handles don't match, or the flush system on the toilet is a combination of two different flush systems. So, when Fernando checks the *butano* bottles to see if either are near empty (by lifting them and testing the weight), he doesn't replace with brand new bottles, but one from elsewhere which just happens to be fuller. The upshot is there's no way of telling how long a full bottle lasts as we never know if the 'new' bottle is actually a full bottle or only a half full one. Fundamentally, I applaud the attitude of the Portuguese in this area. This is not a throwaway society. Items aren't replaced because there's a sexy new model on the market, they're only replaced when they can no longer function. Everything is used and reused until it finally gives up the ghost. It's the same with cars. We think Cindy is old at 14, Dona Catarina's car is 20 years old.

Getting back to the *butano* bottles, the problem with not knowing when they're near empty means we never have an inkling when the hot water is about to stop being hot water. This invariably happens when one of us is in the shower, and it's nearly always Andy who is the victim. In summer, a sudden blast of cold water can be welcome. When it's 5-8C, it's a scream-inducing shock to the system which involves a race-against-time mission where I have to sprint outside to the gas bottle cupboard to try to do a Formula One pit-stop speed changeover of the bottles before Andy succumbs to hypothermia. The clanking of metal against metal during the changeover tends to bring Dona Catarina running, a look of concern across her face as she points in the general direction of the bathroom and asks "*Dona Andrea no chuveiro?*" When I nod back she covers her mouth with her hand and says "Ooh," before bursting into a fit of the giggles like a naughty schoolgirl.

The sudden dip in nighttime temperatures also brings the realisation we don't have the requisite clothes for cold-weather living. Our entire wardrobe, apart from hiking gear and jackets bought for trips to Britain (at any time of the year), has evolved into one which is designed to keep us comfortable in spring and summer conditions. Bathrobes, jumpers, thicker trousers, slippers, and even cardigans have to be be purchased so we can feel relatively warm inside the house during the day. Oddly, the pattern of life in such climates can be turned on its head. When we head outside for lunch we take jumpers off and put sunglasses on. The second we go back into the house, the jumpers go on again.

There are lots of other little nods to this change in seasons. We toast the end of the working day with a warming Port instead of a cooling *cerveja*. As is proving to be a common occurrence, Dona Catarina turns up at the door one afternoon to present us with the fruit of the season, pomegranates, picked from somewhere on the farm. She tells us juicily ripe pomegranate seeds in a glass of Port make for a delicious drink. Seasonal fruits from the farm usually arrive with a tip or two. Cindy continues to struggle to get going on the coolest mornings, so we delay going out anywhere until after 11:00 by which time the sun has warmed her up to the point she's amenable to taking us where we want to be. And there are roasted chestnuts on sale in *Praça do Bocage* in Setúbal where many locals wrap up in thick jumpers, scarves and parkas with faux fur-lined hoods even though it's 23C, just as they do in the Canaries.

THE VILLAGE

Brejos do Assa isn't a pretty village by any means. It's the sort of place you'd drive through on the way to somewhere far more appealing without giving it a second glance. In fact, you wouldn't even drive through it unless you'd taken a wrong turn somewhere. The first time we saw Brejos do Assa our hearts fell; it looked quite depressed, on the run down side. And that was on a sunny day when places should look at their very best. Initially I felt like a fraud referring to it as a village when talking about it to friends and family. I felt to use the term was to break the Trade Descriptions Act, making me guilty of the same crime as folk I'd mentally sneered at over the years for 'bigging up' the urban landscapes they inhabited by referring to them as 'the village.' Some people I'd worked with at Stockport Job Centre many moons ago referred to the district of Hazel Grove as 'the village'. To me it paints an image of a collection of quaint houses set around a lawn where men in white shirts and trousers gaily dance around a maypole whilst other villagers recline on benches drinking frothy mead outside a local pub with a thatched roof. Okay, villages don't have to exactly look like that, but you get the idea. Hazel Grove, although I like it as a place, is just not my idea of a village, especially as the perpetually traffic-clogged A6 dissects its main street. On Tenerife there were some ex-pats who referred to what are basically housing developments as 'the village.' On one occasion, whilst we were scribbling notes for inclusion in our *The Real Tenerife* guidebook, a couple asked us what we were doing. When we told them we were writing a guidebook the woman replied. "Don't mention our lovely village, we don't want the secret getting out."

"Don't worry, we won't," I laughed, wanting to add. "There's no danger of us including it as this isn't a village, it's a soulless, modern housing development."

Whenever I used the term 'village' for Brejos do Assa I felt as though I'd joined their ranks.

But the more we get to know 'the village', the more we

realise those first impressions were on a superficial level; the derogatory labels we initially applied are being peeled away one by one to be replaced by fairer ones. The scruffy, whitewashed cottages lining the main street aren't scruffy at all, they're just not manicured; their gardens allowed to grow with carefree abandon resulting in explosions of flowers cascading over low walls. The 'down at heel' residents sitting outside some homes are just country folk who haven't been sucked into a designer label-fuelled maelstrom; The shifty looking, whip-thin men who congregate outside one of the village's two bars are farm workers whose weather-beaten faces are covered in grime from an early morning shift tending vines or peeling cork bark. This isn't a picture postcard village, it's an honest, hardworking agricultural *aldeia*. Follow any road or track from the centre of Brejos do Assa and we're soon alongside vast vineyards, cork forests, wide open pastures where flocks of sheep graze, citrus orchards, and over-sized allotments brimming with courgettes and pumpkins. People look on the grubby side because they've been working hard.

The village has two *pastelarias* (cake shops); a *frutaria*; two hairdressers; a post office/mini-market/bar; pharmacy; a couple of restaurants; and a fishmonger/butcher. So far our experience of each has been mixed. Twice we've tried the *frutaria*, which looks more like a converted front room than a shop, wanting to spend money locally rather than in the big supermarkets. And twice we've walked back out of the shop having bought not a thing. It's strange, as soon as we leave the *frutaria* empty handed I can't remember anything it had on its shelves. It's a sad wee place and my heart goes out to the elderly woman who runs it, but I guess somebody buys something there. We don't eat cakes much so are never going to be regular customers of the *pastelarias*. We did try for bread and croissants once but bombed out on both accounts. Having seen some of the hairstyles around the village - the same, severe short cut and copper-red rinse for every woman - Andy won't be frequenting the hairdressers anytime soon. The mini-market's bar is the haunt of men who lounge outside most of the time as they all smoke. The pharmacy is useful, as pharmacies tend to be. The mini-market itself is one of the social hubs of the village. Run by the Hobbit-sized Dona Natalie and her husband, it's a decent enough wee supermarket which sells a range of basics (beans, water, pastas, tinned goods, canned fish, soap, washing powder, toilet rolls etc.), some fresh fruit and vegetables, salt cod, fresh bread, and cured meats and cheeses. The Post Office section is behind a counter on which is a display of hunting knives, clocks, flea powder for pets, and what looks like a locally produced magazine whose cover always features a naked woman on it, usually next to a photo of a wee man in a bunnet holding up his prize *calabacín*. The latest edition involved a topless woman directing her breast milk into a tin bucket below a cow's udders. It is just bizarre and so out of place. Nearly every person who uses the shop spends more time gossiping to owner Dona Natalia than actually shopping; there are always a couple of women in housecoats loitering around the till area doing nothing apart from chatting and generally getting in the way as there isn't a lot of space. The husband spends his time serving at the shop's minuscule meat and cheese counter, and popping next door to serve patrons of the bar. It is a great little shop, packed full of character. On the face of it, it's a ramshackle establishment where the owners potter about in an anarchic way. But everything gets done quite smoothly and efficiently. The first time Andy posted a birthday card destined for the UK, Dona Natalia tossed it into a pile of empty cardboard boxes behind the glass counter.

"I'll be amazed if that ever turns up," Andy grumbled when she emerged from the shop.

Four days later the recipient had the card in their hands.

When snails ate most of a delivery slip the postman left in our post box, obliterating who the delivery was actually for, Dona Natalia took the tattered slip from my hands like it was a common occurrence.

"*Caracois*," she laughed, grabbing a buff package from among the jumble of boxes behind the 'post office counter' with barely a glance at the address on it. There aren't many foreigners in these parts, so I guess they quickly got to know who we were.

There are efficient jungle drums, as there are in every small
community. It's how we find out information via Dona Catarina.
Senhor Antonio might phone her to tell her an Englishmen
with many motorbikes is enquiring about renting a property,
or Dona Maria will let her know when the Romani travellers
have pitched up in a nearby field. There's a family which passes
through every so often. They pitch their makeshift tents in a
field a few kilometres away and only stay for a couple of days.
When their simple horse-drawn cart trundles through the village,
children with dark olive faces and bright smiles wave at us from
its trailer.

Although the mini-market is fascinating to spend any time
in, our favourite place is Âncora & Serrano, the village's main
restaurant and bar. In a village where every other establishment
looks as though it has time-travelled from the past Âncora &
Serrano was a revelation. One part of it is a large bar; another
is a Payshop where locals pick up their lottery tickets and top
up phones. It has a wide, covered terrace, but the views from
it are not great. There's also an ATM at the entrance to the bar.
This is extremely handy as you can do all sorts of things using
ATMs in Portugal. As well as using them to withdraw money,
pay utility bills, income tax, and social security contributions,
you can use ATMs to make various purchases, like concert
tickets. When we needed to buy more Portuguese Military Maps
we were able to order them online, and were then given a code
which we punched into Âncora & Serrano's ATM to finalise the
payment before the maps were dispatched. The restaurant is the
best part. Even though we knew the food would be good, thanks
to Susanna the estate agent, we expected a quite traditional,
small town affair, i.e. basic with not particularly aesthetic decor.
We were wrong. Âncora & Serrano's restaurant is surprisingly
stylish; the dining area consisting of chunky, contemporary
wooden chairs and tables whose pine surfaces are given a blast
of contrasting colour courtesy of scarlet, linen runners. Two of
the dining room's burnt orange colourwash walls are covered
with neat pine units filled with wines from the area. The third
wall is made up of mainly windows overlooking the terrace,

plus a blackboard listing *petiscos* of the day. The dining area manages to look both sophisticated and homely at the same time; a nice spot to spend time in. To have somewhere such as this within walking distance is a real bonus; one which is especially appreciated whenever we return early evening from a trip and don't have anything in the house to eat, or can't be bothered cooking after a long day travelling. The first time we ate at Âncora & Serrano was the night we moved into Casa Camelia, it was like striking gold. We immediately hit it off with chatty staff who were happy to answer questions about dishes on the menu we weren't familiar with or couldn't translate; dishes like *pica-pau*.

"I'm not sure what the word is in English," the waitress said as I frantically Google-translated.

"This?" I showed her my phone.

"That's the word," she nodded. "Woodpecker."

"It's really woodpecker?"

"Yes, it's woodpecker."

We decided to stick to a starter of huge puffy, golden *pataniscas* (cod patties) followed by *choco frito*. The *pica-pau* could wait until we were able to establish if it was, or wasn't, woodpecker. It wasn't. *Pica-pau* consists of meat and pickles and is traditionally shared, everyone using wooden toothpicks to spear the food, hence the name. On other visits we've enjoyed chorizo and squid stew, *bacalhau à Brás* (shredded salt cod and straw potatoes embedded in a scrambled egg-like mixture), and Iberian black pork with *migas*. Usually the portions are so generous there's no space left for dessert, but on one occasion we fancied squeezing in something sweet at the end of our meal.

"We've only one dessert left," the young waiter led us to a counter featuring the sole offering, a glass cup filled with what looked like caramel-coloured mousse. "*Baba de camelo.*"

"What is it?" Andy asked.

"It's very nice," our waiter replied, and then laughed a laugh which could be described as being on the nervous side.

"And what is *baba de camelo*?" Andy asked again, now slightly suspicious.

"It is really tasty," again the nervous laugh, and a glance at a waitress who was barely concealing a giggle by this point, raising our suspicions further.

"Okay, there's something you're not telling me, what does *baba de camelo* mean?"

"It's camel…" he pointed to his mouth and laughed.

"Camel mouth?" Andy guessed.

"No," this time he doubled over laughing before pointing to his mouth again and making a gesture as though something was falling from his mouth.

We looked at each other for a moment, both totally perplexed, as he continued to mime something falling from a camel's gob, before the penny finally dropped.

"It's camel spit?"

"Yes, camel spit, that's it. *Baba de camelo* means camel spit."

You've got to love a restaurant that serves dishes like woodpecker and camel spit. Despite visualising a camel drooling into a glass bowl every time I dipped my spoon into it, *baba de camelo* (made from boiled condensed milk) turned out to be delicious.

IMPRESSIONS OF THE ALGARVE

It's the fourth time we've driven the IP1 motorway between the Algarve and the rest of Portugal and it's already a dull journey, especially post-summer when a countryside devoid of rains isn't looking at its best. On the plus side there's not a lot of traffic on the road, so at least it's a relatively quick route. The first time we made it was when we arrived from Tenerife and drove from Huelva to Azeitão. The second and third time was a 'there and back' trip for my sister's birthday celebrations when she'd rented a villa in Albufeira. Meeting up with the family was great fun, but Albufeira hadn't charmed us. Much of it seemed like 'anywhere resort' and the glut of British pubs grated, far too much of a contrast to life in Galegos. It felt as though we'd left Portugal, or at least had swapped it for a theme park version of itself where it had a sprinkling of the basic ingredient moulded to suit those who wanted a hint of a country's personality but not the real thing. I was also a bit freaked by the obsession the resort has with Cliff Richard; although, the life-sized cut-outs around the town of Sir Cliff hawking his wine are so kitsch they're good. Something you find in resorts everywhere around Europe is they have a largely homogeneous character which doesn't reflect life in the world beyond their boundaries. The Canaries are no different. We felt like we'd gone on holiday to a different destination whenever we left the north of Tenerife to spend time in the southern resorts. At least with many of Tenerife's purpose-built resorts nothing of note existed before they were developed for mass tourism, so they hadn't displaced traditional communities. With Albufeira, we could see there was once a quite charming old town before it had the resort makeover. There still is, but much of it has been concealed under a thick layer of gaudy makeup. On the other hand, it does boast gorgeous beaches.

As the plan is to check walking route directions and make amendments to a couple of Inntravel holidays in the Algarve, we expect to see different faces of the region, so we're not going to condemn it yet based on an experience over one weekend.

First stop is the Algarve that's nothing at all like the Algarve many might visualise. Monchique is a pretty-ish little hill town surrounded by a dense, green carpet of pines, cork oaks, chestnut trees and Portugal's scourge, eucalyptus. We stop there to complete a couple of walking routes. It's more like the Portugal we're now used to - beehives lining the path, banks of postal boxes on dirt tracks, yapping dogs excited at the rarity of someone passing the houses they're protecting. One route crosses fertile valleys full of citrus trees and wild shrubs – campanula, rhododendrons, and euphorbias – before we wind through the forest on a more demanding trail in order to share the 360 degree viewpoint at the summit of *Serra de Picota* with Bonelli's eagles. On our return route to Monchique we pass beneath trees laden with vibrant red fruits which, when squished, reveal equally vibrant orange flesh. They're *medronhos*, strawberry trees. When we return to the town we spot signs for *Aguardente de Medronho* (a firewater made from the fruit). It's claimed that the fermented fruit on strawberry trees is so potent that bears who eat them will become inebriated. Madrid's coat of arms features a bear eating from a strawberry tree, there's also a statue of it in the city's *Puerta del Sol*.

It's quite late in the day, and we've still a decent drive to reach the rural accommodation in Odiáxere which will be our base, but it's only 5km from Monchique to the summit of Fóia. At 902m it's the highest point in the Algarve. They say on a clear day you can see the *Serra da Arrábida* from the summit, which would be pretty cool. This is a clear day, but by 17:30 the sky is on the hazy side so we can barely make out the sea let alone hills where we live 250km away. It is, however, cool to the point of being nippy. The *Miradouro da Fóia* is a natural attraction which draws coach loads of tourists from the coastal resorts. And, just like the excursionists we regularly saw in Teide National Park who arrived at 2500m in winter months dressed in beachwear, many are obviously not aware the higher you go the colder it gets.

It's immediately apparent that Odiáxere and surrounding area is no Albufeira. Although there's plenty of evidence of it being an area where tourism dominates, and there are the unmistakable signs of ex-pat communities, it's on a much smaller scale and has a very different vibe from purpose-built resort areas.

The first route we map out takes us from the traditional village of Figueira along country paths to the near deserted and expansive sands of *Praia das Furnas*. Despite temperatures which would have Northern Europeans stripping off everything, there are only a handful of sunseekers on the beach – a few neo-hippies (an ubiquitous ingredient on western Algarve beaches) and a couple of Northern Europeans who have, well, stripped off everything. Although it's an impressive opener it's a mere taster for what is to come. From Furnas, our route leads us across red-earth paths to cliffs overlooking an even more beautiful bay, *Praia do Zavial*, lapped by the sort of deliciously turquoise water which fools you into thinking its caress will be warming. As we stand, transfixed by the scene, finally beginning to understand why the Algarve is such a popular destination, we're roused from our entrancement by an English couple who join us on the cliff-top. They're regular visitors who are happy to share a bag load of useful tips compiled over 30 years of walking visits to the Algarve; the first being the name of a plant with glistening, sticky looking leaves which has been intoxicating us with its perfumed scent - gum cistus.

If one route showcases just how alluring the Algarve coastline can be it's the Seven Hanging Valleys trail, deservedly one of the most popular coastal hiking routes in the region. We join it at Benagil, once a small fishing community where octopus was the main catch. It's still a small community but now it exists more as a tourist beauty spot where people catch boats to get close-up views of the area's sea caves. From Benagil, we head east along a honey-coloured landscape of abstract rock formations; the imaginative creations of the trio of artists known as wind, sea, and rain. The cliff-top trail winds through thickets of wild thyme, rosemary and fennel, skirting cove after cove, some accessible only from the sea. Sheer cliffs and soft sands compete for the title of 'most golden wonder' whilst the sea, with its soft azure shades, provides an inviting contrast. It's unlikely anyone would grow bored of encountering one idyllic cove after another but, just in case they did, both sea and wind have combined to sculpt arches, caves and rocky stacks so that no two Midas-touched scenes are exactly the same. The natural eye-candy changes with each indent in the cliffs – huge rock arches in one; deep, dark intriguing caves in another. Turning up regularly are postcard-perfect golden sand coves – *Praia da Marinha* is considered one of the 100 most beautiful beaches in the world (so an info board tells us). There's no denying it's a looker of a beach. The air around us is perfumed by the increasingly familiar aroma of gum cistus whilst the wildlife includes warblers, egrets, and flocks of ex-pat walkers. At one point we even bump into our information-sharing friends from *Praia do Zavial*. It can be a busy route, but it is a peach of a coastal walk.

Further west along the coast offers similar ingredients but fewer other hikers. Our route heading west from Luz is transitional; a bridge between the world of resorts and a more traditional Portugal. Luz is not a place which wins us over. There are too many bars with Brit names and blackboard menus featuring dishes for folk who like to steer clear of unfamiliar 'foreign' food. However, as we travel west we quickly leave Luz behind, replacing it with a rugged landscape of spiny cactus and agave spikes before arriving at the more traditional and picturesque Burgau. Our route into the village passes a whitewashed cottage whose wall displays a street sign for 'Borough of Islington'. Leaving the village, we see a bus shelter painted with an amusing reflection of life in the area It depicts a trio of women (two elderly and Portuguese, one young and a neo-hippie) who look out from a panel above a washing line on which a huge pair of white bloomers hang next to a pink thong. Beyond Burgau we skirt a headland before descending to *Praia da Almadena* and the stylish Cabanas Velhas Beach restaurant. Normally we don't eat a heavy lunch when walking, but the cuisine in the Algarve hasn't wowed us so far, possibly because many traditional restaurants we passed are closed. Dining experiences have been disappointing, not bad but not memorable, so when we happen across an attractive and inviting restaurant at just the right moment we'd be mad to walk on by. Plus, a blackboard menu shows the dish of the day is fish and chips in a vodka batter. We've resigned ourselves to the fact local specialities aren't going to feature much on this trip, so why not embrace what there is? And it is bloody delicious fish and chips. We could easily fritter away the afternoon at Cabanas; however, our route continues onward, the landscape softening thanks to the green of spurges, junipers and pines, before we descend to a peaceful flat valley split by an estuary, where sheep and goats tug at long, hardy grasses. The transformation is complete.

It seems common in locations which are popular sun and sand holiday destinations that a significant amount of visitors who were originally attracted by the coastal charms of a place choose to live a wee bit inland when they decide to make it their home. We've seen enough evidence to suggest the Algarve is no different. But there's more of a bohemian character to the inland towns in the western part of the Algarve. Barão São João is just 15 minutes from the sea and was once a traditional town. Now it feels more like an artists' commune where strolling the streets is akin to wandering an open-air art gallery - a naked trompe-l'œil pixie climbs out a window on the side of a cottage; two clay cats copulate on the tiles of another cottage. These and others like them are quirky additions to what would otherwise be a typically Portuguese small town. Barão São João is also the gateway for a walking route we're putting together in the *Mata Nacional* (national forest), a woodland consisting of eucalyptus, cork oaks, and stone pines. Part of the route involves following a poets' trail (poems and images are etched into rocks) which embodies the character of the nearby town. We lose time trying to find the legendary *Pedra do Galho Menhir* (cock rock – a name which makes me think of *Priscilla, Queen of the Desert*). The story goes that when you stroke cock rock it's said you'll hear a cockerel crow. The reason we can't find it is it is not a very big

nor striking rock, we walked past it and didn't register it. We're
so taken aback by its diminutive ordinariness we forget to stroke
it. No cock on a rock here.

For all the outstanding beaches on parade, the settings which
carve the greatest impact are the wetlands. *Sitio das Fontes* near
Silves is thirty kilometres from Albufeira, but might as well be
a thousand and thirty. An old mill sits on the edge of lagoons,
creeks and waterways - a haven for birds at the right time of
the year. It's a watery world with a serenity-inducing influence.
Designated paths take us from the old tidal mill to springs, picnic
areas, wooden bridges, and an amphitheatre. It's an area for
locals to enjoy, and accordingly gets busy at weekends and in
summer months. On a weekday in November it remains virtually
empty of people.

We power walk our way around the Alvor wetlands as dusk
is rapidly becoming nightfall and we're racing against a sun
which has slipped into third gear in its bid to reach the horizon.
But the lateness of the hour brings a dream-state quality of light,
creating a magical golden and pastel world which puts the brakes
on our pace. So what if darkness falls and we are still a long way
from our car? The mirror-calm waters glisten with a metallic,
silky quality whilst the sky could have been painted by Monet.
We walk briskly through a descending curtain of darkness
atop grassy dykes. On one side, ghostly flamingos goose-step
in slow motion. On the other, a couple of shellfish fishermen
wade through mud banks with the same slow and considered
movements. It is spiritual, nature's benzodiazepine. It might have
be one of the shortest walks we've enjoyed during the year, but
it's one of the most memorable.

Best of all is the Costa Vicentina, where the Algarve meets
Alentejo. This is a resort-free wild west where sandy paths
which suck the energy from legs link sprawling beach after
sprawling beach. It's empty in November save for a few surfers
and a handful of neo-hippy travellers.

Where our south coast routes were characterised by the
postcard fodder of scenic coves and pretty beaches, the one
route we walk on the Costa Vicentina rewards with sandy

scenes which are even more epic, some of *Lawrence of Arabia* proportions. Amoreira, our starting point, is a huge expanse of sand and a surfers' haven. We climb away from the beach to cross a sandy plateau of low shrubs, farmhouses and stone pines whose umbrella-shaped canopies have to be about the greenest of any trees I've seen. The path winds through kermes oaks and between thickets of cistus, juniper, crowberry and, a favourite of ours when paired with fish, samphire. In these untamed lands are otters, kingfishers, and tortoises. Not that we actually spot any, but I'm willing to trust the info boards which tell me they exist. Our route ends at a steep staircase, made from recycled plastic, which takes us to the wild curves of Carriagem, a beach with a mix of white sand and hard volcanic rocks.

As an add-on we stop for a short explore of *Praia de Bordeira*, more small desert than beach. It's so big you might need directions to find your way to the shoreline. A finger of an estuary splits one side of the beach, creating an inland lagoon which adds to the exquisite beauty of the place. It's basically a mini Sahara where I wouldn't be surprised to discover the bleached bones of sun-seeking tourists who had expired en route to the sea.

Just as we're rounding off our work in the Algarve in the town of Silves - a rather attractive riverside town with an impressive Moorish castle - we get a phone call from James at Inntravel, outlining an extra mission. "This might sound odd," he starts. "I need you to find me a pig and bring it back to Britain with you when you come in December."

The pig in question is a clay pig used to roast chorizo - an *assador de chouriço*. It takes a few repeat descriptions from James before it sinks in what exactly this is. Google images fill in the missing dots. It looks like a clay barbecue with a pig's head and legs. It's being offered as a prize for a travel competition; the details already online even though there's no pig to offer… yet.

"What size is it?" I ask, imagining us trying to lug an enormous pottery pig barbecue through security in Lisbon and Manchester.

"Oh, it's only about six or seven inches long," James replies reassuringly. "You can pick them up just about anywhere in Portugal."

The few shops we try in Silves are a bust. On our final afternoon we've planned to take a quick look around Sagres, surely we'll find a chorizo-roasting pig there? Nope. The closest we get is a souvenir shop which stocks a brightly painted, but non-functional, version that would crack at the first attempt to use it. Our explore of Sagres turns into a wild goose (pig) chase where assistants in one pig-less shop after another suggest other shops which may have or may not stock piggy chorizo roasters. None do. Ironically, Jill and Julio, the owners of the rural hotel we're staying at, *do* own a blackened and much used pig-shaped *assador de chouriço*. Julio even gives us a demonstration of how it works. He pours methylated spirits into its bowl (belly), lights it, and WHOOSH. It is impressive and would clearly be a lot of fun if we actually had a *chouriço* to roast on it. We have one more chance of finding one before we leave the Algarve. Our return route home takes us through Monchique again. If anywhere in the Algarve has a pig-shaped *assador de chouriço* it'll be there. Wrong again. We do get offered quite funky, folding wooden chairs the town is known for making. But no pig. We've failed our final Algarve mission.

24 hours later and we're back in Setúbal at our local supermarket, buying food to restock empty cupboards, when we walk along the kitchen utensils aisle we stroll through every week. At one end we notice lots of clay dishes of various shapes and sizes, including the elusive pig-shaped *assador de chouriço*. We must have passed them on numerous occasions and never spotted them. James was right, you can pick them up anywhere in Portugal, just not quite so easily in the Algarve.

WINTER

The cork forest is absolutely delightful; winter rains have turned the forest floor fresh green, the sea of young grasses broken by the first signs of spring; buttercup-yellow wild flowers. Shafts of sunlight illuminate irritated Eurasian jays, squawking noisily as they relocate to more distant treetops when we approach.

DARK DECEMBER DESCENDS

The litmus test is whether the house feels like 'home' when we return from a trip. Weary from the exertions of hiking every day in the Algarve for the last couple of weeks, we can't be bothered cooking so we light the fire, warm a couple of flatbreads, open a tub of hummus, cut some cheese, throw slices of *presunto* on a board, crack open a bottle of Alentejo red, and flop onto the sofa to indulge in a night of catch-up on Netflix. It feels like the same sensation as snuggling under a warm, fluffy duvet listening to the rain's pitter-pattering against the window. The Litmus test has been well and truly passed.

We're barely 20 minutes into *Stranger Things* when Andy's phone rings. She picks it up and checks who's calling.

"That's odd," she says. "It's Dani."

I watch with growing dread as Andy listens for a few second, puts her hand to her mouth and utters a strangled. "Oh no." I can hear sobbing coming from the phone.

"Mark's dead," Andy finally whispers.

We're pole-axed by news which has come out of the blue like a devastating thunderbolt. Andy's younger brother had been suffering from health problems for many years, but nothing we believed was imminently life-threatening. He had multiple sclerosis, which was mostly in remission. The greater problem was he had become seriously visually impaired in recent years, apparently the result of an incident which occurred when he was a young boy; so Mark had told us when we last saw him in York two years ago. Apart from her brother John, who lives in Stockport, Andy's other siblings live in various disparate outposts around England. Another brother, Ged, lives in rural Devon; Tracy, the youngest, lives in Haverfordwest, the most awkward place to get to in Wales; and Mark lived in Durham. It's not been easy to see them on a regular basis, especially as none of them travel abroad. As a result, we have to arrange 'sibling trips' every now and again. Times like this brutally ram home why it's worth making the effort to see friends and family

on a regular basis. We'd been taken aback the last time we saw
Mark, but that was mainly as a result of how bad his vision had
become. Mark had put on a brave face, typically making light
of his situation and reassuring Andy that all was okay; although,
he wasn't happy in Durham. He hadn't shared everything about
his health; Dani, his estranged partner, reveals he'd suffered
a stroke a few years back. When Dani hadn't heard from him
for a couple of days she arranged for someone to check up on
him. Scant consolation though it is, it sounds as if he passed
away peacefully, sitting in his chair. For the rest of the night we
simply sit and stare into space, numb with shock.

As fate would have it we're due to travel to Britain in a
couple of days. We normally return to Britain at this time of
year to deliver training sessions to Inntravel staff for the new
holidays we've helped design over the previous 12 months,
describing each holiday's ingredients and spouting anecdotal
tales accompanied by images to help give staff more of an
insight and hopefully bring destinations alive. Every three years
Inntravel hold a travel fair called Discovery Day. It's open to
the public and involves stalls manned by representatives from
tourist boards and hotel owners from across Europe. Each
location's stalls usually include a tasty selection of regional food
and booze, making the day educational, interesting, and a lot of
fun. This year it's being held at Cheltenham Race Course and, as
well as helping staff the Portugal stall, we're scheduled to give
a presentation about the Canary Islands. As other presentations
are being delivered by television presenter Kate Humble, and the
ebullient raconteur that is Count Francisco of Calheiros, we're
honoured to be in such esteemed company and had been looking
forward to it immensely. Now it seems unimportant, something
we just have to get through before we can travel to the North
East of England for Mark's funeral.

Difficult though it is to avoid, it serves no real purpose to
allow grief to obliterate all else. Even though there's a surreal,
hazy, going-through-the-motions element to everything, Andy,
always a consummate professional in everything she does,
navigates her way through both the Discovery Day event in

Cheltenham, and the subsequent staff training at Castle Howard near York before we head to Stockport to meet up with the rest of the family. In truth, the work is a welcome distraction, for me at least, especially when two of our dearest friends from Stockport, the Largies, turned up unexpectedly at the Discovery Day event. Coincidentally, they were taking a mini break nearby. In reality, despite the happiness at meeting friends we never see enough off, nothing is going to fully distract Andy from the heart-wrenching anguish of losing her younger brother.

Funerals are such odd affairs. Heartbreaking for obvious reasons, but one of the times many families fully gather together. They can present a rare chance to catch up with loved ones. I guess there has to be some solace, some positive aspect, otherwise we'd just mentally crumble. The last time Andy's family were all in the same location was for her father's funeral over a decade ago. Funerals should be a reminder to make more of an effort to stay in regular touch with those who mean something to us, and promises are usually made about meeting up more often. However, time erodes these best of intentions and far too often it doesn't happen.

The logistics involved in getting all Andy's siblings in one place - in this case Stockport - are head-spinning. Ged travels from Devon on the National Express. We arrive from Portugal via Cheltenham and York. And Tracy has to make her way with her two boys from the backside of Wales. Travelling by train, she has the most convoluted journey of all, not helped by the fact a blizzard has descended and trains are being cancelled left, right and centre. As we sit around the large dining table in John's house in Great Moor we get regular, and often teary, updates from Tracy. With the snow storm being so severe, it looks as though there's no way she can make it north in time for the funeral. The average person wouldn't stand a chance. However, we have a secret weapon in Liam, oldest offspring of John and Karen and our surrogate son. Liam works for the railways and has an encyclopedic knowledge of getting from A to B by train. Each time Tracy phones in floods of tears to say the weather has brought her train to a premature halt in a station she doesn't want to be in, Liam directs her onto another train, one which is continuing north(ish). He even talks her through navigating platforms in various unfamiliar stations. In this way he painstakingly pieces together the jigsaw, each sluggish step bringing Tracy slightly closer to Stockport. For us it's a roller-coaster of hope, disappointment, hope, and then more disappointment. Each time it seems as though he'll be defeated, Liam pulls the proverbial rabbit out of the hat. But the storm proves a stubborn opponent. At Birmingham all options run out. No trains are continuing north, the weather has won. That's it; game over. Tracy is entrenched in snow in the Midlands. And then an angel intervenes. A guard on the train, noting Tracy's distress, offers to drive her, the boys, and another passenger all the way from Birmingham to Stockport. It's a Christmas miracle. The kindness of a stranger is a brightly shining beacon of light on what is otherwise a dark day.

By the next morning the storm has passed, and the sun shines on snowy white hillsides as a successfully reunited family makes its way by train to Durham without incident. None of us know Durham. We don't even know Mark's former partner and daughter very well. The cemetery is an unfamiliar setting with unfamiliar people, save for our side of the family of course. Maybe this makes the funeral slightly more bearable; there are none of those little triggers which prompt the sort of memories which strip the bones from the legs and squeezes the heart till it feels as though it could burst from too much sorrow. As dusk starts to fall, and festive lights add their twinkle to the world, reminding us it's nearly Christmas, what should be a time of family joy, we say our farewells to Mark and depart for home.

Pretty Rita and Marijuana

As we enter the second half of December it becomes
apparent this is a month which isn't going to improve. Andy
has a niggling toothache that isn't going to magically go away.
She needs to see a dentist but we aren't registered with any.
This is another side of living abroad, essentials you build up
naturally in your home country - doctor, dentist etc. - as you
grow up have to be organised afresh whenever you move
somewhere new. I guess that's no different from moving from
one part of the country you live in to another, except there's the
added complication of having to arrange it in another language
combined with the fact we don't know how systems work
here. Whilst we try as much as possible to communicate in the
language of the country we're living in, when it comes to health
we look for someone who can speak English; it's not an area
where it's wise to run the risk of misunderstanding what we're
being told. The internet has made this aspect of life abroad so
much easier; a search turns up a handful of dentists in the area
who can speak English, one conveniently in the commercial
centre where we do our weekly shop. We decide to try them to
deal with Andy's toothache and, if we like them, to possibly
sort a dental problem I've had for the last few years, a loose
bridge. The bridge is my front top teeth (thanks to a punch from
the younger of the McAllister brothers whilst I had my hands
round the older brother's throat when I was fourteen) which
means I can't tear at food; subsequently I eat everything with a
knife and fork, even sandwiches and burgers. There have been
temporary fixes, but they don't last. I can't remember the last
time I was able to enjoy the pleasure of sinking my teeth into a
bacon butty. The sensible answer would be implants, but regular
travel has made undergoing a lengthy procedure difficult to
fit in. That's been my excuse anyway. In truth, I have a fear of
dentists. Dentists, doctors and hairdressers. In 2002 I caused
havoc in a Beijing hospital after collapsing during a visit to
learn about the Chinese holistic approach to medicine. I was at

the back of a small lecture hall watching a doctor work his way around the members of our tour group, examining mouths and feeling pressure points before declaring what ailments each had. As the average age was 70 (we were youngsters compared to nearly everyone else) every one of them had an ailment or two to be 'guessed.' He got it right every single time, much to the delight of the examinees. It was like watching a surreal Chinese version of a magician doing the rounds of guests in a resort hotel's lounge. By the time he reached me I'd worked myself into a right old lather, convinced he was going to look at my tongue and discover a terminal health problem. Almost as soon as he touched my jaw I fainted, scaring the hell out of Andy and causing panic among the hospital staff present who didn't want a tourist death on their hands. Andy told me what happened after I came round.

"It was fantastic," she gushed in admiration of the doctor's technique. "He grabbed your jaw firmly and squeezed a couple of places on your cheeks and you immediately came around."

"Did he find anything wrong me?" I asked groggily.

"Yes, he says you have a severe fear of white coats."

Hairdressers I don't like because whenever I returned from having a haircut at Nadia's as a boy on Bute, my mum would declare it to be unacceptable and would send me back to instruct the person responsible to fix it. I hated having to do it and it has left a lasting uneasiness. Dentists are dentists, who doesn't dread a visit to one? Growing up, we had two on Bute. One was an alcoholic whose hand shook badly, the other was an ogre I was terrified of. Once he slapped my face in anger after I accidentally spat bloody water onto his surgical instruments tray instead of into the sink. In my defence both were enamel and I *had* just come round from having gas.

The dentist is a small practice in a *local* (outlet) opposite the supermarket checkouts. It might sound an odd place for a dentist, but there's all sorts of useful establishments in the long line of these box-shaped shops opposite the tills, ranging from techie hipsters fixing laptops to wee women in pinafores carrying out dress alterations.

We immediately take to Sandra, the receptionist, a straight-talking woman who speaks excellent English. We explain we only speak a little Portuguese badly, and then also do what we do to try to let people know we're not arrogant Brits who have never bothered our backsides trying to speak anybody else's language - we mention we *can* speak Spanish; something which sends Sandra off on a little diatribe against her geographical neighbours. Her mini rant includes observations such as, "We're far more outward looking than the Spanish, we integrate with people from our former colonies, the Spanish don't," and "we can understand the Spanish, but they can't understand us."

We're assigned to two *dentistas* who are in their mid 20s, female, petite, and infectiously bubbly. Andy gets Rita Bonita (Pretty Rita) and I get Marie Juana. Where Rita Bonita is raven-haired and dark-eyed, Marie Juana has a shock of red hair, braces in her mouth and is wearing ripped jeans.

Andy's toothache is dealt with almost immediately whilst I'm more or less talked into having implants by Sandra - "they will change your life for the better."

Andy promptly has the offending tooth extracted without too much fuss and then it's my turn. I have the honour of having both Rita and Marie Juana examining me, with Marie Juana taking the lead. As they prepare for a preliminary assault on my mouth, both sing along to bad Portuguese pop songs. The music is awful but the casual atmosphere relaxes me more than I've ever felt in a dentist's chair. Even so, when Marie Juana starts poking around at my gums I instinctively move my head slightly away from her and in the direction of Rita Bonita.

"Look at me," Marie Juana teasingly chides, "I know she's the pretty one, but I'm the one doing the work."

I've never had dentists like this before, it's almost fun. There's also scope for confusion as I discover when Marie Juana turns to her laptop to set the date for the serious implant work to start.

"You can't smoke beforehand," she warns.

"No problem, I don't smoke." I tell her.

"No, I mean you can't smoke anything," she places an emphasis on the *anything*.

"Ah," I see what she's getting at. She must have decided I was a stoner. "Marijuana?"

"Yes?" She spins round from her lap top and smiles at me. "That's me."

"What?" For a second I'm confused, and then I make the obvious connection. "Ah, no I was talking about marijuana."

"Yes?" She smiles again, but now there's a look of confusion on her face."That's my name."

This could go on forever, lost in translation.

"It doesn't matter," I smile back. "That date's fine."

Marie Juana and Pretty Rita haven't cured my dentophobia but they have at least put a little, err, dent in it. I won't turn up suffering from abject fear next time, just the ordinary run of the mill kind.

SMOKING KIDS AND A GRIFTER GOAT

Christmas is a bah humbug event this year. We're in no mood to celebrate, not that we ever go over the top anyway. But it's our first in Portugal and we had been looking forward to experiencing the festive season, or *Natal* as it's called here, with all its trimmings somewhere new. The stress of the past few weeks finally take their toll on Christmas Day, with Andy feeling nauseous just as we put the turkey on the table; a blow, as having turkey for Christmas is a treat. On Tenerife it could be hit or miss whether we could pick one up or not. If our local supermarket did stock turkeys, it was a limited supply. Here they are plentiful, and cheap. After a couple of visits to the bathroom Andy curls up on the sofa watching *The Sound of Music* on Portuguese TV, whilst I attempt to tuck into the mountain of food by myself. It's not long before I feel a wave of queasiness sweep over me, and Christmas dinner is completely abandoned. Luckily enough our L-shaped sofa is large enough to accommodate two invalids feeling very sorry for themselves as Julie Andrews perkily sings "*Doe, a deer…*"

We don't often watch Portuguese TV for the reasons that a) we have Netflix and b) if anything it's worse than Spanish TV. But it does have one great advantage over Spanish TV, the Portuguese don't dub foreign programmes; there's no shrieking sixty-year-old women who can't act pretending to be the voices of ten-year-old girls. Foreign shows and movies are screened in their original language with Portuguese subtitles. This is possibly a reason why English is more widely spoken in Portugal than in Spain. A friend told us the Portuguese had the choice of swapping the subtitles in favour of dubbing a few years ago but opted to stick with the subtitles. It's an admirable decision; not only does it help teach the population another language, they don't have to put up with the excruciating hell that is bad dubbing. Anyone who's not Spanish who has spent any time watching Spanish TV will know exactly what I mean. We feel so poorly, and are constantly drifting in and out of sleep, that we don't want to waste one of our favourite Netflix shows of the moment; *The Sound of Music* is expendable. When the film ends our groggy attention is snapped out of its haze by a bizarre news report about a festive *festa* in Vale de Salgueiro in the north of Portugal. During the *Festa de Reis*, the town's children are encouraged to smoke. The report shows footage of boys and girls as young as five and six proudly puffing away on cigarettes as their parents talk to the presenter. Nobody can really explain why they do this, just that it's always been a part of the festival. It's so strange to watch scenes of children smoking I wonder if I might be hallucinating or half dreaming.

It became apparent in November that Christmas in this part of Portugal would be slightly different from what we were used to on Tenerife. Where we lived in the north of Tenerife, the Canarios *did* put up decorations, there were carol singers in the streets, and Christmas songs on a loop in the shops. However, *Silent Night* was sung as *Noche de Paz* and the song which invaded our heads most during the festive season was *Feliz Navidad*. In November in Setúbal we walked into a shop to hear *Christmas Wrapping* by The Waitresses blasting out; the first time I'd heard it in years. Setúbal itself does feel very Christmassy, helped by a towering blue, artificial tree on *Avenida Luisa Todi* that we can walk inside and make ourselves dizzy by following the spirals of sparkling lights to the tip from within. There's also a small Christmas Market in *Praça Bocage* where little wooden chalets sell handicrafts and food; the best being a *ginjinha* stall where we have a shot of cherry liqueur in a chocolate cup for 1€. However, our hearts aren't in it this year; we go through the festive motions because that's what you do, but it all feels very hollow and superficial.

Dona Catarina does her best to boost our spirits, turning up on the doorstep with not one but two traditional Portuguese Christmas cakes; a *bolo-rei* and a *bolo-rainha*, the king and queen of Portuguese Christmas cakes. The *bolo-rei* is very similar to the Spanish *roscón de reyes*, a circular fruity cake ring topped by seriously sticky caramelized fruits. The *bolo-rainha* is also similar but without the sticky fruit, and with more nuts in the cakes. We prefer the *rainha*.

The sickness bug (stress reaction) leaves us groggy for a couple of days, but it's possibly had a cleansing, restorative effect. We normally walk off the excesses of Christmas Day with a Boxing Day hike, but this year we're too weak, and there were no excesses anyway. By the 27th we're feeling much better, but don't push it with anything too strenuous, just an amble along the dirt tracks which pass for roads around much of this area. It's a grey, cool day with only a few blue breaks in the sky. Even the ducks, huddled together in pot holes on the track outside the duck farm, look fed up; maybe that's because their numbers have diminished significantly during the festive season. The vines which fill many of the fields around us are still naked and stark; not particularly aesthetically pleasing. All in all it's a dour wintry scene until we pass a flock of sheep being guided along the road. At the rear of the flock, skipping along with enthusiasm and energy, are a handful of snow-white lambs. For some reason seeing them brightens our spirits. New life, new hope perhaps? As we return to the *quinta* I hear the sound of a distressed sheep. Getting to know various 'baa' tones has been a subconscious learning curve; they register as we hear the pattern of the flock's day. There's the 'let us out of our field' baa; the 'it's time we were fed' baa; and the 'where's the rest of the flock?' baa. This is something different. This is a sound of a sheep in trouble. We find Dona Catarina at her little 'pottering about' shed and ask her if there's a problem with the sheep. She cocks her head to one side and listens for a moment before announcing.

"That's not one of mine, but it sounds as though there's a problem," and setting off in the direction of the cries.

Andy and I traipse after her as she runs (she always runs everywhere) through the small pine forest and citrus grove to a fence at the edge of her property, passing her flock who are happily munching grass around the trunks of the orange trees. The source of the plaintive cries is a lone sheep in a field on the other side of a track which separates DC's farm from her neighbour's.

"That's Senhor Antonio's sheep," Dona Catarina tells us.

"But why is it crying?" Andy asks.

"Because it's lonely," Dona Catarina motions toward her flock. "It can see them and wants to be with them."

Sure enough, the solitary sheep is staring at DC's flock whilst crying incessantly.

"I'd throw it some oranges to cheer it up," Dona Catarina says. "But I can't throw that far."

I take the hint, pick an orange from a tree and lob it toward the sheep. My throwing arm is a bit rusty and the orange doesn't quite clear the fence, hitting the top wire instead. It doesn't impede its trajectory too much, in fact the wire slices off a section of peel. That's a bloody good service if you ask me, having a partially peeled orange delivered directly to hooves. The sheep should be happy. The orange thuds to the ground a few feet in front of the sheep, but instead of trotting forward it looks at it in a dozy 'what am I supposed to do now?' sort of way. Whilst it dithers, a small goat appears from behind a low stone wall off to one side and steals the orange.

"Oh!" Cries Dona Catarina, covering her mouth and giggling.

I grab another orange and throw it, this time my arm is looser and my aim better. The orange lands closer to the sheep. Again it simply stares at the fruit in that stupid sheepish way. And once again the orange is pilfered, this time by a second goat which appears from behind the wall. After the same thing happens a third time I begin to think we're the victims of a farmyard animal scam. The crafty goats have put the sheep up to it, hiding behind the wall until some juicy fruit came their way. The lone sheep wasn't alone at all. But there was no way we could tell that from our position.

"She just wants to be with her own kind," Dona Catarina says wistfully.

How strange. I'd never really thought about animals being able to distinguish one from another in this way before; not to the extent of a sheep in a field of goats actually yearning to be among other sheep. Sometimes the animal kingdom can reveal much about our own behaviour.

My birthday falls on the 30th December. It's a horrible
day (Andy groans whenever I say this, accusing me of being
a grump). Nobody wants to do much on the night before New
Year's Eve, and places are generally quiet. It's a damp squib of a
day on which to have a birthday. The annoying thing is, had my
mother held on for just 16 minutes more I'd have been a New
Year's Eve baby; that would have been the coolest day of all for
a birthday. Just 16 minutes more, was that too much to ask? We
decide to celebrate by spending two nights at a boutique guest
house in Setúbal so we can toast my birthday and New Year's
Eve without the hassle of trying to find a taxi to get us back to
the farm. As expected/predicted the town is quiet. The upside of
this is we get a table at 490 Taberna STB without a reservation.
A good meal accompanied by some wine is my ideal way of
celebrating birthdays these days, and 490 Taberna STB is reliable
for good food and a warm ambience. A generous selection of
petiscos to pick at - the quail eggs and *presunto* on toasted bred
is a must here irrespective of whatever else is on the menu -
combinned with a bottle of Bacalhoa red are apparently enough
to prise me out of my grumpdom.

On New Year's Eve day we take another opportunity to get
to know parts of Setúbal we're less familiar with, starting with
a coffee and mini *pastels de nata* under the gaze of Maria Pó's
witty sculptures at *Parque do Bonfim*. The biggest omission so
far has been the *Forte de São Filipe*, a star-shaped fortress above
the bay. Like all the castles and forts in these parts, entrance is
free. People use them as leisure facilities as they all have cafes or
even restaurants within their walls plus, being castles, they tend
to come with pretty special views. Built in the 16th century, the
fort is as solid a castle as I've seen; its walls look impenetrable.
The entrance is a revelation, an arched hall rises, via stone
steps rubbed smooth over the centuries, from the large portal
to the ramparts. We enter at forest level and emerge high above
Setúbal, overlooking the Sado, the Atlantic, and the Alentejo
plains stretching south. It's a commanding position for sure.
At the top of the steps is a gorgeous little chapel whose walls
and ceilings are completely covered in *azulejos* depicting the

life of Saint Philip. It's only when we emerge into the light we can appreciate just how solid the fortress is. There is no interior courtyard as such, the castle floor is at nearly the same level as the top of the walls, giving the impression the six arms of the star are completely solid. Buildings have been constructed on top of the walls rather than within them. I've never seen another castle quite like it. Some arms point over the coast, others over the town, and the rest toward Arrábida's verdant embrace; walking to the tip of each rewards with contrasting views. The fort's cafe has prime position, tables and chairs placed along the solid ramparts mean drinks and snacks come with views across the Sado. One of the buildings was once a *pousada* but Setúbal didn't attract enough visitors to sustain it. People don't know what they're missing here.

Local advice is best isn't it? Not always. There's a given within the travel writing business that locals, any locals, are destination gurus with unrivalled knowledge of the places they live. It's a questionable belief. Pick the right local and the reward is an invaluable insight into a destination. However, pick one at random and it's a lottery. I can recount any number of examples where locals have proved clueless sources, including a postman on Tenerife not having any idea which of the streets of the town where he delivered mail had once been (and still was at one part) a *camino real* - a former merchants' way. It's logical when you think about it. We're all locals somewhere but how many of us actually have an in-depth knowledge of the history, culture, traditions, gastronomy of the area where we live? There's a belief that 'locals' know all the best places to eat. Some do, some don't. A couple of years ago I spotted a sign outside a restaurant/bar in the town where I grew up which proclaimed it was 'where the locals eat.' I know the place and consider that sign as being more of a warning.

The owners of the guest house in Setúbal assure us there are lots of food stalls around the harbour for the New Year's Eve celebrations. We know the score in traditional towns where there's a culture of locals eating out; restaurants on New Year's Eve are booked by big groups of families and friends way in advance; places will be rammed with revellers. We try to avoid restaurants on nights like these, big crowds all eating at virtually the same time can result in the quality not being of the same standard as usual. Wandering and grazing at food stalls serving local goodies suits us just fine.

Strolling alongside the harbour area, the place where crowds will gather to watch a firework display ring in another year, it's clear we're right about two things. The first is that restaurants are packed to capacity. The second is advice from a random 'local' isn't always as reliable as it could be. The 'lots of food stalls' turn out to be a hot dog/burger van and a *farton* bar (*fartons* are sweet, pastry fingers from Valencia which are traditionally dipped in *horchata*, a plant-based milk sweetened by tiger nuts). With no other obvious options we order sad excuses for burgers and I amuse myself, and embarrass Andy, by posing in such a way I obscure the O and N of the sign which says FARTON BAR. Still hungry, we scour the streets nearby hoping to find somewhere we can supplement what was an unsatisfactory and meagre haul. We pop into wine bars in the hope we can have some *petiscos* with a drink, but without success. With the effects of alcohol on top of a small amount of food making itself felt, we spot one free table in a pizzeria and order a large four-cheese pizza. After an hour we still haven't been served. I ask about the order and am assured it's on the way. But I can tell they'd forgotten it in the New Year madness. Five minutes later and a plate appears on the table. On it is a small, flat, round of garlic bread. I take it back to the counter and, in stuttering Portuguese, suggest they've made a mistake. The woman behind the counter insists not, that what I have in my hand is a four-cheese pizza. It's laughable... but I'm not laughing. I try to argue but the woman turns away. We have two choices. Dump it and walk out without paying, or shut up and eat it. Hunger wins. It is the only bad experience we've had in a restaurant in Setúbal. Not only did they cheat us out of our pizza, the service took so long we only just make it back to the harbour in time for the clock to strike midnight. As we clink plastic glasses filled with sparkling wine, we're treated to a double dose of firework displays; Setúbal's, which are launched from boats just offshore, and that of Troia across the estuary. It's a spectacular end to an unusual and eventful year.

Waiting for Jo

When we moved to Tenerife our first visitors arrived ten days after we did. In Portugal it's been eight months and still nobody's bitten. We're eager to show friends and family around a part of Portugal which isn't well known outside of the country, so are giddy with excitement when our friend Jo, who lives in a remote valley on La Gomera, is able to stopover for a week on her way back to Britain. Because we've turned our second bedroom into an office, we don't have a spare room. But we'll happily sleep on an inflatable bed in the living room for the duration of Jo's visit. Dona Catarina is having none of it when she hears this.

"Dona Josephina will sleep in the *casinha*," she puts her foot down, inisting Jo will have one of the little houses.

When we ask her how much it'll cost, she waves the question away.

"Dona Josephina is family, and family don't pay."

We'd already told Dona Catarina a lot about Jo and how much she meant to us as soon as we heard she was planning on visiting. After numerous such 'arguments,' we know it's unlikely we'll win, so relent… for now. We usually find a way to reach a compromise in the long run.

Lisbon is only a couple of hours flight time from the Canaries, and the main local airline there, Binter, runs a twice-weekly service (Thursday & Sunday) from Tenerife Norte Airport. In theory, getting to Tenerife Norte Airport from La Gomera is relatively easy as there are numerous daily flights between the two islands. It's only a hop of a flight; barely enough time to eat the legendary, to anyone who's flown with the airline, Binter biscuit which is handed out to passengers on inter island flights. Tenerife Sur is the busier airport on the island, the majority of flights involve transporting holidaymakers to and from the island from various European destinations. But it's the resort airport. From the second you walk into the departure hall you feel as though you've left the Canary Islands behind at the front door. Tenerife Norte, on the other hand, handles mostly internal flights to the Spanish mainland and the bulk of flights to other Canary Islands. As a result it has more of the ambiance of a business airport. Whenever we travelled to any of the other islands from Tenerife Norte our fellow passengers were mainly made up of business people and politicians. We far prefer it to Tenerife Sur's homogeneous, mass tourism destination ambiance. But Tenerife Norte does have a major drawback, its location. The airport sits at 600m above sea level in a valley that is a magnet for *bruma* (dense, low cloud) during some months. In March 1977 it was the site of the worst aircraft crash in history when, in a blanket of fog, two Jumbo Jets collided on the runway. Whenever we had to fly from Tenerife Norte between January and April it could feel like a lottery we didn't want to participate in; every year there are numerous delays and cancellations due to misty mornings. The *bruma* usually buggers off mid morning and flights resume, but not always.

On the Thursday Jo is due to hop across to Tenerife from La Gomera we wake, turn on our laptops and, with fingers crossed, check the flight situation. What we see is exactly what we hoped not to see - '*retrasado.*' All early morning flights between La Gomera and Tenerife are shown as being delayed. Having left the leg from La Gomera till the day she's due to catch the Lisbon flight, Jo has no chance of getting to Tenerife in time for her onward connection. Her only other option is a ferry, but that would take her to the Port of Los Cristianos in the south of the island, 80km from Tenerife Norte Airport. We're gutted, Jo is gutted. But there is not a damn thing we can do about it. We have to resign ourselves to Jo catching Binter's Sunday flight and us only having four days to spend together.

Sunday dawns blue skies and sunshine in Brejos do Assa, but not in the Canaries. Once again it's foggy at Tenerife Norte. It's a rerun of the previous Thursday. Our plans are scuppered for the second time. There would be no point in Jo coming to Portugal at all, except she booked her onward flight to Britain from Lisbon.

Last chance saloon is the following Thursday. Thankfully

there's no *bruma*. It's the day before Jo's due to catch her flight to Manchester from Lisbon so she'll be on Portuguese soil for less than 24 hours. It doesn't make sense to waste time on two journeys transporting her between our house and the airport, so we decide to spend the night in the city.

Jo's predicament is a reminder of some of the drawbacks of island living. I was aware of this growing up on a small island where we were reliant on the ferries running to get us anywhere we wanted to go. A poetic local wit once compared successfully getting off Bute to the movie *Papillon*, where Steve McQueen's Henri Charrière figured out a way to escape from Devil's Island by studying the waves.

"The only way to escape from here is to catch that seventh wave," the local wit would muse.

Additionally, getting back to Bute could occasionally take on Phileas Fogg type proportions as it might involve a race to get to Wemyss Bay before the final ferry of the day set sail. On one occasion, queues on the motorway between Blackpool and Glasgow caused a friend and myself to miss the last ferry. We found ourselves stranded in Wemyss Bay, a ghost town after the ferries have gone, without any money; having spent it all during a boozy week in Blackpool. As it was January we really didn't fancy spending a night in the open air. With no options open to us, we flagged down a passing police car and asked the *polis* if they'd put us up in a cell for the night. They laughed and refused, but advised us to 'break into' the train station/ferry terminal where we'd at least have some shelter. Breaking in simply involved climbing over a fence; they weren't suggesting any damage to property. A trailer covered with a green tarpaulin became our makeshift bed for what was a bone-chiller of a night. Somewhere in the wee small hours we were woken by noises and a flashlight being shone on our bleary faces.

"Just thought we'd check you lads are okay?" Asked one of the policemen we'd flagged down. It was an act which left a lasting impression and was one of those many lessons in life which taught me not to blindly apply stereotypes to anyone.

Travelling to and from Tenerife wasn't quite as bad as that, but it could still prove a pain in the backside, especially when doing it on a regular basis. We never knew exactly how we were going to get home whenever we flew into Tenerife South Airport. Hitting the jackpot was when the timing was just right and we could jump on the direct bus to Puerto de la Cruz. However, that was a rarity. Fate in the form of Tenerife baggage handlers had it we usually missed this bus by just a few minutes, leaving a two-hour wait for the next. Other options were to catch a bus to Santa Cruz (these were more regular) and then change to one to Puerto de la Cruz. The whole process could take nearly as long as the flight time between Britain and the Canaries. Alternatively, we'd negotiate a seat on a coach/minibus taking holidaymakers north. As the majority of holidaymakers head south when they land on Tenerife, there were usually seats to be had. All in all it was still mostly a faff completing this final leg after a reasonably long flight.

By contrast, travelling to and from the farm to Lisbon is easy and cheap. There are a number of ways we can do it. Our favourite is a 35-minute drive which takes us across the Vasco da Gama Bridge. At 17km in length, it was the longest bridge in Europe until the Crimean Bridge was built, and is a modern wonder of the world. Most of the bridge sits low on the Tagus like a causeway. Driving from the southern side it feels very close to the water as we pass flamingos in salt pans on one side and an army of fishermen wading in the low tide mud on the other. The bridge ends amid the ultra contemporary buildings of *Parque das Nações*, Lisbon's dockland area sexed up to host EXPO '98. Humbert Delgado Airport is easily accessed from this northern end of the bridge, meaning we can zip across to the airport without having to negotiate congested city streets.

However, we normally take the train into Lisbon. Palmela train station is a ten-minute drive from the farm and has a large, free car park where we can leave the car for as long as we want. From there we have the luxurious choice of two trains to Lisbon. One runs hourly, the other every half hour. Which one we catch depends on whether our objective is a jaunt to Lisbon, or to the airport to travel further afield. The double-decker Fertagus train trundles past the outstretched arms of the Cristo Rei statue, inspired by Christ the Redeemer in Rio de Janeiro, to cross the Tagus on the *25 de Abril* Bridge. From Entrecampos station it's a short taxi ride to the airport. To spend time in Lisbon, we catch the Comboios train to Barreira on the southern bank of the Tagus and jump on a connecting, commuter catamaran ferry which drops us right in the city's historic centre at Terreiro do Paço, not far from where visiting dignitaries would have once stepped from their boats on the Tagus onto *Praça do Comércio*. The cost of this journey for one person is less than we'd pay a taxi to take us to the bus station in Puerto de la Cruz to catch the bus to Tenerife South Airport. Having access to such a richness of transport options was one of the factors we'd looked forward to from living in mainland Europe. Plus, Portuguese trains are a pleasure to travel in, all the more appreciated when compared with the stressful, cramped ones we'd endured in Greater Manchester, Yorkshire, and the North East during December.

Jo's flight lands on time, although a suitcase damaged on transit delays her exit from the airport. After a lot of hugging and an excited cascade of jumbled words as we talk over each other trying to catch up eight months in thirty seconds, we take the underground back to Terreiro do Paço. Andy booked us all into a hotel in the Baixa district on the edge of Alfama, only a few minutes from the station. Jo is somewhat of an internet Luddite, and still considers Facebook to be a dating app. As a result, we're not as up to date with her life as we are other friends who have embraced social media. Subsequently, a whistle-stop tour of Lisbon involves much stopping in bars so we can simply relax and have a natter. In Peruvian Qosqo we pick at a trio of ceviches, *causa rellena*, spicy prawns, and thick, fried sweet potato fingers whilst getting merry on far-too-easy-to-drink pisco sours. In the simply, but appropriately, named Wine Bar we sip smooth, red wines from Alentejo and talk incessantly as a couple of musicians strum at their guitars and sing melancholic songs. La Gomera; life in Portugal; Hay-on-Wye; Tenerife; Manchester United; the Tories; Labour and Jeremy Corbyn; the plight of the NHS (Jo's a nurse); and, most importantly of all, the wellbeing of family all bounce in and out of an erratic conversation. Time unravels far too quickly. We've enjoyed many adventures with Jo over the years; in a way, she was responsible for us choosing Tenerife as a home. Like many people we'd have dismissed it out of hand as being over-developed for mass tourism had she not urged us to "take a look at the north". Time spent with her, even when it's a smidgens like this, invariably adds quality to our lives.

Although the weather gods have deprived us of the amount of time we should have had, as well as the prospect of introducing her to our new surroundings, this has been a much needed tonic. Her convoluted journey just to get to us has also been a reminder what sheer pleasure lies in just being able to jump on a train whenever we want to visit one of Europe's most beautiful cities. Fourteen years living on an island makes us consider things which form part of everyday normality in many people's lives as possessing a wondrous novelty.

Taking A Peek at Palmela

Palmela is down-to-earth, working class, and historic, as well as being gastronomically interesting. There are lots of disparate aspects to the town which, when moulded together, make for a meatier offering than at first might appear. It is the sort of place which divides visitors. Some recognise it for what it is, an authentic Portuguese town with a rich history; a place that was once prosperous but now, superficially at least, looks down on its luck. Others pass through and think 'nothing to see here, move on.' It is, of course, a 15 minute drive from our house. The route we take to get there, along rural country lanes, reveals aspects of the municipality's character - cork trees give way to vineyards and in-between them is the occasional, out-of-place, factory. Just before a large supermarket on the outskirts of the town is a domestic garage turned into a mini-market selling fruit, veg, and snails. We often get caught in a small traffic jam caused by an eccentric shepherd moving his flock who waves his arms about theatrically and shouts as though in a fury. With the windows rolled up, and sound cut off, he has the appearance of a sun-wizened conductor of an orchestra. With the windows down it sounds as if he's throwing a hissy fit; whether at disobedient sheep or drivers who don't respect his flock and try to inch past without stopping, it's hard to say.

Palmela's centrepiece is its Moorish Castle. Not only is the castle the focal point of the town, it lies at the hub of a network of castles built by the Moors to defend Lisbon and the Tagus Valley. Even though it sits at only 240m above sea level, from the ramparts it's possible to see the *Forte de São Filipe* in Setúbal, Sesimbra Castle, *Castelo de São Jorge* in Lisbon, and Sintra's impressive *castelo*. Palmela is the only one of this list of castles from which all the other key fortifications are visible. Unlike other Portuguese hill towns such as Marvão, Monsaraz, and Óbidos, Palmela's historic centre doesn't nestle within protective walls. The old quarter lies outside the fortifications, flowing down the north face of the hill like a bustle under a

245

Victorian skirt.

The first time we visited Palmela we parked at the bus station in the lower town and walked up steep, cobbled streets to reach the castle… where we found decent car-parking and a road which completely by-passed the confusing-to-navigate narrow lanes we'd just puffed our way up. It didn't really matter that we could have driven closer as the climb proved a good workout and gave us an initial feel for the character of the town. Along the way, sun-bleached information panels in Portuguese and English point out historic spots such as the 17th century Town Hall which was formerly a court, prison, stables, and a butchery; Market Square once bordered by taverns, coal merchants, cobblers, and barbershops, and where street hawkers sold fish, vegetables, milk, and sweets; the main commercial street snaking upwards which would have bustled with townsfolk popping in and out of tinsmiths, bakers, and dressmakers; and *Praça Marquês de Pombal* through which farmers brought their products on a daily basis. In the centre of this square was a fountain which, until the mid 20th century, acted as a source of fresh water for those residents who still didn't have water piped into their homes. All of these help paint a vivid picture of past life that isn't too difficult to visualise as the old streets haven't changed that much over the years. Some small shops don't look as though they've changed their window displays in a couple of centuries. Painted on peeling walls in the upper part of the town are evocative political images; one depicts a naked woman in a cell and has the message "*Não ao aborto clandestino.*" There's no need to read social history books to learn this part of Portugal is resolutely socialist in nature.

Overall, I wouldn't describe Palmela as a charming town, but it is a town with charm. It has no airs and graces yet, perched on the fringes of Arrábida Natural Park, it boasts riches from the land. There are a handful of *adegas* to be found in and around the streets, wineries you can pop in to sample *vinhos* produced from the valleys which spread out from the last row of old houses. In September, stalls are set up in the streets to celebrate the *Vendimia* (wine harvest). Themed gastronomic fairs and weekends throughout the year showcase the area's wines, sweets, breads, cheeses, stews, fruit, and dishes involving rabbit.

The main reason we visit Palmela is to eat lunch with a view. On the southern flank of the hill, just outside the castle walls, is Casa do Castelo which has views across the Sado Estuary and Arrábida Natural Park. After dark at weekends it becomes more of a wine bar, something not uncommon around these parts. At lunchtime it's a superb venue with a menu which mixes traditional with contemporary - Azeitão cheese; stuffed mushrooms; guacamole; and *ovos rotos com farinheira* (scrambled eggs with Portuguese sausage). The dessert menu includes local speciality *fogaça de Palmela*, a biscuit made with orange zest, lard, sugar, cinnamon, and fennel which is shaped like the battlements of the castle and has a gastronomic festival all to itself. On the northern flank, with views toward Lisbon and the Tagus, is the Culto Café which serves decent burgers and a small selection of other dishes.

However, the castle is the real draw and whatever reason we have for visiting the town, we like to have a wander around it. Entrance is free of charge and within its walls are the ruins of the church of St Mary, a Gothic tower, a Moorish clock face, the Tourist Office, archaeological exhibits, a couple of handicraft shops, and the Taverna Bobo da Corte, a great little *petisco* restaurant where the owner told *us* what we wanted to eat on our first visit. It doesn't have views as such, but with its wooden benches and tables it feels exactly like the sort of place you want to eat when inside a Medieval castle, and their sweet potato fries are sensational. From the castle's ramparts, courtyards and terraces, extensive views open out over the Lisbon plains, the Sado estuary, the Tagus estuary and Arrábida Natural Park. There's also been a pousada inside the grounds since 1970, the building it's located in originally built to house the Order of Santiago until the Order's dissolution in 1834.

The irony when it comes to Palmela is, even though it stands head and shoulders above all other towns in the Tagus Valley, and therefore acts as a beacon from miles and miles away, it remains invisible to many who pass this way.

Return to the Fortunate Islands

"Do you miss Tenerife?"

It's a question we get asked on a regular basis by family and friends.

Eight months after we set sail from Santa Cruz, we fly into Tenerife Norte Airport. Is it really only eight months? It feels significantly longer. So much has happened in that time, and we've seen more of Portugal than we could have imagined. As we still regularly write about the Canary Islands and have Tenerife walking guides and travel guidebooks to keep up-to-date, return visits are always on the cards. Additionally, a UK newspaper has commissioned some Tenerife hotel reviews.

Although our return visit is mostly for work reasons it's also an opportunity to catch up with friends as well, starting with one of our dearest *amigas,* Arantxa, who lives in the island's capital, Santa Cruz. Arantxa was one of a trio of people on Tenerife who helped influence the path our travel writing careers took. When travel blogging was still in its infancy she had a major role in organising the first blog trips. She already knew our travel websites and was a fan of our writing. As a result, she arranged for both of us to be invited on a blog trip to Costa Brava which included meeting, and getting to enjoy the culinary creations of, superstars of world gastronomy such as Ferran Adrià and the Roca Brothers; skydiving above Empuriabrava; and feasting on Palamós prawns in a fishermen's hut in Tamariu. It was a groundbreaking trip, setting a sky-high benchmark for all others to try to reach, and was supremely organised by a travel industry visionary, Jaume Marin, at the time Director of Marketing at *Patronat Turisme Costa Brava Girona*. Arantxa had recently suffered from health problems so we are especially pleased to be able to spend some time with her.

We meet her on the terrace of Strasse Park, a cafe overlooking *Parque García Sanabria*, the green lungs of Santa Cruz and one of our favourite parks anywhere. It's an instant tonic to see Arantxa looking fabulous; we all hug and immediately launch into non-stop conversation, topics zipping about all over the place and banging into each other like dodgem cars. We've had lots of fun experiences with Arantxa over the years; one involved heading to a secret location to interview a carnival queen dress designer who was working on his latest flamboyant costume. All we knew was his workshop was located right beside a sex shop in a back street in Santa Cruz. I'm still amazed we weren't arrested when Arantxa, her young daughter on one side and me on the other with my DSLR around my neck, stopped a passer-bye and asked, "can you direct us to the sex shop?"

After Santa Cruz we travel south, pausing at El Médano, a laid-back coastal town which is a haunt of windsurfers and kite-boarders and one of our favourite towns in the south of Tenerife, to meet up with another friend, Linda, for lunch, before continuing to Puerto de Santiago in the south west of the island where we're due to stay at the first of the hotels we'll be reviewing, the Barceló Santiago. We've stayed at the hotel a couple of times in the past and like the place; it has hypnotic views of the Los Gigantes cliffs as well as the island of La Gomera, the vistas are especially captivating as the sun drops behind La Gomera. But resort hotels at this time of year make me uncomfortable for one reason, the shocking hygiene displayed by far too many guests. I find myself obsessively watching and stalking people as they wander around buffets prodding at fillets of meat; touching dishes they're unfamiliar with before sniffing and discarding them; not using the spoons and forks provided to pile cold meats on their plates; snuffling, coughing, and sneezing as they hover over trays laden with food.

During the day we escape the sniffling masses to check walking directions for some of our hiking routes in the south of Tenerife are still accurate; one follows a former merchants' trail, a *camino real*, through traditional hamlets above the south west coast. Another winds across the hills to a hidden valley where there was once a thriving agricultural hamlet. For many years the stone cottages there lay abandoned, but since the last time we walked it there are signs farmers are moving back

into the valley; a couple of the old buildings look as though
they've been recently spruced up. A third route climbs through
a volcanic landscape, passing old lime kilns and threshing
circles, to a viewpoint high above Tenerife's south west coast.
At one point we pass a small cottage, Cabaña La Galipani,
whose whitewashed walls are decorated with faded newspaper
cuttings. As we move closer to read the snippets, a man with the
weather-beaten look of someone who has spent decades outdoors
in a sunny climate appears and introduces himself as being
the subject of the articles – Pedrito, a Portuguese footballer.
There's a lithe youthfulness to him which makes it impossible
to guess his age, something we try to do out of curiosity because
photos of him at the height of his career date from sixty years
ago. Pedrito eases onto a bench in front of his open air photo
album and shares a few tales from a very different life; a time
when he pulled on the national strip of his homeland Portugal
to play against such masters of the game as Edson Arantes do
Nascimento – Pelé – during the Brazilian football team's tour of
Europe, just before they went on to lift the World Cup in 1958.
He's more than happy to shoot the breeze with us, reminiscing
on his Tenerife hillside on a warm January day, and he's a joy
to listen to – as well as being somewhat of a curio. It's not
every day you bump into a former international footballer on
a quiet hiking trail on an island in the Atlantic. As we say our
farewells to Pedrito he asks us to wait and ducks back inside
the gate to his house where we glance a shady courtyard. He
returns a couple of moments later with a handful of mandarins.
We smile and thank him for his time and generosity, and then
wonder about preordained paths. Twenty minutes earlier we'd
eaten two juicy oranges we'd brought in our rucksacks from the
farm in Portugal. There's a satisfying equilibrium to the fact our
Portuguese oranges have been replaced by mandarins grown on
a Spanish island by a Portuguese football player.

   During our return route to our car I mention to Andy that
I feel the going tougher than I should do. It's a warm, sunny
day and there's no shade, but it's not that difficult a route. She
replies she feels exactly the same and had put it down to a mix

of us being out of practice and not challenged enough by less hilly Portuguese terrain. By the time night falls we're both exhausted to the point we can hardly keep eyes open, and take to our beds early. The follow morning we feel worse and don't have the energy to drag ourselves out of bed. We've picked up a bug, and I'm willing to bet one, or more, of the buffet-fingerers are responsible. Under normal circumstances it would be bad enough, but because we're on Tenerife for a limited time to get work done it's a disaster. Months previously we booked a meal at our favourite restaurant in the Canary Islands, El Rincón de Juan Carlos - a one star Michelin restaurant in Los Gigantes - for this very night. The idea we'll be too ill to go is tragic. We sleep feverishly throughout the day, shivering one moment, sweating buckets the next and feeling generally shocking. By evening we both rally enough to drag ourselves to our dinner date. We'd be absolutely devastated to miss this opportunity. We've been fans of Juan Carlos ever since we interviewed him a few years ago for a magazine article after learning he'd been awarded runner-up in a prestigious, 'best young chef in Spain' competition. As soon as we tasted his food we knew he was destined for Michelin star greatness. The restaurant is a family run affair, two brothers and their wives, which makes it quite homely despite the theatrical, avant-garde creations which come out of the kitchen.

As usual Juan Carlos's tasting menu is a whirlwind of a ride for the taste-buds, even our below par ones. An *amuse-bouche* of artisan bread and Canarian black pig with chicken skin *coca* is followed by a tasty parade of the sort of works of art on a plate we've come to expect from Juan Carlos, including Gillardeau oysters with coconut and galangal; smoked eel, ponzu, corn, and yoghurt; crayfish and sriracha; pigeon with pumpkin and couscous; violet, banana and *palo cortado* (aged sherry); and coconut dumplings. The final, theatrical flourish is a bonsai-sized, whimsical candy floss tree. It's pure culinary brilliance and his creative flavours manage to bypass taste-buds which are dulled by whatever it is we've picked up. However, we know they're not in enough shape to appreciate the experience as much as they would have been had we not fallen victims to the slavering undead who patrolled the hotel buffet.

Still feeling weak, but not feverish anymore, we swap the southern side of Tenerife for the north, driving from one micro-climate into another at Puerto de Erjos, a gap in the hills 1117m above sea level where one side of the hill can be in full sunshine whilst the other is shrouded in *bruma* (low cloud). It was around this spot we first started to take Tenerife seriously as having potential to be somewhere we could actually live. The south and the north are very different places for a variety of reasons which are not just to do with the fact the bigger tourist resorts are based in the south. On both the western and eastern roads north, there were specific spots where we could feel the change, points where, after returning from travelling, one of us would say to the other "now we're home."

Having spent time in Portugal, we notice more connections between the Canaries and Portugal than we did when we lived there. The old road from the south west to Puerto de la Cruz via Icod de los Vinos passes through a small town called Ruigómez, a place I always thought sounded like a Portuguese footballer. One of the hiking routes we walked in the south passes above a town called Aldea Blanca. Dona Catarina always refers to Brejos do Assa as the '*aldeia*', the Portuguese word for a small village. It's also occasionally used in Spain, but mostly in Galicia where Portuguese and Spanish words can overlap. *Mojos*, spicy green and red sauces, are favourite Canarian specialities yet the Spanish word for sauce is *salsa* whereas the Portuguese word is *molho*. *Mojos* are also anomalies in that they are often spicy and the Canarios/Spanish don't really 'do' *picante*. The Portuguese, on the other hand, enjoy spicy food, chicken *piri piri* being one of the most obvious examples. These links pop up regularly, no surprise really as the people who settled on the Canary Islands after the conquest weren't just Spanish, they were a mix of European nationalities, Portuguese being one of them.

We're booked into the Hotel Monopol, an iconic colonial building which has been around since 1881. It's in a peach of a position in the historic part of Puerto de la Cruz, the old rooms

with their carved wooden balconies overlooking one of the best
looking squares on Tenerife, *Plaza de la Iglesia*. Unfortunately
we're staying in one of the rooms in the newer annex at the rear
of the building, and these are anything but charming. They *are*
antique in that the decor looks as though it's from the 1980s
- all tired scarlets and yellows. Maybe the walls were once
sunbeam yellow, but now they come across more as nicotine.
It's a depressing room, and it's cold. A cold front has rolled in
to the Canaries, bringing snow to Mount Teide and along the
ridge which splits the island in half, the snow line descending
to around 1500m, which is low for the Canaries. The room
isn't a comfortable place to spend time in, not aesthetically nor
in temperature terms. I hate to write this as we really like the
Monopol, it's a family run hotel with bags of character… in
parts. The atrium lounge is wonderfully sub-tropical; and for
years the owner's mother, dressed in traditional Canarian dress
and with a big smile for anyone who spoke to her, decorated the
steps at the hotel's entrance with vibrant hibiscus flowers. It's
the annex rooms which let it down, they desperately need a nip
and tuck.

It does feel good to be back in Puerto de la Cruz, a place
where many fond memories were made over the years. Another
friend of ours is in town. Bob is what's known as a swallow,
someone who spends winter months in a warmer climate. We
got to know Bob whilst watching Manchester United games
at the Beehive Bar. He's a Wolves fan and doesn't really like
Manchester United but, bless him, tries to be objective because
we *do* like Manchester United. Bob has an infectious enthusiasm
for Tenerife's countryside and is a pleasure to walk with as a
result. Before we left he joined us on a number of hikes during
the months he spent on the island. Unfortunately, thanks to
the mystery bug we're still not up to any serious walking. But
there is one annual tradition we can manage, the *Fiesta de San
Antonia Abad* in La Matanza which takes place at the end of
January. La Matanza is a traditional northern hill town which
lies way below the radar of most visitors to the island. It takes its
name from the area where the indigenous Guanche thrashed the

better armed Spanish conquistadors in 1494. What's interesting is the islanders identify more with the Guanche than they do the conquistadors. A mural at one end of the town depicts a triumphant Guanche warrior blowing into a conch shell. At his feet lies a stricken conquistador knight. The *Fiesta de San Antonia Abad* is an agricultural gathering where animals are brought from miles around to be blessed by the local priest. Thousands of people turn up for it, very few are non-Canarios. Most of the animals are livestock; oxen, goats, a handful of sheep, hunting dogs, and horses (quite a few people still get around on horseback in these parts). But there are also oddities like birds of prey, iguanas, and pythons. It's not uncommon to find yourself ordering *cerveza* at a beer stall next to someone who has a snake wrapped around their neck. The pleasure of this type of *fiesta* is the atmosphere; the Canaries are friendly islands and, presumably being used to centuries of travellers passing through on their way to or from the Americas, nobody bats an eyelid at strangers. We simply wander through the bustling throng of people and animals listening to a soundtrack of traditional Canarian folk music blasting out from loudspeakers on the church's spire; stepping out of the way when burly oxen are driven through the crowd; pausing to watch the goat-milking competition; admiring dressage on streets which are steep enough to sled down without needing a snow coating; squeezing in between *caballeros* to order *pinchos morunos* (seasoned pork skewers) or fried rabbit from a food stall; and sending Bob off on a mission to acquire a litre of *vino del pais* (rough but eminently drinkable country wine). Some people would be intimidated by the surroundings, this is a Tenerife which is light years away from the one of the resorts. But Bob has no qualms about trying to communicate in Spanish in a place where even some mainland Spaniards might struggle to be understood. Canarian Spanish is not only more in line with South American, in the hills the dialect is thick as butter and consonants are often discarded haphazardly.

The journey back to Puerto from the *fiesta* is always interesting, and slow. We get stuck for a while behind some horses where the riders have clearly enjoyed too much *vino del pais* which prompts the question, can you be fined for being drunk in charge of a horse? Once we're past the horses we find ourselves slowed by a herd of goats being let by a girl wearing ripped jeans, a baseball cap, and a camouflage parka. This is what life is like in the real Tenerife.

Our final port of call on the island is at the former capital of La Laguna, a UNESCO World Heritage Site thanks to the perfectly preserved colonial architecture of its old quarter. It's one of those cities we never tire of visiting no matter how many times we pound its streets. It's both the theological and academic centre of the island; as well as historic buildings and churches you get trendy restaurants and bars. When we first moved to Tenerife there weren't many tourists exploring its streets, now there are more but most are day-trippers and local life still dominates. Being located at 600m above sea level, La Laguna is considerably cooler than coastal level in winter months. Thanks to the current cold front it is positively chilly, and very wet. A giant has upturned a huge bucket of water over La Laguna. Rain plummets onto the old streets like it has an aspiration to be Niagara Falls. At lunch time we look for somewhere warm and dry to shelter from the mini monsoon. With heavy drops machine-gunning our backs forcing us to chose the first place we pass, we scamper into the aptly named El Refugio del Abuelo Miguel and grab a booth away from a perpetually open front door. Three men sit at the bar chatting and singing along to traditional folk songs between sips from squat glasses of *vino del país*. We order a couple of *arepas* (Venezuelan filled cornflour pancakes which are a common snack on Tenerife) and listen to water cascading down the historic street outside. La Laguna is not a particularly warm place in late January when the sun isn't shining. But we know that and have dressed accordingly. However, the cold front has caused temperatures to plummet. Our fleeces and light rain jackets are not enough to combat a damp, chilly wind. Even inside El Refugio we don't warm up as much as we'd like.

There's a gap in the rain and we take to the streets again,

managing to cover a couple of hundred yards again before
Monsoon – the Sequel starts, forcing us into the first bar
we pass, located inside another old town house. It's stylish
and contemporary in a way which compliments the colonial
architecture. On a cold, wet day it should be full of shoppers and
sightseers sheltering from the inclement weather. It isn't. Only
one other table is occupied, by two women who, despite wearing
heavy coats, huddle over two cups of *café con leche*. We order
a brace of warming *barraquitos* (an addictively good speciality
Tenerife coffee) accompanied by red wine chasers, and then take
up the huddle position ourselves. Generally speaking, bars and
restaurants in the Canaries aren't geared up for cold weather,
even in somewhere like La Laguna where it's no stranger. I can
think of a few places where there are warming fires, but mostly
bar and restaurant owners don't adjust their environment when
the thermometer drops. Doors that are wide open in the default
setting of warmer weather remain wide open when it gets cold.
They completely lack that cosy element. We've huddled in
bars and restaurants on most Canary Islands, it's just a thing.
Canarian bars and restaurants are missing an obvious trick. There
are plenty of people on La Laguna's streets scouring the old town
for a cosy haunt with closed doors and the merest semblance of
warmth. Instead of being filled with refugees from the cold and
damp, bars sit mostly empty. The one cafe we passed which had
heating was packed to capacity. But La Laguna isn't the sort of
place to visit if all you're looking for is warm weather. However,
this is extreme and not conducive to reacquainting ourselves
with streets which acted as a blueprint for a number of South
America cities.

Thankfully our hotel, the newly opened La Laguna Gran, is
cosy, warm and no hardship to spend time in. It's more along
the lines of the sort of hotel we prefer to stay in; a smallish,
stylish affair located in a renovated colonial building in the old
quarter. The decor is an attractive blend of old and new - plush
leather sofas complementing contemporary globe lighting, and
the hotel has a great little bar in which to pass the time until the
rain lets up. It should also be home to Tenerife's latest Michelin

star restaurant, NUB, but its opening has been delayed so that instead of it being ready to coincide with our visit, it'll open the week after we leave. Hey ho, this is Tenerife and things rarely happen on time here, it's part of the charm.

The inclement weather means we spend much of our time in La Laguna in bars and restaurants; tapas of *ensaladilla rusa* and various croquettes in Rincon Lagunero; a glass of red wine in a *tasca* which was the birthplace of Spanish surrealist Óscar Domínguez; dinner consisting of *almogrote* (a pungent cheese pate from La Gomera), steak tartare, and spinach and mushroom lasagne at the wonderfully named El Jinete Sin Cabeza - the Headless Horseman. La Laguna is full of atmospheric *tascas*, so the weather doesn't impact on our experience anyway, and it's not as though it's our first visit.

Tenerife Norte Airport is next to La Laguna, so only a few minutes away by taxi. As we wait for our flight back to Lisbon, thankful that despite the bad weather there isn't any fog, we talk about how we feel to be leaving again, and whether our first return visit prompted any regrets.

"I'll miss the *barraquitos*," says Andy.

"I'll miss Canarian wine," I add. "Although Portuguese wine more than compensates."

"And *miel de palma*," Andy throws in a delectable syrup from La Gomera called palm honey which elevates everything it's added to.

"Good one. I definitely miss not being able to get hold of bottles of that." I agree. "But will you... do you... miss Tenerife?"

"Nope," Andy replies without any hesitation.

"Me neither."

Tenerife is the past. And we prefer to look forward rather than backwards. It's as simple as that.

THE PEOPLE WHO LIVE IN THE SHADOWS

I know it confused Dona Catarina initially, but we'd
explained what we did for a living as best we could to Susanna,
the estate agent who'd arranged the rental. Presumably she in
turn passed that information on to Dona Catarina. However,
she still must have wondered at first why her tenants 'hid away'
for days, even weeks, on end, especially when the people she
was used to renting the houses to in summer lived all their
lives outside, and usually in swimwear. When we finally do
emerge from the shadows, we disappear for a couple of weeks
or so before returning to retreat back into the darkness again.
On Tenerife a neighbour once asked us if we were spies; our
anarchic pattern intriguing him. It was rich coming from him
as he'd regularly more than hinted he had been, possibly still
was, involved in espionage. If we were spies surely he would
have been the ideal person to find us out? But then, if we were
exceptionally good ones, maybe not. As we try not to bore
people with the finer details of our work, I know even friends
and family don't fully grasp what our occupation actually
involves, and I understand that. One friend more or less
described us as walking for a living, which wasn't technically
incorrect but did over-simplify things a little.

Basically, writing has remained the foundation of our work
over the last 16 years. As the online world muscled its way onto
the travel writing scene, virtually shoulder-barging traditional
print into the sidelines, what that writing has involved has been
fluid.

Thanks to a combination of learning from our own
experiences the hard way as well as listening to, and following,
the advice of people who knew a lot more than we did about a)
travel writing b) the potential power and rise of social media
c) the coming ascendancy of online travel writing/blogging,
we've kept our fingers in a number of pies over the years. These
include commissioned travel writing and photography for print
and online publications; managing our own trio of specialist

258

Slow Tavel/walking websites (Buzz Trips, The Real Tenerife, Walking Tenerife) where we showcase our writing and sell our own travel guides; and, as Slow Travel consultants, helping create walking/Slow Travel holidays around Europe. In the case of the latter we're involved in planning new holidays; have responsibility for mapping out walking routes and compiling essential information; we write bespoke guidebooks; provide photographs for travel brochures; pen descriptions for web pages and brochures; and compile marketing material such as travel articles about the off-the-beaten-track destinations where we've helped create holidays. How all this translates in real terms when it comes to the balance between being on the road and sitting in front of a laptop is we might travel for a month, then spend the next couple of months writing... and then repeat. It's not quite as prescriptive as that and the pattern isn't necessarily concurrent, as work trips tend to be like that old saying about London buses; you can wait for ages for one and then three arrive at the same time. What it all translates to in Dona Catarina's eyes is that we're absent for big chunks of time and even when we're at the *quinta* we're mostly hidden away in our wee office, only emerging once or twice a week to prevent ourselves becoming stir crazy by going shopping, walking, or exploring somewhere nearby we haven't visited before. When deadlines are looming we're pretty much in lockdown and human contact amounts to our daily Portuguese lessons with Dona Catarina, aka brief chats prompted by her passing our 'office' window each morning enquiring "*tudo bem?*"

Mostly things are indeed *tudo bem*, but sometimes they're not.

Like the time when far too many wasps started to regularly appear around the house and we tracked the source of entry to them coming straight through the roof tiles into the living room and kitchen, presumably seeking somewhere cooler to escape the sizzling weather. Luckily they tended to be dozy from the heat and seeing them off the premises without being stung wasn't difficult.

"*É a natureza*," Dona Catarina shook her head in a resigned, seen-this-all-before manner when we told her about the wasp invasion, before arranging for panels to be fitted inside the roof, blocking the wasps' route, and helping insulate the house more in the process; something we really came to appreciate when the cold winter nights arrived. The local man she hired to fix the ceiling did a good job; he and his son (the young waiter who'd introduced us to camel spit at the village restaurant) nearly completing the work in one afternoon. I say nearly because toward the end of the afternoon he sliced through his thumb with a Stanley knife which abruptly stopped play. He still hasn't returned to complete the finishing touches.

Then, one night, a nicotine-coloured scorpion appeared on the living room floor, scuttling into the centre of the room from underneath a cabinet, its tail raised and stinger brandished. It gave us quite a turn, you don't expect to find a scorpion heading toward you during *Line of Duty*, adding to the already unbearable tension. I carefully, and nervously, trapped it under a sieve, slipped card under the wire to secure the prisoner, and escorted it outside. Dona Catarina happened to be staying over at the farm that night and when she heard us outside the house (the people who live in the shadows never emerge after dark unless something is wrong) came out to see what was the problem.

"*É a natureza*," she sighed, shaking her head as she brought a rock down on the poor creature, explaining she had to execute it as she was worried it might sting the toddler of a couple holidaying next door to us. Dona Catarina claimed it was the first time she'd ever seen a scorpion at the farm. We'd just been lucky. Very lucky it would seem, as it happened again. On two more occasions during the following week, scorpions just appeared on the living room floor. From where, who knows? Our wood basket was the initial suspect, but I always check the logs as I fill it and wasn't convinced. I thought it more likely they were coming under our back door. Following the forest fires the previous summer, the Portuguese Government introduced stringent measures to try to reduce the risk of future fires. These included landowners cutting down trees that were within a specific distance of buildings. A rigid timetable of action to be taken during certain months was drawn up. If people hadn't complied with the new regulations when inspectors called, a hefty fine was levied. What this meant for the farm was a thinning out of the pine forest behind our house. I'd read the fires and subsequent loss of trees had resulted in processionary caterpillars taking up residence in trees closer to urban centres than was normal. Maybe the loss of pine trees had also prompted scorpions, who'd had their homes disrupted, relocating elsewhere, and our back door was closest to the pine forest. Whatever the reason, they were only attracted to our house. Dona Catarina's little *casinha* remained scorpion free. After witnessing how she'd dispatched the first intruder, I didn't tell her about the others. Instead, I released them back into the pines and hoped they'd stay there. For a while after this, the daily *"tudo bem?"* became *"tudo bem? Nao escorpiões? Nao Vespas?"*

Now and again rain can short the electricity, leaving us without any until the main fuse box dries out.

"É a natureza," sighs Dona Catarina when this happens, her eyes rolling upwards to the heavens.

Or one of the sheep might sustain injuries trying to get at leaves on branches that are too high; one of its spindly legs buckling as its barrel-shaped body crashes back to earth after attempting to reach forbidden fruit.

"É a natureza," accompanied by a sad shake of the head.

When the water pump stopped working, resulting in no running water as the electric pump brings the precious liquid from a bore hole, it prompted Dona Catarina's second favourite sigh-accompanied saying.

"Sempre problemas."

Conveniently, the farm's other some-time handyman, Marcelo, works full time as a heating engineer and knows about such things. As far as I can see, he is the closest thing to a professional worker in the entire area. Normally the smaller *'problemas'* are fixed by Fernando, when and if he shows up. Fernando has what you might call a flexible approach to his working hours; he turns up when he turns up. We like Fernando a lot. He's always got a smile on his face, never gets rankled by

261

anything, and has proved a good source of information. But he's only got one gear when it comes to work and that's Fernando speed. However, there's a hare and the turtle element to his approach, Dona Catarina being the hare in this partnership. She runs about everywhere; her body sometimes overtaking her feet so that she falls over now and again, resulting in occasional facial cuts and bruises. No matter how many times we tell her she needs to slow down, she insists on haring it around the place. Fernando is in no danger of ever falling over, except if he falls asleep as he rakes the grass. However, even with his slow and steady approach, he still gets things done pretty efficiently.

After a couple of months at the farm we realised we hadn't seen Fernando pottering around for a couple of days. We asked Dona Catarina if he was okay.

"He's got a job at a factory."

We were sorry to hear he'd left and we hadn't had the chance to say goodbye or wish him luck in his new job. We'd grown very fond of Fernando and his easy-going ways. Whenever he saw us he'd always ask if we needed anything done. At Christmas we bought him a bottle of whisky (we didn't tell Dona Catarina as she wouldn't have approved. She already thought he drank too much) and in return he presented us with a bottle of *Moscatel Roxo* from a nearby vineyard, informing us it was the best of the Moscatels. He'd regularly turn up at our door with a basket of whatever fruit was ripe on the farm - tangerines, pomegranates, loquats, plums etc. We'd miss him for a number of reasons.

"But he'll be back before long," Dona Catarina added.

She was right. Fernando was back chopping logs and tending to the sheep the very next day. The shock of moving from self-regulated hours at the farm to ones set in stone proved too great a challenge apparently. Since then Fernando has left to take up a number of other work positions, and returned to his farm work within a few days at most.

As we are used to solving our own problems, we're not comfortable having to rely on others. We regularly try to wrench some aspects of DIY back under our control, but usually with limited success. The door handle to the bathroom had been temperamental since we moved in, threatening to imprison one of us inside the bathroom. The idea of having to exit via the window wrapped in a towel and coming face to face, or worse, with Fernando concerned Andy for some time, so I decided (was encouraged) to replace the lock myself. However, when we tried to buy a replacement at AKI, a large DIY store in Setúbal, none of their locks had the same measurements. In the end I had to tell Dona Catarina about the problem handle.

"That's strange," she remarked. "It's quite a new lock."

She took the mechanism to an ironmonger where she lives in Seixal, returning with a new one the following day.

"The man in the shop was surprised when I showed him the mechanism," she told us. "He hadn't seen one like it in 15 years."

15 years in this part of the world is still considered 'relatively new.'

The bigger issues that occur around the farm are generally dealt with by neighbour Senhor Zé, or whoever else Dona Catarina can round up. These guys clearly all know the rudiments of self-sufficient living and are able to patch up just about any problem which arises. But the result can be, even to my limited eyes, a patch up or, as Andy coined it, B-I-Y (botch it yourself). Things do tend to work after being fixed, but often not in the way they might if a professional had been involved.

The biggest disruption so far has been when the ground above the cesspit collapsed, revealing the concrete walls of the pit had crumbled and the whole system would have to be replaced. In most places this would be a job for experts. Here it was a task for Senhor Zé, a friend of his who was able to get hold of a JCB, and a motley crew of other neighbours. There were two bits of bad news for us regarding this unsavoury turn of events. The first was the original cesspit was located right at the rear of our house and we had no plans to travel anywhere during the time the cesspit was open and 'perfuming' the air. The second was that until a new cesspit was constructed, our temporary cesspit consisted of a large bucket, placed in an open hole below a pipe extending from the ground at the rear of our

263

house. Senhor Zé, or one of his cronies, emptied this bucket on a daily basis which seemed above and beyond the call of duty for him, and was seriously off-putting for us. That sort of thing is just too personal, especially when the demands of nature can't be ignored and I'd no choice but to visit the loo whilst Senhor Zé and cronies were actually working in the temporary pit directly outside our house. At such times I tried my best not to imagine the scene outside when I flushed the toilet, but it insisted on forcing its way into my thoughts in glorious high definition images to embarrass me.

Where Fernando, Marcelo, and Senhor Zé get things done, albeit unconventionally in some cases, other workers brought in to solve *problemas* can be more hit and miss.

We currently have two electrical sockets hanging off the wall. These are new sockets which were were recently fitted. The old ones were replaced after virtually going on fire when we plugged the oil heater into one. Dona Catarina engaged the services of an 'electrician' who lived in the village; a diminutive man with an impenetrable dialect, a Sex Pistols haircut and a single gold ring earring – a punky pirate who reeked of booze and tobacco. He turned up without an electrician's screwdriver and had to borrow one of the only two tools I currently possess (the other being a hammer). When Dona Catarina asked him if he wanted her to turn the electricity off he laughed and told her no need, before sticking my screwdriver into the socket and shorting the electricity all over the house. He's responsible for the wayward sockets.

In cases like these Dona Catarina shakes her head in despair before ironically uttering the third of her top three favourite sayings.

"*O charme do sul.*" - the charm of the south.

The great beauty of all this is even during the time we spend in the shadows banging away at keyboards, quirky events unfold right under our noses. We get to experience a rich tapestry of life in this rural part of Portugal without even having to leave our 'office.'

PORTUGAL AND THE ORIGINS OF POPULAR DISHES AROUND THE WORLD

There's a question which has been niggling away at me for some time. Why does just about every cafe in Portugal sell samosas?

A thought-provoking book I'm reading reveals the answer, and has me pondering the origins of popular dishes in various countries. The book in question is *The First Global Village – How Portugal Changed the World* by Martin Page. A couple of pages relating to the exchange of cooking techniques and the movement of ingredients from one country to another illustrates how trying to pinpoint 'ownership' of specific dishes can be a minefield.

Cultural appropriation is a buzz term of the moment. Like other current trends which have their origins in something worthy and important, it's been bandied around recklessly to the point casual accusations of it often distract from serious cases of, well, cultural appropriation. This seems especially the case when it comes to food. A number of chefs have found themselves in the cultural appropriation firing line from people who aren't chefs, and who often don't really have any connection with the food preparation industry. You have to be extremely knowledgeable about gastronomy to jump into a culinary arena and fling cultural appropriation accusations around. Either extremely knowledgeable, or completely ignorant when it comes to food. Recipes change and evolve from chef to chef, cook to cook, frying pan-wielding granny to frying pan-wielding granny (or grandpa). Expand that to an international level and you discover a veritable smorgasbord of influences to be found in some popular traditional dishes.

Take tempura, the famous Japanese dish of seafood and/or vegetables which is lightly battered and deep fried. It's not Japanese at all. It was introduced to Japan by the Portuguese in the 16th century.

Then there's the Indian snack samosa. According to the book, the Portuguese picked up the method of wrapping light pastry around a savoury filling from North Africa, took it to India and hey presto, the samosa came into being. The Portuguese then brought this snack with them back to their homeland and that's why you can buy *chamuças* (samosas) in just about every cafe in Portugal.

The Portuguese also took chillies from Brazil to Asia, bringing about a radical transformation in the cuisine there. Even the post-pub pain threshold tester, the vindaloo is down to the Portuguese. It seems obvious when pointed out, but it means garlic wine (*vinho de alho*) – a reference to the Portuguese method of marinating meat in barrels filled with wine and chillies.

In Troia, on the other side of the Sado Estuary from us are the remains of Roman *garum* 'factories'. *Garum*, a fermented fish sauce which was highly sought after in the age of the Roman Empire, is said to be the forerunner of the pungent shrimp paste used extensively in South-east Asian cuisine.

The book goes on to list a range of fruit, vegetables, spices, and cooking methods whizzing back and forward between various countries across the globe. In Alentejo we were introduced to *sarapatel*, a savoury and slightly spicy meat and offal Portuguese dish. It's a dish which is popular in parts of Brazil and Goa in India.

Staying on an Indian theme, historians claim that some of the sauces we know as 'curries' were created for British during the days of the Raj. Just to highlight how confusing the whole thing can be, it's said Chicken tikka masala was invented by a Pakistani chef in an Indian restaurant in Glasgow. Try unravelling cultural appropriation out of that spicy little nugget.

A few years ago I read a satirical article in a Spanish magazine which suggested all the Italian restaurants on the island of Fuerteventura were run by Argentinians pretending to be Italian. A relatively common dish on the Canary Islands is *arroz a la Cubana*, which allegedly doesn't come from Cuba at all but was created by the Spanish. It's also popular in the Philippines. *Ropa vieja*, one of Cuba's national dishes, originated in the Canary Islands.

In the Caribbean, much of the cuisine owes its existence to influences from Africa, Asia and Europe – *sofrito* from Spain; callaloo and ackee from West Africa; salt fish from Europe and North America. I've even seen one suggestion that Jamaican patties have their origins in Cornish pasties.

Trying to figure out who has 'ownership' of what is bewildering, and also rather pointless. Tracking the journey of dishes is, however, fascinating.

One of Britain's favourite dishes, fish and chips, may have been introduced by Italian or Jewish immigrants. The Scotch egg came from India or North Africa. Pizza began life as flatbreads with toppings in Greece. Pasta was brought to Italy from China. And on and on it goes.

Any map showing the historical movement of food products and dishes across the globe is like a spaghetti junction of tracks which mirror exploration and trading routes, with culinary influences spreading to and fro in all directions.

The joy of travel and trying the cuisine of different cultures often involves shared experiences. As a lover of good food and trying new things, I'm eternally grateful so many ingredients, techniques and dishes have been 'shared' between cultures and nations in the past. Without this exchange the world, gastronomically speaking, would be a much poorer and blander place, and we wouldn't be able to snack on *chamuças* whenever we had a yen for one.

THE STORK FARM

After four months of living at the *quinta* we have yet to turn left after we exit the gate. Why? We just never got around to it. The *quinta* is at the end of a dirt road, but a rough track (two furrows at either side of a grassy central reservation) does continue into a cork forest beyond a rusty old fence with a red and white *zona de caça* (designated hunting area) on a post; possibly one of the places our neighbour Senhor Zé goes to hunt wild boar. It's an area we've dismissed as being private, but during the course of a stilted conversation with Dona Catarina about walking she asks if we've walked to the Sado Estuary via the *Estrada Nacional*, the network of roads which connected various parts of Portugal before motorways were built. Whether it is private or not remains unclear; however, Dona Catarina insists it's absolutely fine for us to walk through. Knowing where we can and can't walk is proving somewhat of a head-scratcher in this area of Portugal as there is no walking infrastructure (no officially designated routes with signposts or markings). As there's no right to roam in Portugal we're never sure whether we're on public paths or trespassing. But landowners don't seem to bother so…

February is warm and sunny south of the Tagus. Dona Catarina tells us she often wears short sleeves when she's pottering around the farm in February which she claims is a warmer month than March. The nights remain cold but days are extremely pleasant, spring-like even. We take the opportunity to finally turn left when we exit the *quinta's* gates.

Within a few steps we're in a forest of low, twisted and gnarled trees whose lower trunks are smooth and russet-coloured whereas their upper trunks and branches are knobbly and light sage - cork oaks. Portugal produces over 60% of the world's cork. Every July and August the bark is stripped by traditional methods, leaving the characteristic russet-coloured trunk. Each stripping gang consists of several experienced strippers and some apprentices. First a circular incision is made high up on the trunk with an axe, followed by two or more vertical ones. These are made very carefully, so as not to damage the tree's internal 'bark' (phellogen). The outer bark is then carefully levered off. When done by experts, the cork comes off as two semi-cylinders, the shape of roof tiles. It's an eco-friendly and sustainable industry as it doesn't damage the tree, with trees only being stripped once every nine years to allow for re-growth of the bark. Numbers are written on the trunks of stripped trees to show the year the tree was last harvested. As bark re-grows from the inside, these numbers remain visible until the tree's next harvest is due. We've developed greater respect for wine with traditional cork stoppers since learning about the cork industry in Portugal, and now sneer at nylon and screw-top substitutes. There are concerns that both of these pose a threat not only the livelihood of cork-strippers, but also the ecosystem which has developed over the centuries around cork oak forests. It's good to know that by drinking Portuguese wine we're doing our bit for the industry and nature. In recent years the cork production industry has diversified. There's now a wide range of cork products on sale in Portugal, ranging from handbags and shoes to hats, coasters and even umbrellas; cork can be surprisingly soft, almost leather-like. One of the biggest purchasers of cork is one of the most unexpected - NASA. A taxi driver told us this. We were highly dubious until I researched and found it to be absolutely true. Cork is used in spacecraft because it's a natural insulator and cools down rapidly. It's staggering to think such an old product, still harvested in traditional ways, is a key to the success of the most cutting edge transport we have. Continuing on from their voyages of discoveries, the Portuguese connection to boldly go where no person has gone before seems still relevant.

The cork forest is a revelation; winter rains have turned the forest floor fresh green, a sea of young grasses is broken by the first signs of spring, buttercup-yellow wild flowers. Shafts of sunlight illuminate irritated Eurasian jays, squawking noisily as they relocate to more distant treetops when we approach. The path curls alongside a small orchard beside a sprawling field where skeletal industrial irrigation sprinklers sate the thirst of a land still recovering from last year's long, hot, dry summer. We emerge from the cork forest into an open pasture decorated by a few puffball-shaped stone pines; in the distance Palmela Castle adds its Medieval presence to the scene whilst a huge flock of sheep, with a handful of goat interlopers, moves imperceptibly across the grassy expanse. On the backs of many are hunched, white riders - egrets. We've only walked a couple of kilometres and it's already a cracking little route. Our path takes us through the centre of an attractive, and badly dilapidated, colonial-style farmstead. It must have been quite a place in its heyday, a circular dovecote with domed top is more lookout tower in appearance than bird abode. There are numerous outbuildings, most with partially collapsed roofs. An open courtyard has the dimensions of a small town square bordered by porticoed buildings. It's a fascinating place in its own right, but it has a feature which elevates it into wide-eyed wonder territory; the old farm is home to a colony of storks. There must be 30 or more, their over-sized nests clumped together on rooftops, chimney stacks, the dovecote, and every telegraph pole leading to the run down yet still elegant property. We gingerly walk through the courtyard, half expecting some outraged farmer to emerge from one of the buildings. But the only creatures not happy about our presence are the storks. Some take to the air to circle above, casting pterodactyl shadows which momentarily blot out the sun. Others clack their disapproval with their long beaks, creating a noisy drum beat which could be the opening intro to Adam Ant's *Ant Music*. Some storks stand sentinel in the field, appearing nearly as tall as we are. They're beautiful birds, bigger than I'd realised. We've spotted them gliding gracefully overhead plenty of times; seeing *cegonhas* (storks) above the farm always brings a smile to Dona Catarina's face. They're revered in Portugal, as they are in many countries, and encouraged to nest by farmers. Dona Catarina's husband converted a concrete pole into a potential stork nest, but none took the bait. Despite them seemingly preferring human-made constructions to trees they're timid creatures, taking to the air whenever they deem us as being too close. It astounds me they build nest besides busy motorways, completely ignoring the noisy metal monsters which roar past nearby, and yet when we tiptoe past quiet as church mice, they're offski in a shot.

The stork farm is only a couple of hundred metres from the N10 *Estrada Nacional* which separates us from the Sado Estuary. By Portuguese standards it's a busy road, but we're able to cross it without feeling as though we're risking life and limb. We've mapped out a route which takes us along back roads through small agricultural hamlets where painted tiles on houses illustrate the working life of an area; one shows women harvesting wine; another depicts men stripping cork oak; yet another portrays labourers shovelling salt. A road sign informs us we're entering Gâmbia, a fitting name for the area as there are flamingos at the estuary and ostriches in a field not much further along the N10. We ponder which Gambia came first. The Sado makes its presence known quickly after crossing the *Estrada Nacional*, our route follows muddy channels and skirts rectangular basins filled with water as we wind closer to the estuary itself. It's sleepy farming and fishing country; a world where dogs laze in the shadow of tinny Piaggio Apes, the mini-me truck which is the Vespa's bigger relation, and white herons high-step their way around beached, flat-bottomed river boats. Once ensconced in the maze of the Sado's tributaries it's impossible to know which paths end at locked gates, which end at water-filled trenches, and which lead onward and out of the confusing network of tracks. It's both beguiling and frustrating; on the one hand a gentle terrain of salt pans, fish farms and oyster beds inhabited by cormorants, egrets, heron, stilts, and spoonbills. On the other, it's a mocking maze which is difficult to negotiate as there are just so many dead ends. All we can do is meander anarchically and hope we'll eventually work our way back to the N10. In a way it doesn't matter, this is the sort of walking route which provides a greater insight into life in the area. Although there's no structure to it as such, it's packed full of pieces of a jigsaw which, as each segment slips into place, reveals more about this part of Portugal. We eventually find a dirt track heading back in the right direction through cork oaks when Andy spots a thin rope lying across the path.

"Stop!" She shouts as I'm just about to step on it. "That's not a rope."

I retreat pronto, realizing what I nearly put my foot down on; a convoy of processionary caterpillars. We know all about them after Fernando pointed out their cotton wool-like, puffball nests on the pine trees behind the house and warned us about how dangerous they can be when they descend from the nests in long nose-to-tail convoys during January and February. These are the first we've seen up close. They are quite incredible to observe; each two-inch, striped creature connected to the one in front, like a string of hairy chipolatas stretching right across the wide forest path. It is truly a procession. We watch it from a respectful distance as this is a parade which packs a nasty punch. When threatened, the caterpillars release fine, toxic barbed hairs which can cause itchy rashes if they come into contact with the skin, but pose a far greater threat if inhaled. They can result in inflammation and irritation of eyes and throat, coughing, vomiting and all manner of unpleasant symptoms. At worst they can trigger a serious allergic reaction. Basically, avoid them at all costs, and don't let pets near them. We give the line a wide berth and continue, spotting and avoiding two more processions before we safely return to the *Estrada Nacional* and make our way back home.

Discovering Arrábida Natural Park...
Finally

Its beaches are so renowned around the country it draws Portuguese holidaymakers in their thousands during summer months. For three months its coastal road is reduced to a single track lane such is the volume of cars parked on the verges at either side, blocking the progress of anything bigger than the average car. And yet, apart from a couple of brief forays, we've still to explore Arrábida Natural Park even though it's virtually on our doorstep.

Lying forty kilometres south of Lisbon and forming the southern strip of the Setúbal Peninsula, Arrábida stretches from Sesimbra in the west to Palmela in the east; part of it is a limestone massif which falls from 400m to sea level, forming the highest sea cliffs in Portugal. Its highest peaks are just 500m above sea level, low-lying compared to the topography of the island we recently left but lofty by Portuguese standards; this is a landmass which can be seen from the Algarve. Having now become acquainted with a reasonable chunk of Portugal, we can see that Yann Martel's book *High Mountains of Portugal* has an ironic title. Arrábida's hills and vales are coated with a rich *maquis* of low, open scrubland; its south-facing slopes are wooded with varieties of oaks and pines; sequestered valleys are carpeted in rows of vines and olive groves, and it's generally accepted Arrábida's coastline boasts some of Portugal's most beautiful beaches. The area consists of three main hilly ranges which create folds and ridges that are hidden from the world outside the park area. As a result, Arrábida feels remarkably rural, remote even, despite its proximity to Lisbon.

The Natural Park label in Portugal is a curious one. It tells us an area is known for outstanding beauty and often scientific interest, but these are not Natural Parks in the sense we might think. Most of Arrábida is privately owned (around 97% according to one source; although, we haven't been able to verify this figure). That's one of the reasons we haven't explored

273

it more on foot. We expect a Natural Park to be a rich source of walking routes and Arrábida is touted as such, yet when we stayed in Azeitão and enquired at the tourist information office about walking in the park we were gently discouraged, in a concerned 'you might get lost, fall down a hole, or attacked by a wild boar' way. Locals who know the terrain, and where they can or can't hike, *do* walk trails in parts of Arrábida; visitors don't. There are few official walking routes. However, there had clearly been routes at one time. Last May, from our Azeitão hilltop base just inside the park, we'd explored dirt tracks leading into cork oaks. One initially had faint red and yellow waymarks but these faded out, deserting us in the depths of the forest. As route-finding is part of our job, navigating our way through a forest where tracks run off in all directions didn't pose too much of a problem. But for those who aren't accomplished map readers it might be a story with a different ending, especially as one tall tale I heard locally involves an alien who lives in one of the many tunnels which run below the ground, and who emerges on Thursday's to drag an unsuspecting human back to his lair. Why only Thursday I have no idea. I guess we all have our preferred food-shopping day.

We'd also previously walked from Setúbal town centre to *Praia de Albarquel*, a beach which would be one of the world's exceptional town beaches if it weren't for a huge rock barrier jutting into the sea separating the beach from the town. It requires heading slightly inland and an 'up and over' in order to get to the beach. Albarquel barely gets mentioned in travel articles about the beaches of Arrábida, and yet it is a stunner of a *praia*, one of the best looking beaches I've seen anywhere. With angular limestone rock formations and white sands backed by a dense wall of greenery, it reminds me more of a beach in Krabi, Thailand than anything I'd expect to find close to a major European city. Remember, this is adjoined to a town which doesn't have any beaches according to some Portuguese. Spoilt for choice is the phrase which came to mind when we set eyes upon the glorious sands of *Praia de Albarquel*.

However, along with our windmill ridge walk in Palmela,

these have only been tentative first bites around the fringes of Arrábida Natural Park. After five months of living in the area, a more thorough exploration is long overdue. A mini road trip seems the most logical way to get a decent feel for the park before we attempt to get to become better acquainted with it off road and on foot.

The N10-4 road heads west from Setúbal's harbour, where the town ends abruptly and the forest begins; an instant and dramatic transformation. One second we're in a bustling town, the next we're engulfed by trees; gaps in the forest allowing glimpses of a calm, sparkling Sado and an equally bejewelled Atlantic beyond the estuary's mouth. Arrábida's protective arm seems to keep the Atlantic at bay; the water outside the entrance to the estuary is often as glassy as that inside it. The first spot which entices us to pause comes after only a few minutes; *Parque da Comenda*, a leisure area beside a tributary. A narrow footbridge leads from a rough car park to a picnic area beside a small river/large stream lined by squat palm trees. At the car park is a wooden shed of a kiosk. The tables outside it are occupied by a troop of septuagenarians. Inside, a woman of similar age serves her customers with exactly the same two drinks; a cup of coffee and a glass of something murky poured from a five-litre plastic water bottle. The liquid is the same colour as the water in the muddiest part of the stream; some sort of local firewater no doubt. I make a mental note to research what it might be (i.e. ask Fernando). It's a shabby picnic area, but ramshackle in that charming Portuguese way. I like it, it oozes personality. But then I'm still in the 'thrilled to see a river' stage. We work our way along the riverside, passing a clowder of feral cats, a white heron, and some kayakers preparing to take to the water, to the iconic building which makes *Parque da Comenda* an intriguing spot. Half hidden by the trees on the slope at the mouth of the tributary is the *Palacio da Comenda*, a derelict, 26-room palace built for the prosperous Albino family in the 19th century. It was sold in 1870 to Count Ernest Armand, the diplomatic son of a Parisian politician whose own son had it redesigned to look like an Italian villa. In the 20th century it became renowned for its parties, and a favourite summer haunt of the rich and famous. Truman Capote, author of *In Cold Blood*, spent the summer of 1965 there with his friend Lee Radziwill, the sister of Jackie Kennedy. Locals claim Jackie Kennedy herself stayed in the house, recuperating following the assassination of her husband. Now it's a sad, crumbling, rundown shadow of its former self. The people who lounge on its elegant balconies over the sea are intruders - graffiti artists and Instagrammers. (*Update: in 2019 the Palacio da Comenda and surrounding lands were purchased by a mysterious buyer who immediately incensed the local population by giving notice they were closing the picnic zone, dug up the public car park at Praia de Albarquel, and put up 'Private' signs on tracks through the forest, some of which were freshly marked official walking routes newly created by Setúbal council*).

Another few minutes of winding along the coast and we drive through an eyesore of a sprawling cement factory. It would be far more of an eyesore if it actually stood out more than it does. The cement factory is enormous in size, spreading for some distance inland, yet nature does an admirable job of concealing much of its bulk. Even from a short distance away it can be mostly hidden from view. Still, it shocked us to see a concrete monster in such a scenic environment and in an area labelled as a 'Natural Park'.

"Why on earth would the authorities allow this to be built here?" We asked one person when we first saw the factory from Setúbal. They were more shocked by our question than by the presence of the factory.

"It brings jobs," came the pragmatic reply. "And that's good isn't it?"

As outsiders who don't have to rely on employment in the area it didn't feel appropriate to push the issue.

Beyond the factory, Arrábida really begins to cast its spell. It's a want-to-feel-the-breeze-in-your-hair road to drive; the steep cliffs hemming us in on one side, pristine turquoise waters at car level on the other, before we arrive at what is ostensibly a wide sandbank of a white beach, *Praia da Figueirinha*. On a pleasant sunny day in February the sands are virtually empty. In summer they are rammed to capacity with sunbathers. Following the devastating fires of 2017 the local council don't want to leave anything to chance regarding the risk of forest fires in Arrábida. If a fire had broken out during the previous summer, the fire services wouldn't have been able to reach it due to the volume of parked cars clogging the road. As a result there are new restrictions. From summer 2018, Arrábida's coastal road will be closed at *Praia da Figueirinha*. From Figueirinha, shuttles will transport sun-seekers to the beaches beyond, the ones which regularly make it into travel articles listing the top ten beaches in the world. For me, Figueirinha doesn't have the charm of Albarquel, but it's an impressive beach nonetheless. As we warm our toes in the soft sand, I begin to understand why the Portuguese can be so picky about what constitutes a beach. Anywhere else and Figueirinha would be considered a cracker. Here it's merely okay when compared to its neighbours. There's a lone, funky beach restaurant which becomes a chill-out bar in the evening; it must be a special spot to sip a sundowner on a warm evening. We make do with a black coffee and sit for a while, watching fishermen moor their small boat on one of the desert island-like sandbanks which lie between Figueirinha and the finger-thin peninsula of Troia just cross the mouth of the Sado. It's a tranquil paradisaical beach scene, one which is juxtaposed by a gargantuan merchant ship heading through the narrow mouth of the estuary on its way to Setúbal Port.

From this point the scenery changes gear, slipping seamlessly into overdrive. The road curves into the folds of the coastline, obscuring views of Setúbal and the unsightly apartment blocks which corrupt the tip of Troia. Instead, there are unspoilt bays and teasing glimpses of wild beaches, Coelho and the one which earns the most accolades, Galapinhos, backed by verdant mountains which sweep right down to the water's edge. We follow signs for a car park and find ourselves not exactly where we hoped to be, but at the opposite end of a beach which curves all the way to the picturesque fishing hamlet of Portinho, our intended destination. We decide to walk to the hamlet, immediately stumbling upon the ruins of a Roman fish-salting site overlooking a bay as alluring as just about any I've set eyes upon; the handful of white houses perched on the water's edge at Portinho contrast with the carpet of dense greenery that threatens to engulf them. It's captivating, not in the slightest bit manicured and far wilder than we expected. Images from last year's hot, hot summer showed a family of wild boars cooling down alongside human bathers in the water here. Looking over this beguiling landscape it doesn't seem as unlikely a scene as when I first saw the photo. We descend to the shoreline and stroll along soft sand to Portinho where there are a trio of restaurants, two of which jut out over the clear water. It turns out parking at the 'wrong' end of the beach was a wise, if unplanned, decision. There are only a few parking spaces to be had in the hamlet itself - access to the place is via a single lane track controlled by traffic lights - and even on a quiet day in February all the spaces are taken. Another benefit of parking some distance away is that by the time we reach Portinho we've entered the lunchtime zone; a restaurant on stilts above crystal waters teeming with fish seems like too good an opportunity to miss. Plus we haven't had *choco frito* in a while, and every restaurant by the sea serves fried cuttlefish . Only one of the two is open, so that removes any difficult decision making. D'uportinho it is. The terrace is enclosed which makes it perfect for February, large windows allowing panoramic views whilst both protecting from a cooling sea breeze and boosting the warmth of the sun's rays. The scenic setting adds extra flavour to a tuna salad given a fresh zing by the addition of strawberries and orange segments, followed by a slate of *choco frito* and a basket of French fries. Prices are slightly higher than back in Setúbal but this is an exceptional location in which to eat Setúbal's favourite dish, and D'uportinho serves good *choco frito*.

From Portinho, the road heads inland and upwards to a junction where we can either continue west or turn back on ourselves and head across the *Serra da Arrábida*. We turn right. Where the coastal road was a gentle sea-level amble of a route, the twisting curves rising to the *serra* are a rally driver's dream or, in one particular case, a spy's nightmare. This is where James Bond's new wife, Tracy (Diana Rigg) was gunned down at the end of *On Her Majesty's Secret Service*. Despite George Lazenby not quite being up to the job of filling Sean Connery's shoes, it's one of my favourite Bond movies. Subsequently it's a thrill to be in such an iconic spot. This upper route is an exhilarating stretch of road; one which deserves to be on a top ten travel list. It's often compared to the Amalfi coast, but is so way below travellers' radar we hardly encounter any other cars. Lined by low stone barriers which allow sensational (aka dizzying) views down to the azure sea, the road snakes in and out of Arrábida's lush crevasses. Rough parking areas along the way allow Andy (the driver) an opportunity to enjoy bird's eye view of coast and beaches without running the risk of driving off the cliff. The best of these *miradouros* overlooks the *Convento de Arrábida*, a rambling monastery built by Franciscan friars in the early 17th century which is so nestled into the undulating hillside it's not easy to spot from the coastal road below. The *Convento* is the size of a small village and looks immaculately maintained, even though there is only a handful of monks living there. Also intriguing are a row of ancient monastic cells perched precariously on the ridge which rises from the viewpoint.

The *Convento* isn't the only surprise along this road. After finally reaching the ridge, the road levels out for a few kilometres. We stop intermittently just to gaze down one side of the *serra* toward the coast and across the golden sandbanks to Troia, and then cross the road to look north over the Vale dos Barris to the great city of Lisbon in the not so far distance. The descent when it comes is as much of a white-knuckle ride as the climb; there's no need to look around to see panoramic views, the sandy mouth to the Sado fills the windscreen as the car goes into a nose dive. On one switchback we notice rusty open gates set just back from the road and decide to take a breather and have a nosey around. A track leads us to an abandoned building which has the appearance of a mock fort, beyond which is a trio of huge coastal battery guns, their long, graffiti-decorated, barrels still pointing out to sea. Beneath the guns, a network of tunnels lead to barracks, armouries, and storerooms. It's a gun emplacement, built in the 1930s to defend the entrance to the Port of Setúbal. It's fascinating in a Marie Celeste way in that it's relatively well preserved, as though it had only recently been abandoned. It's a notion which isn't that far off the mark as research reveals it was manned by the military until the end of the 1990s. There's an eerie, disquieting air to the place. I'd expect the tunnels and rooms to be vandalised, even used by vagrants, but a brief explore - it becomes pitch black after only a few feet and is a confusing maze of corridors - shows that few folk venture far beyond the entrances. The rooms I make it to, directly below the big guns, are untouched and clean; large iron racks looking ready to be loaded with shells. I don't hang about long though, or stray too far from the entrance. I've played too many *Silent Hill* type video games to not have my brain conjure up images of mutant monsters whose fangs are dripping with blood-tinged saliva waiting for me to take a look around just one corner more. I retreat back to the safety of the light and we continue on our way. From the gun batteries, we twist and turn till we return to sea level, emerging back at the monstrosity of the cement factory.

When we return home, I publish a few photos on Facebook highlighting the best of our mini road trip. It's not long before we get a phone call from James at Inntravel, and a question we half expected after sharing on social media some of the revelatory landscapes we saw in Arrábida Natural Park.

"Do you think there's scope for us to develop a Slow Travel holiday in Arrábida?"

SPRING AGAIN

The cape contrasts with the lush and lovely landscapes further east along the coast in Arrábida. It's devoid of trees, a windswept plateau of low-lying Mediterranean scrub jutting out into a rumbustious Atlantic. Thanks to Portugal's sunny disposition it's not bleak as such, but it is raw and battered, and yet still beautifully compelling in the way capes can be.

Dinosaurs and Opera Singers

We've been invited to join a group of 30 journalists/bloggers/influencers specialising in outdoor activities to spend three days walking the last stages of the *Camino de Santiago* in Galicia, in the process testing jackets/boots made with GORE-TEX. We don't tend to accept press trips now as a) we prefer to explore places under our own steam and not follow an agenda set by someone else, and b) they're too restricting and don't always result in the authentic and impromptu experiences we relish most. But we've talked about walking the *Camino de Santiago* at some point and this sounds like it could be the perfect taster. Plus, we've already dipped out toes into *Camino* waters, albeit Portuguese ones when we criss-crossed the route to Santiago de Compostela whilst putting the Minho Slow Travel holiday together. However, our limbs have become lazy over the winter months. Normally we use the cooler winter months to notch up a lot of hikes, but not this year. It's time to shock them back into life, and we haven't explored our surroundings on foot anywhere as extensively as we'd hoped. Researching ready-made official routes reveals the municipality of Sesimbra shows most potential.

Sesimbra lies at the western tip of the Setúbal Peninsula, separated from both Setúbal and Palmela by Arrábida Natural Park. The town is the closest thing to a resort on the peninsula even though its character is quite clearly that of a fishing community. Mention Sesimbra to any Portuguese person and the first thing they're likely to say is "great fish and seafood." They're right, the town is full of fish and seafood restaurants, many with barbecue grills built into the side of exterior walls, sending forth the aroma of sardines, bream, and bass being grilled - which is intense and near impossible to resist. Beach front restaurants boast the sort of views visitors lap up, but it's the restaurants found in the narrow maze of tiled back streets which tend to serve the tastiest fish, and at lower prices. The beach is wide, golden and runs the length of the town, all the way to the substantial fishing fleet at the harbour. There are two things which make the beach stand out from the crowd. The first is the *Fortaleza de Santiago*, a honey-stone fortress embedded in the sands of the town beach. It's home to a neat little Maritime Museum (featuring evocative images from the days when the sands beside the fort were covered in rows of fish, laid out by fishermen), the tourist office, and the Tap House which serves tapas and craft beer on the battlements overlooking the sands. Greedy Sesimbra doesn't have just one castle, there's an even more impressive affair, *Castelo de Sesimbra*, on guard on the hill above the town. Known as the Moorish Castle as it was originally constructed by the invaders in the 9th century, it's a Knights of the Round Table type castle with turrets and crenellated walls which hug the hill's undulations. Visually it's not dissimilar to Sintra's Moorish Castle, and was considered one of the most important fortifications south of the Tagus, responsible for helping protect Lisbon from invasion from the sea. The second interesting curio about Sesimbra's sands is part of it is called *Praia da California*, named after a stream which ended at the sea here. What's particularly intriguing is the name existed before the eastern US state was founded. The accepted explanation regarding how California was named attributes it to Spanish explorers who took the name from an obscure 16th century tome titled the *Adventures of Esplandián*, by Garci Rodríguez de Montalvo; California being a mythical island in the work of fiction. However, an alternative explanation involves Sebastião Rodrigues Soromenho, a Portuguese navigator who, in the 16th century, charted coastlines around China and the Philippines before crossing the Pacific to sail south along the coast of the area now known as California. This Portuguese captain hailed from Sesimbra. Coincidence or not? I guess we'll never know for sure. But I know where I'd put my money.

The first hike we attempted from Sesimbra didn't exactly inspire us. It involved walking south west from the town centre and into the *maquis* to reach a ravine which descended to a hidden beach. The outward route was okay, but not spectacular; however, the return route was not up to the standard we expect from a good walking route, especially as it involved ducking through a hole in a high wire fence into a working quarry where there were signs galore warning of the possible chance of us being blown up.

We have high hopes for our second attempt as a) it's recommended on Sesimbra's official website and b) it seems to feature many quirky ingredients. We park in the village of Azóia and walk a few hundred metres along the country road leading to Cabo Espichel to a point where we can join the official circular route. It's not a promising start. At the exact point the leaflet we've downloaded shows us we can pick up the route, there's a sign warning we're entering private property and anyone caught trespassing could be punished with imprisonment. It's a sign which provokes a loud rant consisting of the 'best of' Scottish expletives. It's not the first time we've found ourselves face to face with an unexpected blockade due to historic paths being fenced off by a new landowner. It baffles, and annoys the hell out of me, that a country with a socialist government can be guilty of selling off so much of its land. This is especially frustrating as it's one of only a couple of walking routes Sesimbra council showcase on their website. In defiant mood we decide to ignore the sign and follow the path anyway. If the GNR (National Republican Guard) appear we'll wave the downloaded route at them and accuse the council of misleading potential visitors as well as encouraging people to trespass. It quickly becomes evident that an imminent arrest is highly unlikely. The reason for the sign is a half-built house beside the path which hasn't been touched for quite some time. Somebody obviously purchased the land with designs to construct a cottage and then ran out of money. Beyond the building there are no more private signs, fences, or any evidence we're on anything other than the *Chã dos Navigantes*, a marine path that around 100,000 years ago would have been at sea level. As the views open up to sweep back along the coast toward Sesimbra and the green curves of Arrábida beyond, the rocky and potentially vertiginous path descends to a ruined building in prime position just above a sea which is sparkling silver in the sunshine. The *Forte de São Domingo* is a coastal defence from the 17th century and a good spot for an energy-boosting cereal bar. Although not particularly challenging, the narrow path was precipitous enough to wake slumbering muscles from their winter reverie. From the old fort we follow a maze of narrow, earthy tracks which traverse the hillside, leading through thickets of scratchy broom. It might be a known old path but, apart from occasional blue daubs, there are no signs to show it's an official trail. Although ruddy tracks galore criss-cross and veer off in various directions, walkers would have to be directionally challenged to get lost. Keep the sea on the left and continue heading west is all we needed to know. Eventually the white and red tip of *Faro de Cabo Espichel*, peeking above the *maquis* ahead, does what it was designed to do, acts as a beacon we're heading in the right direction. The lighthouse sits just back from the most westerly point of the cape, guiding sailors away from the possibility of shipwreck on the treacherous *Costa Negra* - the black coast. It was commissioned in 1790 by the Marquis of Pombal as part of a network of lighthouses created to make the black coast safer to navigate, and is one of the oldest lighthouses in Portugal.

The cape contrasts with the lush and lovely landscapes further east along the coast in Arrábida. It's devoid of trees, a windswept plateau of low-lying Mediterranean scrub jutting out into a rumbustious Atlantic. Thanks to Portugal's sunny disposition it's not bleak as such, but it is raw and battered, and yet still beautifully compelling in the way capes can be. Lighthouses are hypnotic for various reasons; the obvious being the light that draws our gaze toward them. But their very presence also stokes the imagination; invoking thoughts of what life must have been like for the sentinels who kept them working. Normally they're solitary figures, the lighthouses that is; although it might apply to their keepers as well. Not in the case of the *Faro de Cabo Espichel* though. On the adjacent headland lies a rather unusual neighbour and rival which completely upstages the *faro*. We already knew about the *Sántuario de Nossa Senhora*

do Cabo Espichel, it was one of the reasons we wanted to walk
this circuit. But knowing about the existence of something
and seeing it first hand are two very different things. We're
completely blown away by the old sanctuary, and that's nothing
to do with the wind sweeping across the cape. On the cobbled
streets of a Portuguese city, the ornate, baroque facade of this
17th century church wouldn't warrant a second glance; these
fancy churches are ten a penny in Porto, Braga, and Lisbon.
However, the impact of seeing one perched on the top of
amber cliffs on an exposed headland is like a punch to the
solar plexus; it's completely unexpected, a structure which is
completely out of place, and all the more captivating because
of it. What adds to the drama is the *Sántuario* is no ordinary
church. Two arms stretch out from the main building, creating
a long narrow courtyard which ends at a stone cross. Each arm
consists of a two-story long-house, the upper half being for
lodgings, the lower a covered arcade of what was once shops
and stalls. The *Sántuario de Nossa Senhora do Cabo Espichel*
is a place of pilgrimage; the compound itself more of a small
village created to meet the needs of the hundreds of worshippers
who once journeyed there. The most astounding feature of this
extraordinary place is it even boasted an opera house where
entertainers from across Europe performed for the gathered
masses. The opera house lies in ruins and the shops and lodgings
have been boarded up with breeze-blocks, but it's impossible
not to feel the presence of the ghosts of pilgrims past; to see
them applauding fire-eaters in the courtyard; hear their bartering
for oranges and cheeses; and imagine them entranced by sweet
voices in the opera house as a barrage of Atlantic rollers pound
the cliff face below. What a place this must have been in its
heyday; a bustling, buzzing religious village at the very edge of
Europe. And the reason it all exists? A woman on a giant mule.

The story goes that in the Middle Ages a brace of fisherman
saw Our Lady riding a huge mule up the cape's sheer cliffs,
leaving footsteps in the rock. The story of the sighting spread
throughout Portugal, drawing pilgrims to the area as a result. Its
popularity grew to the extent Dom João donated the land where

the woman on the mule had been spotted to the cult of *Nossa Senhora do Cabo*, later to become the Marian cult, and a small chapel was built on the spot. The original is no more, but its replacement, built in the 15 century, houses some of Portugal's oldest *azulejos*. There are still annual pilgrimages to the *Sántuario de Nossa Senhora do Cabo Espichel*, but on a March Sunday, when it's unclear whether the rain clouds or the sun will win a seasonal skirmish, there are a few modern pilgrims, all are dressed in leathers and astride motorbikes. There's clearly a Sunday scene here. A couple of tables covered in handcrafts have been set up in the red earth car park beside two food trucks, each selling exactly the same snacks -*bifanas*, *farturas*, *churros*. Our route takes us beyond the sanctuary, following the indent of the coast to one further headland to see if we can spot the *Pedra da Mua*, dinosaur footprints. One hundred and fifty-five million years ago great herds of dinosaurs roamed these parts, some leaving their mark on the land. In 1976 palaeontologist Miguel Telles Antunes discovered various sets of tracks belonging to sauropods and theropauds. One of these sets, made by a family of herbivores, climbs the cliff toward the *Sántuario de Nossa Senhora*. It begs the question - what exactly did those fishermen see making its way up the cliffside all those years ago?

Information boards in Portuguese mark the best spots for viewing the dinosaur tracks, but bugger me if I can see anything. Eventually Andy spots some; a track of evenly spaced, elephant foot-sized circular indents making their way across the rocks. As soon as she sees one her eyes know what to look for and, as I'm still struggling to make out the first set, she's quickly pointing out another and another. Once my own eyes lock on as well, I can make out tracks all around. It's mind-boggling to think we're standing where these great creatures once roamed. Seeing their footsteps etched into the land for eternity makes it feel all the more real, bringing the grazing dinosaurs much closer to us; the term 100 million years becoming a meaningless number. This circuit might have started out as a bit of a damp squib, but it's more than delivered the quirky goods since we were stopped in our tracks by that 'private' placard.

287

SHOCK FREET, POR FAVOR

"*Shock freet, por favor,*"
It was the first time I've ordered it the way the locals pronounce it. Up until this point I've always asked for "*chocko freeto.*"

Recently, whilst ordering a hit of what has become a firm favourite of a dish, a waiter confirmed my order by saying the words "*shock freet*" so quickly they whizzed past my ears before I could fully register them. By the time my ears tuned in they were faint, just ghost words on the breeze. But I caught them.

It's taken a while, but more and more we're picking up some nuances of dialect. On Tenerife, it took some time to realise the letter S tended to go AWOL at the end of sentences, so '*dos*' would become '*daw*','*gracias*' was '*graciah*', and '*más o menos*' (more or less - a phrase used a lot) came out as '*mah o menoh*'.

Here, south of the Tagus, it can be the last vowel which does the disappearing act. Trying to ask an assistant in a supermarket where the plastic cups were proved difficult even though we knew the Portuguese for them was *copos de plastico*. Eventually the penny dropped and she exclaimed, "*ah, copsh plasht.*" Subsequently, *choco frito* (fried cuttlefish) sounds like *shock freet*. Considering we've eaten masses of the stuff, we've been slow on the uptake regarding how to actually order a dish which is somewhat of an obsession in Setúbal. I recently saw a Portuguese website which said "*Setúbal is much more than choco frito, but choco frito is Setúbal.*"

I'd eaten cuttlefish semi-regularly in the Canary Islands, but none were like Setúbal's. In the Canaries, cuttlefish tends to be simply served, still looking like a cuttlefish. I enjoyed it when it was done well - simply grilled - but it was never a 'wow' of a dish. Andy was never much of a fan. In Portugal it's a completely different eating experience. *Choco frito* is boiled with bay leaves and garlic, marinated in wine and lemon juice, then coated in savoury, seasoned cornflour before being cut into strips and fried, the crispy batter contributing a satisfying crunch. We tried it on our first visit to Setúbal, ordering it not because we'd done any in-depth research into culinary specialities of the area, but because just about every restaurant we saw advertised *choco frito*; restaurants with names like the Taverna do Choco Frito and the Rei (king) do Choco Frito. There's even a Museu do Choco – a restaurant specialising in different ways to cook *choco*. Cuttlefish is such a part of the town's character that witty statues to the revered *choco* bookend the town. One is a mischievous take on the statue of Fernando Pessoa sitting outside Café A Brasileira in Lisbon, where Portuguese visitors sit on the empty bronze seat opposite to have their photo taken with the famous Portuguese writer. In Setúbal, a *choco* takes the place of Pessoa, so passers-by can have their photo snapped sitting next to a human-sized cuttlefish cartoon character. The *choco* sculpture at the opposite end of the town is a similar cuttlefish sprinting on its tentacles to escape a frying pan. It's not in the best taste, and made us feel a bit guilty the next time we faced a plate of cuttlefish after seeing it for the first time, but it is amusing.

The obsession with *choco frito* is said to have started in the days when cuttlefish had no commercial value. The fishermen who sailed the waters south of the Tagus, from the Sado Estuary down to Sines, tended to keep *chocos* for themselves; taking them into Setúbal's bars where they were fried and served as an accompaniment to post-fishing drinks and lively conversation. It was a tradition which grew and grew until *choco frito* became synonymous with the town. Now it is in such demand some of it has to be imported from other places. Restaurant owners in the town, even ones not specialising in fish and seafood, claim they have to have *choco frito* on the menu otherwise they'd never get any local custom if they didn't; there's always someone among any group of Setubalenses who will insist on ordering *choco frito*. And if it ain't on the menu they'll simply leave. We understand why, it is an addictive dish. After a few weeks without eating it we develop a yen, a need to have a *choco frito* hit. Over the last few months we've compiled a list of our favourite places to eat it. In truth, we haven't had a poorly cooked *choco frito* in Setúbal, but some restaurants have stood out for serving exceptionally good versions, Kefish on a small square in the backstreets is one, Restaurant Galeão in Portinho is another. The service can be painfully slow at the latter, but the setting is extra special, the portions are ridiculously large, and the batter they use is lip-smacking good.

This week whilst wandering around Setúbal we saw posters which made us smile. One of the things we love about both Setúbal and Palmela is there are often themed gastronomic weeks. Palmela's tend to reflect the land. There are gastronomic weeks and weekends based on rabbit - *coelho à moda de Palmela*; festival biscuits made from sugar, flour, brandy, oranges, cinnamon and fennel - *fogaça de Palmela*; and an intriguing concoction called *sopa caramela* - a hearty, stew-like soup consisting of fennel, various types of cabbage, potato, turnip, carrot, onion, garlic, pork, bacon, pig ear and chorizo. The name is said to come from a nickname given to itinerant rural workers who ate it in the fields and whose skin was a rich coffee colour due to the time spent labouring under a fierce sun.

In Setúbal, themed gastronomic weeks tend to involve gifts from the sea; *caldeiradas* (fish stews) in early spring; mackerel in late spring; sardines in late summer; mullet in autumn; oysters also in autumn. And this week, posters around Setúbal tell us it's the *semana do choco* (cuttlefish week). The town has a special *choco frito* week, which seems ironic as every week is *choco frito* week in Setúbal. What can you do? We pop into the nearest seafood restaurant. When in Rome, do as the Romans do. When in Setúbal, eat fried cuttlefish.

Marching on the Camino de Santiago

March continues to meander along in fickle fashion, not quite able to make its mind up what it wants to do; the seasons involved in a tug of war where some days winter wins and we're shrouded in a cool, grey, damp blanket. On other days spring triumphs and bathes perky grasses and budding wild flowers in warm sunshine. It was in March we first visited Setúbal last year. Daytime temperatures were around 24C, warmer than the ones we'd left in the Canary Islands. After dark; however, a bitter wind howled around the streets. Dona Catarina says February here is a better month for weather than March, it's more settled and warmer. The month ends with a jaunt to Galicia, to spend three days walking the final stretch of the *Camino Francés*. If we were doing it under our own steam, we'd drive directly and it would take us around six hours to get there. But as this is the trip sponsored by GORE-TEX, the participants all have to meet up in Madrid before setting off for our *Camino* starting point in the small, sleepy Galician town of Melide. It might not be the most direct route for us, but at least we get to spend an afternoon and night in Madrid, and eat some tapas.

Stage 1, Melide to Arzúa: The black bubble tent looks like a UFO which has touched down in Melide's tiny Medieval plaza. Around 30 journalists, bloggers, and Instagrammers from Germany, Spain, Italy, France, Norway, Sweden, Britain, South Korea and Japan line up to collect maps, water flasks, and a compact camera. In return we hand over our mobile phones, to be returned when we complete the stage. Although our objective is to test GORE-TEX jackets and walking boots we've all been issued with, the organisers are also keen participants experience the *Camino* without the distraction of social media. This is something which doesn't go down well with a trio of German Instagrammers whose phones are essential for what they do.

The plan was to start walking at 12:45; however, the bus

journey from Madrid took longer than estimated. At 14:30 we're just starting lunch, a hearty affair consisting of noodle soup and a schnitzel. The cutlery has gone missing en route so we drink the soup from its rectangular container and treat the schnitzel like finger food, watched by a couple of police officers who are clearly bemused at the sight of an international gathering sitting cross-legged in their town square. At 14:50 we finally take to the *Camino de Santiago*; it's 16km to our destination. In the hilly destinations we normally walk, a 16km hike could take most of the day so, aware of the lateness of the hour, we set off at a brisk pace. The path is relatively flat with only slight undulations, making the going easy and fast. Soon we swap the town's stone cottages for gently rolling farmlands, excited when we see the first sunburst scallop sign confirming we're on the pilgrims' path.

Almost immediately the group thins out and we find ourselves virtually alone on the *Camino*. We cross streams, pass through dappled forests and skirt hamlets with narrow constructions which look like hen houses raised off the ground, but are actually designed to dry vegetables away from the gnawing mouths of rats and mice. We recognise them as being the same as the *espigueiros* we saw on our trip to the Minho. The new boots we were issued with in Madrid feel comfortable and light as air; a relief as we had concerns about heading out on a long trail wearing untested boots. Even at this early stage it's noticeable there's a tranquil aura along the *Camino*. Cats and hens share the same patch of sunlight and dogs don't go into a barking frenzy when we pass. Anyone who's walked in Spain will know how unusual this is. Three hours after leaving Melide, the *Camino* takes us through the older part of the town of Arzúa to our accommodation, Hotel Suiza. The final section reveals the answer to a question which has been bugging us for years - why do some people stray from the path?

Every quaint country pub should have a Brian Glover, a rough diamond with a Yorkshire accent who sits in a corner nursing his pint of real ale and only springs to life whenever any hikers enter or, more importantly, prepare to leave the premises.

"Don't stray from the path," BG will shout gruffly as they open the door to take to the moors/hills/ forests... whatever.

The hikers will stop in their tracks and turn slowly, concern spreading across their features.

"Why, is there a werewolf out there?" One will ask, only half joking.

"No, cause you'll get bloody lost if you do," Brian will reply before returning to quietly sip his Golden Goblin.

Most of the time the feedback we get about the route directions we write is hugely helpful. But there's one type which has us scratching our heads with bemusement. It tends to go something like this.

"We came to a bridge where there were two paths, one continuing past the bridge, the other veered off our route to crossed the bridge. We took the one crossing it but after a while realised it was the wrong way and returned to follow the other route which turned out to be the correct path. Why didn't your directions tell us not to cross the bridge?"

The simple answer, and the one which has us head-scratching, is if the correct path crossed the bridge we'd tell you to cross the bridge. Route directions would be endless if they were full of instructions telling people what *not* to do.

We arrive in the town of Arzúa at the same time as a trio of other walkers in our group and follow scalloped shells embedded in the pavement through the town until we arrive at a junction where one fork stays on the *Camino*, the other heads to a plaza in the centre of town. As we check our map, the trio continues. By the time we conclude the directions don't tell us to leave the *Camino* till we reach our hotel on the other side of town, the trio have disappeared. As we continue on the *Camino*, with no other members of our group anywhere to be seen ahead or behind, alarm bells start ringing loudly. Something isn't right. However, we tell ourselves over and over that, as route direction writers ourselves, we know only too well you never ever stray from the path unless instructed to do so. But as we leave the town and there's still no hotel in sight that conviction wavers.

And then we see it, a wonderful exonerating sign on a post. It has GORE-TEX written on it and points through the woods. We follow it for 100m to emerge right at the hotel, to see others in our group arriving by road.

Apart from us, and a group of four French participants, everyone else had strayed from the path in the town and decided to follow signposts for the hotel rather than stick to the map which showed they should stay on the *Camino*. The fact that the majority of people needed to be told not to do something was highly illuminating and a valuable experience for us as route writers.

The hotel is comfortable, clean and quite basic. There's a problem with the water on our floor, it refuses to heat up. A rapid, icy shower isn't the most pleasant way to get rid of the day's grime.

"You're experiencing the *Camino* properly," quips one of the organisers when we moan about the cold shower.

Stage 2, Arzúa to O Pedrouzo: It's -1C when we take to the *Camino* after a Spartan breakfast. The sun is shining once again, slightly disappointing the GORE-TEX crew who hoped we'd experience their product under more challenging conditions. Persistent rainfall up until the day we started walking has left sections of the path muddy, so at least the boots get some of a test; although, as I don't want to get my new footwear dirty, I gingerly pick my way through the squishiest sections. The sun might be shining, but baby it's cold outside. Not that I feel it. A combination of snazzy new jacket, fleece-lined trousers bought for a Chile trip and gloves and hat picked up in Germany's Black Forest a couple of years ago have me feeling as snug as a bug in a rug.

There's a different vibe to the path this morning. We're regularly overtaken by groups of walkers aged around 15/16; a school or college expedition. The *Camino* feels crowded - a contrast from the calm meandering of the previous day. We're used to walking lesser known paths where other walkers are few and far between. Subsequently, I find myself resenting the presence of other pilgrims. Comparing the *Camino* with other places we've spent a week or two walking every day, it feels like a walkers' highway. At this point I tell Andy I've lost the desire to walk the full *Camino*. But I'm out of step by judging it as though it were just another walking route.

Approaching a refreshment point after 6km, we catch up with a trio of young girls (not from our group). They're dirt-splattered, limping and look tired even at this early hour. They're also smiling and chatting, clearly relishing the challenge. Whereas we stop for a drink of Aquarius and to munch a Twix, they continue to hobble onward. There is no well-stocked refreshment stall for them. The scales begin to fall from my eyes. More fall with every weary, muddy, joyous pilgrim we encounter. At one point we pass a British couple of similar age to us. They're almost hobbling along, their clothes showing signs of the bad weather they've endured whilst ours are, accusingly, pristine. I feel compelled to confess to being a fraud, telling them we'll only notch up three days in total.

"At least you're walking some of it. *Buen Camino*," the man laughs, his generosity of spirit making me feel even more of a *Camino* charlatan.

With every signpost showing the kilometres to the final destination lowering, there's a corresponding notion the levels of achievement and excitement at nearing the end of the path are rising. With it, even to part-time pilgrims like us, comes a sense of having shared something special. The evident camaraderie among walkers is inspiring, heart-lifting.

We arrive at a junction in O Pedrouzo and, with no sign telling us otherwise and like the previous day, continue on the *Camino* as our instructions suggest. A kilometre or so after leaving the town behind we are 99.999% convinced the *Camino* was never going to lead to the hotel, so backtrack to the junction and search the surrounding area to see if we've missed the GORE-TEX sign. We haven't, but we do eventually find a wooden board on a lamppost which has a sign pointing the way to our pension. This time the organisers hadn't actually left a sign at the point we should have strayed from the path. It's a misunderstanding which adds an extra 4km to our route.

Ironically, and in contrast to yesterday, our experience of writing and following route directions worked against us. Sometimes you just can't win.

We arrive at cosy Pension Maribela at 15:00. It's far too early to stop walking, we should have taken more time. I don't want the stage to end. In complete contrast to how I felt in the morning, now I want to experience the *Camino* like a real pilgrim; to walk it from start to finish.

Stage 3, O Pedrouzo to Santiago de Compostela: It's a grey, drizzly morning. Having enjoyed two unexpected sunny days I don't mind, in fact I'm keen to see how our gear performs in damp, windy conditions. Whereas on other stages our group split into small groups almost immediately, for the final day we seem to subconsciously stick closer together. There are some fellow GORE-TEX 'testers' we've particularly hit it off with; a couple of German journalists; a brace of Japanese bloggers Massa and Yasuke; and especially the delightful Amjoo (Choo), the only participant from South Korea. Choo cracks us up; she's a natural storyteller, recounting tales of life in South Korea in a way which puts Cheshire Cat beams on our faces.

"My mother says I'm not to return without a European husband," she declares at one point.

When Andreas from GORE-TEX asks her during dinner on our second night whether it's true South Korean couples have to have blood tests to make sure they're compatible she responds as if outraged at the suggestion.

"You seem to know more than I do about dating in South Korea," she shoots back.

"So it's not true?"

"Well, yes, it can happen," she laughs. "But not just to go on a date."

For the ultimate stage we walk together. She tells us about South Korea, we show her eucalyptus cups and warn about processionary caterpillars, chatting endlessly as we wind down the kilometres to Santiago. Everyone's pace appears to be slower today. It's not deliberate, perhaps our collective subconsciousness is delaying reaching the end of the road. Lunch is taken at Monte do Gozo, a hill where pilgrims gather for their first sighting of Santiago de Compostela. We know we're drawing close to it when we hear singing; apparently the tradition is for pilgrims to vociferously express their joy at seeing the end of their journey, 5km down the road.

The Monte is buzzing with pilgrims, a small army in multi-coloured hiking gear, eating and chanting. Whereas a couple of days previously I might have muttered something about it being overcrowded, now their unbridled joy makes me beam. I'm happy for them; privileged to witness their achievement. I'm also jealous of the wave of emotion which will surely engulf them when they finally arrive at Santiago's Cathedral. As we tuck into our final lunch on the road we watch the last two stragglers from our group walk toward the Monte. Massa and Yasuke aren't last to arrive because they're slow walkers, they are simply taking their time to appreciate the journey. It's a bit of a *dreich* day, but their smiles are bright as they stride along the path. Each day Massa has walked with a neat, black umbrella as a walking stick. Finally, he has a reason to put it up. The umbrella is more like the type you'd expect to see over the arm of a stereotype of a London commuter than a young Japanese, hipster hiker with a shock of unruly black hair. It makes for a wonderfully surreal image.

As we descend to Santiago's urban outskirts the world suddenly seems more brash and full of jarring, mechanical noises. Instead of sharing the trail with other pilgrims and curious cows we have to make way for cars and trucks. Rather than striding confidently across quiet country lanes, we pause on the edge of pavements, waiting for a break in the traffic at busy junctions. At one we find ourselves marooned on an island in the middle of a busy road when a thought strikes Choo. We crossed at a spot where there were no traffic lights.

"Oh my!" She puts a hand to her mouth. "I'm jaywalking. I'll be arrested. I'll just tell them I'm Asian and don't know any better."

"Don't worry," Andy laughs as she steps into the empty road.

"It's fine to do this here."

"This feels really bad," Choo's head swivels around, not convinced, on the lookout for the policeman she still thinks will arrest her.

The sense of loss at nearing the end of our brief time on the *Camino* weighs heavily. I really don't want to stop walking. Ahead we can hear faint singing and cheering; the sound of mass exhilaration lifts my spirits. Brass shells embedded in the pavement lead us to Santiago's old town where tranquillity is resumed and modernity replaced by suitably historic edifices. Providing a musical welcome to pilgrims as they approach the final arch leading to *Praza do Obradoiro* is a Galician piper. Being Scottish, the rousing sound of the pipes automatically prods my heart, and the hairs on the back of my neck stand up. We stride through the arch to join a mass love-in of people laughing, crying, hugging. We spot some other members of our group and spontaneously throw arms around each other. I was worried we'd be outsiders when it came to being greeted by a wave of emotion at journey's end. A constricting throat and welling in my eyes tell me otherwise.

If I feel like this after three days, I can't imagine the intensity that comes after a month of walking the *Camino de Santiago*.

The Cats of the Quinta Parte Dois

During February we nearly kill Lily, the farm's hitherto sweet and friendly little black cat - as opposed to the black cat known as Bad Boy Ricky, or the third of the black cat trio, Poombaloo with his/her emotional issues. With hindsight, it would have been best for everyone if we had succeeded.

Daily, we're serenaded by an orchestra of countryside sounds around the farm - a melodious feathered choir of anonymous crooners in the morning; jarring squawks from Eurasian Jays when they're not impersonating something else; happy hoop hoops of jaunty hoopoes; excited bleats from the cartoon-cute dwarf goats across the way as they're released from their pen at daybreak, and immediately called back again for breakfast - causing even more excitement; storks clacking out drum beat solos; neurotic yapping from scruffy mongrels or baritone booms from their bigger *amigos* whenever anyone strays within a hundred metres of the property they're protecting; a reverberating, thunderous bray from a mule many fields distant; the chatty meh-ing of the sheep as they complete endless circuits around the farm; nerve-shattering screams when Ricky, with spring most definitely in the air, takes a fancy to any of the female cats who react with extreme prejudice when he makes his move; and so on. We *did* register hearing faint, feeble mews from somewhere beyond the pine woods next to our back terrace, but only as one of many other contributors to nature's soundtrack. We noted the noise and ignored it. When the sorry mewing continued for three days alarm bells eventually went off, especially as we realised Lily, who always turns up for a belly rub whenever we spend any time on our back terrace, hadn't appeared for her dose of daily pampering for quite some time.

"Have you seen Lily recently?" Andy asked Dona Catarina.

"Yes," the reply was instant and assured. "I saw her yesterday."

The problem when you have three cats who look exactly the

299

same from a distance is you can never be *that* certain which one you're looking at. Which is the seed that must have sprouted in Dona Catarina's mind. Thirty minutes after the question was asked, Dona Catarina and Senhor Fernando were doing a sweep of the farm, shouting "Leely, Leely." It didn't take them long to find 'Leely'. She was stuck at the top of a pine tree, her home for at least the last three days. We were wracked with guilt. The poor cat must have been able to see us from her lofty position and had tried to alert us to her predicament numerous times, and we'd completely failed her. Fernando swiftly swung into action, getting the longest ladder on the farm to try to manoeuvre himself as close to the terrified moggie as he could get. It took a lot of coaxing, but eventually Lily gathered the courage to gingerly attempt the descent from her tree-top prison. Initially she tried to shimmy her way closer to Fernando, but then momentum gathered and, as her nerve broke, she spun round and launched herself at his outstretched arm, shredding it as she lashed out to grab on to something, anything. Fernando's bloodied arm slowed her fall enough for her to gain control, and use his back as a ledge before she control-dropped her way to the forest floor, landing, of course, on all fours. She was skinny, exhausted and completely freaked out. But at least she was alive, no thanks to us.

A few weeks further down the line and we regretted mentioning Lily's absence to Dona Catarina. We should have left her to rot up that tree. There's been a complete reevaluation of the cast of cat characters. Even when it comes to the animal world we shouldn't make judgements based on first appearances. Felix unsurprisingly died. Bad Boy Ricky is now Uncle Ricky. Princesa, although still a sweetheart of a cat, revealed a sexually deviant nature. And sweet little Lily has become known as Darth Lily (by me) or She Who Must Not Be Named (by Andy).

This recasting of roles came about after Princesa gave birth to two kittens, Bella and Leo, the father of whom turned out to also be their brother Bob, Princesa's son and lover. I guess this sort of behaviour is common in the animal world, or in *Game of Thrones*, but it's not something we tend to think about. Although we're talking about a community of farm cats it's proving impossible not to apply human sensitivities to their scandalous behaviour.

"Princesa's had kittens by her own son?" was the shocked, joint reaction when Dona Catarina told us the news, prompting her to put her hand over her mouth and laugh.

"*É a natureza.*"

Bella and Leo injected new life to the farm's feline world, two cutesy bundles of fun with contrasting personalities; Bella, a shy, mottled grey and white who stuck close to her mother. Leo, a bouncy, adventurous, ginger and white ball of energy. Lunchtimes were brightened up no end as the kittens put on a daily show, playing king of the castle on rotting tree stumps, and launching ninja assaults on each other from behind our herb border. Each day Leo would wander a little bit further from his mother, following us all the way to the car park whilst he was still a tiny little thing. Sadly, he was too adventurous, straying too far on his own too quickly. Returning from our Friday shopping we came face to face with a crestfallen Dona Catarina.

"Leo's dead," tears welled in her eyes. "Fernando found him outside the gate this morning, his stomach had been sliced open."

We were rocked. We'd grown extremely fond of the kitten, his antics had reminded us of the sheer joy of being young and discovering a brand new world in which everything caused wide-eyed wonder and even the smallest journey felt like an adventure. That had all been snuffed out by a cruel and vindictive act. And we believed we knew the culprit; Lily.

Lily had shown a different side to her personality after the birth of the kittens; she bullied them at every opportunity. Both Dona Catarina and us had to shoo her off on numerous occasions after she'd launch an attack on them for no reason. She also took to viciously assaulting Princesa regularly, tearing chunks out her fur during frenzied, unprovoked assaults. Risking descending into amateur cat psychology, the motive seemed to be jealousy. Lily couldn't have kittens of her own and appeared to harbour an uncontrollable resentment of both Princesa and her offspring. A resentment which apparently culminated in the murder of little Leo. We had no firm evidence, but we knew it was Lily. She was nowhere to be seen for a couple of days following Leo's death, another sign of guilt in our book. When she came slinking back, and slink she did, she had a limp and a bad gash just above her right eye, so bad it left the eye as little more than a slit. Leo hadn't succumbed quietly, it was scant consolation to know at least the wee tiger had put up one hell of a fight.

We never mentioned our suspicions to Dona Catarina, but we could tell from her actions, and the things she left unsaid, she also knew who the culprit was; however, Lily was a favourite of hers so accusations were left unspoken. What was most interesting to observe was it quickly became clear the other cats had no doubts as to who'd killed Leo; their behaviour toward Lily completely changed. From being more or the less the top cat, she was virtually ostracised.

Even though we'd lived beside a cat sanctuary on Tenerife and thought we were old hands at understanding cat shenanigans, we witnessed some quite remarkable examples of a community of cats bonding together to protect their young from a malevolent force. The first example was immediate. After Leo's death the remaining kitten, Bella, was never allowed out of the company of two adult males. Wherever she went she was marshalled by Ricky and Bob, or Lord Greyjohn, who'd protectively lie either side of her. Tellingly, whenever Darth Lily appeared, the cats would take up position between her and the kitten. She wasn't allowed close, and was forced to watch peevishly from afar. Ricky's behaviour in particular was a revelation. The cat we had unfairly thought to be the farm bully allowed himself to be bitten, swiped at, and jumped on by an over enthusiastic kitten without so much as the slightest hint of angry reaction; he simply lay near anywhere Bella was playing, a protective guardian — aka Uncle Ricky.

The most unbelievable incident took place a few days ago following the birth of two more kittens, who we've named Sonny and Cher; another pair of bubbly innocents who are discovering how much fun the playground that is the farm can be. These two are also watched over by a designated adult cat, but their arrival has made it more difficult for the grown cats to keep tabs on all the younger felines. To counter this there's been a shift in strategy. Now Lord Greyjohn sticks like glue to Lily, shadowing her wherever she prowls. The other day Lily sat in the pine forest, glaring at Sonny and Cher as they bounced around our back terrace chasing butterflies. She was unable to do anything to vent her anger because Lord Greyjohn took up position between her and the kittens. It's a brilliant tactic apart from one flaw. It's possible to keep Lily away from the kittens, but impossible to keep curious kittens away from her. Seeing the two cats in the forest, Cher ventured closer to Lily. Frantically we called her back, knowing what would happen if she got within paw range. We saw what happened when Leo or Bella had accidentally wandered within Lily's reach; she swiped at them, sharp talons fully extended. The problem was there's a fence around the forest. It keeps the sheep in, but also prevents us from getting in. As soon as Cher went under the fence we couldn't get to her quickly if Lily attacked. It turned out we had nothing to worry about. As Cher drew close Lord Greyjohn did something remarkable. He took a couple of steps toward Lily and knocked her to the ground, then stood with his two front paws on her side and neck until the kitten became bored and scampered back to safety. As soon as that happened, Lord Greyjohn stepped off the prone black cat and took up position between her and the kitten again. We wouldn't have believed it had we not witnessed it for ourselves. With Lily virtually under house arrest, life for the kittens has become what it should be, idyllic.

FROM THE ORIENT TO ATHENS

Em Abril, águas mil. Basically, it rains a lot in April. Many
countries have a variation of this saying. In Spain and Chile it's
virtually the same - *en abril, lluvias mil*, whereas in Britain it
can be equally poetic - *March winds and April showers bring
forth May flowers*. Whether the land around us will be drenched
throughout the month, we won't know as we're due to spend
a good chunk of April in Greece, on the island of Andros to be
precise. Spring is one of our two busy travel periods in the year,
the other one being autumn. Subsequently we regularly spend
virtually the whole of April/May and September/October away
from home.

The months starts sunny and warm enough, with spring
flowers already putting on impressive displays in the fields
around us and in those parts of the farm which are out of bounds
to the sheep. This year Easter Sunday falls on the very first day
of the month. It's a novelty to actually get to celebrate it (i.e. eat
lots of chocolate) at home for a change. Around midday Dona
Catarina turns up at the door with a bouquet of sunny gerbera
daisies; it's a nice gesture, one which again makes us feel part of
a little community.

Four days later, we swap the tranquil, spring meadows
around the farm for the bustle of the big city. Our flight to
Athens is an early morning one and rather than endure an
unsatisfactory toss-and-turn night's sleep and then risk being
stuck in commuter traffic heading to Lisbon, we book into a
hotel at *Parque das Nações*. One of the airport hotels would
be more convenient but, as it's Easter week, they're full.
Parque das Nações is only a couple of underground stops
from the airport, so it's an easy, stress-free journey. Plus, we'll
enthusiastically grasp any excuse to spend time in *Parque das
Nações*. The transformed docklands area contrasts sharply
with the grand architecture of the city's historic centre - this is
Lisbon's ultra contemporary face and doesn't attract anything
like as many tourists as the city centre. The buildings along the

five-kilometre strip beside the Tagus have a pleasing, futuristic equilibrium to them; all showcase works created by visionary architects for Expo 98. We enjoy charming historic centres as much as the next slow traveller, but there's something elegantly beautiful about *Parque das Nações*. There's a futuristic element to the place which promises airy brightness and hope rather than the post-apocalyptic gloomy claustrophobic streets of the likes of *Blade Runner*. Among the stand-outs of modern architecture is the Altice Arena, the biggest indoor concert venue in Portugal and a cross between a spaceship and a giant crab which has scuttled on to land from the Tagus. Also standing out and looking like two bricks folding a freshly washed white sheet is the *Pavilhão de Portugal*, whilst Lisbon's Aquarium is a cube of an urban island in the centre of a human-made lake. The Oriente Station, the jewel of Portugal's rail network, is a typical Santiago Calatrava masterpiece - meant to represent an interlocked network of glass and steel trees. Maybe I can't quite see wood for the trees, but it *does* look magical when bathed in the golden light cast by the setting sun. I'm not so keen on the beneath ground part of the building though, it comes across more like an underground car park than a work of architectural genius. Saying that, I like the station overall, it even has a permanent book fair. Spending time in it is far preferable to being stuck in Entrecampos, the station we use when travelling back from the airport, which virtually shuts down at 20:00, including the toilets. The biggest attraction for us at *Parque das Nações* is the The Old House, the best Chinese restaurant we've eaten at anywhere, including China. The name is a reference to a place where friends and family would get together to chat and eat, and the menu is based on Sichuan cuisine. But, as the restaurant's Facebook page says, 'you won't find Chinese crepes or chau chau rice here.' The food at The Old House is outstanding - bursting with flavours and exquisitely presented; sauces are freshly cooked from scratch without a hint of MSG in sight. The downstairs dining area is always buzzing with Chinese and Portuguese diners as well as a handful of non-Lisboans - often delegates at a conference. We eat moreish gyozas and steamed won-tons followed by seriously spicy, and addictive, beef plus crunchy rabbit served in a wicker boat, and finish off with a brace of elegant pastry swans filled with sweet, red bean paste. It's an experience which makes catching an early morning flight worthwhile.

Stopovers are the worst ways to experience a city. They're wham, bam, thank you ma'am travel one night stands which ultimately leave you unfulfilled. And so it is with Athens, the ancient Greek capital where the east meets the west. I read a great line on satirical website Uncyclopedia - "*The city is where the west meets the east, mugs it, and makes it inhospitable. The west doesn't belong in Athens...*" Even from a whirlwind of a visit it feels as though there's a grain of accuracy in that. With limited time there is one thing we have to see, and one thing we definitely have to do. The 'see' is the Acropolis. When I say see I mean that literally – there's no time to enjoy its ancient embrace, just enough to stand on the same hill as the one on which the citadel reclines and take a couple of dull snaps. It's a gloomy, damp day (*em Abril…*); the Greek Gods clearly having a barney, their furrowed brows creating bruised ripples across the sky. All that's missing is Zeus flashing his lightning rod. The other 'must' is annoyingly mundane. One of us has forgotten to pack the cable for the laptop and, as we're on a week's mission to walk across, record and photograph Andros, one of the islands in the Cyclades, having a powered-up laptop is an essential tool of the job. So we go shopping.

A pedestrian walkway, *Apostolou Pavlou*, lined with cafes and stalls, leads from the Acropolis to Ermou, the main shopping street in Athens. It's a street which illustrates why the 'east meets west' tag is so justified. Its western end is a manic hotchpotch of ramshackle market stalls and messy stores spewing their goods onto the street – the sort of places which would have Maria Kondo either in ecstasy or therapy. It's an area where it feels, as the blurb said, the west doesn't belong. A compelling place to lose yourself in, but not when time is short. Half-way along and the street becomes familiar, depressingly so. Where the western end (ironically with the eastern vibe) exudes a unique personality, the eastern end, except for a couple of out-of-place Byzantine churches, morphs into one of those homogeneous European city centres (H&M, Marks & Spencer, Zara, McD's). Dull, familiar, and the ideal place to pick up a replacement cable.

To get to Andros we have to catch a ferry from Rafina, about 30 kms from the centre of the city. There are a couple of ways to get there; the easiest one is to jump in a taxi which takes about 1hr 15 mins and costs approx. €60. We're guinea pigs when we're on these missions. We have to experience what customers will so we can prepare them in advance for anything which isn't clear. And there are always aspects to travelling through unfamiliar places which are ambiguous. In this case, one was exactly where to catch the bus to the port. We know it's at Pedion Areos but, as that's one of the biggest parks in Athens, there's a lot of scope to turn up at the wrong part. It's not the most salubrious areas of the city either. Bus stations are often unattractive for some reason, at least this one is in the open air beside a park, albeit a seedy one. It takes some asking around and then asking around a bit more to discover which is the Rafina bus. There's confusion about how to pay; nobody seems to be interested in taking any money. About 45 minutes into the journey the passenger in front of us stands up and rummages around in an old carrier bag for a few moments before pulling out a small antiquated machine, cerca 1971 – he is the ticket collector. The coach is comfortable and only half full, the journey takes about the same time as a taxi to get to Rafina and costs us €2.60pp.

We arrive long before the ferry, but it doesn't matter. Rafina is a bustling and not unattractive town. The port area is home to plenty of fish and seafood restaurants, whilst just behind the harbour is a big square also lined with bars and restaurants. It isn't in the slightest bit touristy. There are some attractive bars overlooking the harbour, but they are filled with an unpleasant fog. A decade after a smoking ban was introduced and it's still being ignored in Greece. There's a threat of hefty fines, but the law isn't enforced. We've even seen waiters in restaurants lighting up between serving customers. We adore visiting Greece, but it's a country which does things its own way. Despite the smoky bars, there's a pleasing down-to-earth character to Rafina. It's not the most picturesque Greek harbour going, but it is friendly and the restaurants, where staff aren't smoking, are good. We ensconce ourselves in one with panoramic views of the sea, order a shedload of mezes with Fix beers and relax. Well, one of us does. As the rain splatters the windows and grey waves lashed at the harbour wall, Andy remembers she hasn't packed any seasickness tablets, expecting the Aegean to be mirror calm. She asks the waitress if there's a chemist in town. There is, but it's shut. However, she comes up with an unexpected alternative.

"Ask the man at the kiosk."

The kiosk is a typical tobacco/newspaper kiosk yet, sure enough, he reaches beneath the counter and produces two seasickness tablets for 0.50 cents. Rafina is just that sort of place.

As the ferry arrives, the clouds dissipate, the sun smiles and the sea calms down.

In Andros the ferry disgorges a sea of people from its open bow. We're met by Irini, the owner of one of the small, family run rural hotels where we'll be staying. How she picked us out from the crowd of people emerging from the bow is a mystery.

"How did you recognise us?" I ask as she walks us to her car.

"Yeeees," Irini replies with a big smile. She must have misheard my question. It is quite noisy to be fair.

"No, how did you know it was us? There were a lot of people coming off the boat."

"Yeeees," Irini replies again.

We've been told Irini is the only one in the family who speaks English. Communications over the next couple of days could be on the stilted side.

Easter Again: The captain of the flight had said an odd

thing when we landed - "have a happy Easter." Except it wasn't an odd thing at all as Orthodox Easter in Greece falls a week after ours. We just hadn't realised it. We've arrived on Andros the night before Easter Sunday. Irini, being a generous soul, invites us to her family's Easter Sunday meal. We have a hiking route to walk and record which makes it difficult to fit in, but it would be extremely rude to turn her down. We have to almost run around the route in order to make it back in time for our 2pm lunch date, and just have enough time to change out of grimy clothes before we're introduced to various generations of Irini's family and friends. None, apart from our hostess, can speak any English. One woman can speak French. Andy makes the mistake of saying she knows the language reasonably well, so the woman addresses her in French all afternoon. Every so often I ask Andy to interpret what the woman is saying, to which I receive an annoyed glance and a sharp kick under the table. For all the nods, smiles, *oui, oui, oui* and *non, non, non* Andy's been answering, she's busking it and my "what did she say?" interjections draw attention to that fact. Not that anyone would notice anyway. I'm seated opposite the family granny who insists on talking at me non-stop. Whether she's saying nice things or berating me who knows? It's all Greek to me. I get a brief reprieve from the awkward non-communication when Irini invites me into the kitchen to photograph the centrepiece of the meal - a whole lamb which has been cooked in a pit in the ground. The lamb is still in the wrapping it was cooked in; basically, the thing Irini wants me to photograph is a lamb-shaped piece of aluminium foil.

"It's good, yessss?" Irina beams proudly.

"Beautiful," I reply, snapping dutifully away at the crumpled aluminium.

Thankfully all embarrassing attempts at trying to communicate are interrupted by the Easter Sunday feast which includes the full lamb (this time unwrapped and sliced), buckets of tzatziki, country sausages, fried liver, Greek salad, trays of spinach and feta pies, and potent, throat-burning home-made wine. Throwing in a few approving "Mmms" ever now and again is communication enough. The conversation may be fuzzy, but the generosity of Irini and her family is as clear as the water in Andros' springs.

Glorious Paths: Many of the paths on Andros have us in raptures. The first time we notice how uniquely beautiful they are is walking the wide *steni* (a path lined by dry-stone walls) between the abandoned former capital of Paleopoli and the coastal town of Batsi. We've tread many former merchant trails in various countries; most have had us bitching about their unevenness and toll they take on the soles of feet after many kilometres. Not so on Andros where many paths consist of wide, flat stones - veritable avenues you could stroll along in your walking finery. Flanked by the most elaborate dry-stone walls we've seen, they are works of art and beautifully maintained by a group of dedicated, passionate volunteers, Andros Routes. Being spring, the island is looking its colourful best; a scarlet poppy army wave at us as we walk. Perfumed orange blossom and the sweet aroma of ripe figs are fragrances I associate with Greek islands anyway, but on an island with a thousand types of plants, 400 species of mushrooms and over 170 varieties of herbs; the Andros air is scented with so much more than orange blossom and figs. On one route which involves passing honey farms, herb-munching goats, a lookout tower from the third century BC, and stepping over a tortoise, it might seem odd to single out a place where doves hang out, but the the dovecotes on Andros are no ordinary dovecotes. They are beautifully constructed; white rectangular towers whose upper tiers are decorated with upside down V symbols. Owning an elaborately decorated dovecote was a status symbol for wealthy landowners who allowed peasant farmers to use the pigeon droppings which accumulated in their interiors as manure. Underground springs keep Andros green even when there hasn't been a cloud in that intense Greek blue sky for weeks and the gurgling from springs and streams is a common accompaniment on our walks across hill, dale and ravine after ravine. There are oaks, chestnut trees, maples, hawthorns and poplars as well as figs and that proud evergreen which adds a distinctive Mediterranean stamp to vistas, cypress trees. Whilst streams and springs are common companions on some routes, one stands out; the Sariza spring in the mountain village of Apoikia. Given its water is believed to have curative properties, and that it fills many of the bottles in supermarkets on the island and beyond, the fountain is understated; a lone lion's head spouting precious liquid. It's said people queue to fill containers from the spring; we only have to wait for one local man to top up his bottle before we replenish ours. It's the first time I've refilled a bottle bought in a supermarket with water from the same source.

By day three, crossing from the north west of the island to the east, we still haven't passed another walker. Andros feels like undiscovered country.

Big Personalities and Orthodox Priests: Dino, owner of Iro Suite - our second base on the outskirts of the Chora, aka Andros Town - is a larger than life character. Although hailing from Andros, he worked for many years in New York where he became known as Dino, and he does have a look of the wine-loving crooner. As a result, he speaks English like he's a character in *Goodfellas*. He also makes a mean French toast with maple syrup for breakfast. Dino's stories are as big as his personality. He tells us one about driving a sports car from Britain back to Andros and racing it at high speeds along the island's narrow country roads.

"Weren't you worried about attracting the attention of the police?" I ask, to which there's a wry snort.

"We don't have police here, we sort ourselves out."

When we tell him we'll be climbing to the Panachradou Monastry he regales us with tales about the generosity of the old priest there, and how he and his friends would phone ahead to ask the priest to have steaming bowls of stew ready when they arrived; the priest has a reputation for feeding souls who wander his way. The path to Panachradou is a challenging one, especially in unseasonably hot temperatures of 30C (those *águas mil* would be very welcome). The final two kilometres are possibly the longest we've sweated our way up in our walking careers. Finally, after crossing a Venetian bridge and climbing beyond an ancient abandoned settlement, we stagger into the grounds of the monastery high above the Mesa Choria valley to find a young priest lugging a sack of flour on his back. The old priest is away on one of his wanders which can last for days on end; it's something old Greek priests like to do apparently. However, the younger priest proves no less hospitable. On seeing us lapping up the views from the terrace beside Panachradou, he invites us into the monastery for coffee and *loukoumi*, a floury sweet which is like the Greek version of Turkish delight.

"Whatever you do, don't say that to the old priest," Dino had laughed when I made that comparison as he described *loukoumi* when telling us about the food at the monastery.

The young priest leads us to a small room with carved wooden benches and ancient religious prints on the wall. He lifts the lid off two porcelain bowls. One is full of bread-sticks covered in sesame seeds, the other is brimming with floury *loukoumi*.

"Help yourselves," he gestures toward the food. "And when you're rested and ready to leave, just close the door behind you."

As he makes to leave, he turns back to bid us farewell.

"Have a good day, have a good week, and have a good life."

This is the first time I've been in a place of worship that actually felt like a welcoming sanctuary.

When we've completed all the routes we need to hike and gathered all the information we need for the guide we'll write, Dino drives us back to the port to catch the ferry. As we retrace our route backwards, and in the comfort of a car seat, Dino asks us a question.

"Have you visited Greece before this?"

"Yes, many times," Andy replies, reeling off the places we've visited. "We've been to Zakynthos, Crete, Corfu, Samos, Symi, Rhodes, and Lesbos."

"So Andros is your first visit to a proper Greek island?"

That's us put in our place. But his frank reply does sort of sum up the difference between Andros and those Greek islands which are popular with many travellers.

WAVING AT SHEEP

"The world's favorite season is the spring. All things seem possible in May." - Edwin Way Teale

It feels to me as though the year begins in May. March and April reflect a tempestuous love affair between winter and summer, with both taking turns being the dominant force in what is often a stormy relationship. May is their beautiful offspring. It is one of our favourite months for hiking; the countryside responding in flamboyant fashion to preceding months which brought a fusion of wind, rain, and sunshine. September is our other favourite month because, with summer's heat abating, walking temperatures are warm, but not oppressively so. It's a reliably sunny month for taking to the trail. That was in the Canaries at least. Here in Portugal September is still too hot to trot. What May has over September is the post-summer landscape in some southern European locations, where rain over summer months is a rarity, isn't the most pleasing to the eyes; the terrain looking thirsty, brittle and vaguely scorched. The countryside in May, on the other hand, looks as though it has awoken, bursting with energy, after a rejuvenating slumber. Whereas September is a parched soul dragging itself through the desert in search of water, May is fresh, perky, and eager to put on its most colourful carnival costume and dance a lively lambada.

Having to put together walking route directions and a travel guide for Andros; finish writing *Rough Guide's Pocket Guide for Tenerife and La Gomera*; and completing a spread about the Canary Islands for French travel magazine GEO keeps us chained to our desks for much of early spring, with all forays whenever we become too stir crazy being close to home. At this time of year, the scenery is particularly beguiling.

The displays of wild flowers we walk through are dazzling, the floral performers changing depending on where we meander. The network of tracks criss-crossing the cork forest and fields next to the farm are a riot of colour. Some wild flowers we recognise from spring displays on Tenerife - Mediterranean thistle and viper's bugloss. Others are different - common vetch, sheep scabious and a plant we've come to consider as providing the perfumed aroma of Portugal, cistus. The skirt of the hill on which Palmela Castle sits is dramatically blood-stained by a rippling ocean of poppies, and the valleys, meadows, and ridges within Arrábida would have green-fingered walkers in a lather. As well as being home to almost 1500 different types of plants and flowers, many of them endemic, there are wild orchids galore; over 30 variations in total. We're no flower experts and have to rely on poring through books and online images to try to identify plants (recently we've started using the Plantnet app which has proved an invaluable time-saver). We get excited by anything bright and pretty which sprouts from the ground, even invasive weeds. However, people we've walked with who do know their flowers have been wowed by the unusual orchids to be discovered peeking out from Arrábida's hedgerows. We've seen bee and yellow orchids sharing grassy verges with grape hyacinth, shrubby gromwell, and Narcissus. One quirky orchid we've yet to spot, but which the schoolboy who lurks inside desperately wants a photo of to share on social media, is the snigger-inducing *Orchis italica* - the naked man orchid. We don't even have to leave the farm to enjoy colourful displays and heady scents (but only in those areas the sheep can't get their greedy chops to); amid bubblegum-pink oleander, papery camellia petals, and fragrant roses are exotic strelitzias (bird of paradise) and snowy jasmine waterfalls which add their intoxicating perfume to the early evening air. Everywhere is pretty as a picture. The long grasses even conceal one of the few Portuguese traits we're not so keen on - casual littering. In summer, when the roadside grasses are sparse, the verges between Brejos do Assa and Setúbal are full of discarded rubbish. There are litterbugs amongst all nationalities, but it seems worse around here than anywhere else I've seen in Europe. Some nationalities just respect the countryside less than others.

Our daily routine throughout the year when at home is we

finish writing at around 17:30. In May, in order to wallow in the
warmth of the late afternoon sun, we decamp to our back terrace
at this time. This month, the wallow is accompanied by a *Porto
tónico* to toast the end of the working day. What our post-work
drink consists of changes depending on the season. Autumn
called for refreshing craft beers; a warming glass of Port was
more suited to winter months; and spring's freshness seems
to compliment a zingy Port and tonic. Following its revamp,
the back terrace has become a favourite spot to relax, read and
quietly appreciate the natural surroundings. We've decorated
an earthy border around the terrace's tiles with solar lights and
various herbs - oregano, basil, thyme, chives, cilantro, lovage
(Dona Catarina's addition) - some of which fare better than
others. Learning of our enthusiasm for cooking, Dona Catarina
asked Fernando to create a couple of mini allotments beside
the terrace in which to grow lettuce. The terrace also doubles
as a comfortable bird hide without walls. It's a super spot for
observing both the wild and more domestic world around us.
It remains a thrill to observe storks passing overhead, circling
in long, lazy circles as they ascend on warm air currents.
Sometimes the storks are replaced by large, pale birds of preys
with feathered wing tips. I think they are kites but Andy believes
them to be eagles. Dona Catarina isn't much help when it comes
to bird and flower identification. Whenever we ask her if she
knows the name of one or the other, the answer is invariably a
shrug and a "*nao sei.*" Fernando *does* tend to know such things,
but he's usually finished work for the day by the time we're
in chill-out mode, and there's no way we could successfully
describe the birds to him in any detail in Portuguese when he
turns up the following morning, afternoon, or whenever he
feels like it. The most common visitors to the sheep's field are
blackbirds and Eurasian jays but, as the temperatures warm up
more, they've been joined by a couple of hoopoes, hopping
around the grass industriously, their fanned-out crowns bobbing
up and down as they stab at insects in the grass. Both keep
just out of pounce range of the ever optimistic Batman. Very
occasionally the birds will be joined by a rabbit bobbing through

the pine forest. The cats don't pay any attention to the bunnies. Rabbits and cats get on reasonably well according to Dona Catarina. She says when she puts out food for the cats near the orchard grove she'll occasionally see cats and rabbits sharing bowls.

Generally, the most distracting entertainment on our rear terrace entertainment zone is provided by the farm's cat population which has swelled in recent months thanks to a combination of further incestuous couplings and Dona Catarina being a wee softy. Not only has she rescued five multi-coloured kittens from a neighbour who was going to 'get rid' of them, she found a pure white kitten abandoned beside a refuse bin and brought it home. He's called Kikou and has the *gallus* swagger of an alley cat. The refugee kittens have no names yet, but we've christened them 'the Jets'. This is because they amble around in a gang, causing havoc wherever they appear. The home-grown kittens of varying ages (Claudius, Leonardo, Mimi, Sonny and Cher) tend to look horrified at this intrusion by the rowdy outsiders, so we've named them 'the Sharks.' We tried to explain why to Dona Catarina but she'd never heard of *West Side Story* so it fell flat. All of them seem to crave human company (although no cat would ever admit that) as, whenever we settle ourselves into our chairs on the terrace, they stroll up one by one until there's a full circus of them, launching rough 'n' tumble assaults on each other from behind low bushes, or playing king of the castle from the top of tree stumps which were once dragon palms.

And then there's the sheep. We've changed our opinion that sheep are the most stupid creatures in the universe... up to a point. They have personality in their own quiet way. Overall they live a harmonious life, unlike the cats, quietly going about their business and spending day after day circling the farm eating grass with no drama. At Quinta Novesium the sheep are more like pets than livestock, Dona Catarina doesn't use them for anything - no wool, no milk, and definitely no meat. They get let out their field in the morning, spend the day doing circuits of the farm, eating as they go, then get 'officially' fed and put to bed around 19:00 when Dona Catarina goes home to Seixal. She talks to them in the same way she does the cats and has names for each. When she's out of sight we can never tell the difference between her talking on the phone or conversing with the sheep. She's also able to identify individuals by their bahs. Although Dona Catarina refers to the *quinta* as a *fazenda* we've never been sure in what way it is a farm. I guess it technically fits the bill if we apply the definition of a farm being "*an area of land and its buildings, used for growing crops and rearing animals.*" Crops are grown on it - we currently have a bowl of *nísperos* (loquats) courtesy of Fernando - and animals are most definitely reared on the farm. But for what purpose other than company remains a mystery; the ducks don't even produce duck eggs.

With the temperatures rising and the sheep increasingly looking like over-sized woollen barrels, it's the time of year they hate the most; the sheep shearer is due a visit. I've read some misguided articles about sheep-shearing being cruel. I've no doubt there are some unscrupulous farmers who are guilty of cruelty to their livestock, but I struggle to believe it's the norm. Partly this is because I spent many school holidays at my aunt's farm in Dumfries & Galloway, including during sheep-shearing, and never witnessed any animal cruelty there or at neighbouring farms. It simply doesn't make any sense for farmers to deliberately damage their livelihood. Admittedly, these were small farms. I don't necessarily trust industrial-sized farms to behave in quite the same way. When it comes to domestic sheep, shearing is essential, especially in countries with hot climates. Unlike their wild relatives, domestic sheep don't automatically shed their thick winter coats. To not shear them would be cruel and potentially life threatening when temperatures are touching 40C. But they don't like it one bit.

Dona Catarina stays at her main home in Seixal most nights, arriving back at the farm around mid-morning. As the sheep shearer is due early morning she has to stay over so she's here when he arrives; the sheep won't come near him without her around. She worries they won't come near him *with* her around, but she has a plan to trick them. The shearing is due to take place in the lower field next to the duck shed. The sheep shearer will hide in the shed until Dona Catarina lures the sheep closer with the promise of oranges, pouncing as soon as they stray within his reach. As the sheep tend to follow her around like little, well, lambs, they should automatically come trotting down to the duck shed when they see her offering the forbidden fruit.

The sound of frantic and distraught 'bah-ing' accompanied by frustrated shouting at dawn's first light suggests all has not gone as hoped. By the time we get to the sheep's 'hairdressing area' it's obvious the sheep haven't been fooled in the slightest by DC's cunning plan. The flock has retreated to the lemon orchard on a mound overlooking the duck shed, where Dona Catarina and sheep shearer are calling the sheep to come closer, holding out oranges as bait. They aren't having one bit of it. The funny thing is they don't run away from us and are happy to let us stand right beside them among the lemon trees.

"They recognised the sheep shearer from last year and wouldn't come close once they'd seen him," Dona Catarina explains later.

The sheep shearer couldn't hang around long as he had more sheep to shear elsewhere. Not a single sheep was sheared, so a rematch has been arranged. Part of the problem is Dona Catarina doesn't want to stress the sheep in any way, so won't use 'assertive measures' to encourage them (i.e. drag them).

A couple of days later and a second attempt is made; the sheep shearer arriving by a different entrance, one which doesn't involve passing a field of sheep who are clearly proficient at face recognition. This time the sheep fall for it and wander into the trap. One is grabbed. The others; however, scatter and take to the high ground once again. From a safe distance they look on in horror as their comrade has her coat sheered from her, revealing an anorexic stranger underneath. I can imagine how brutal it must appear to the poor creatures, but sometimes you have to be cruel to be kind. There's no chance of any of the others going near Dona Catarina after witnessing this. The sheep shearer leaves having removed the fleece from a grand total of one animal. With the shearer unable to return for a few weeks, by which time it will have become extremely hot, those animals are going to rue this day.

Whilst we wonder the purpose of the sheep, it occurs they might be pondering the same about us. Because she's insistent we shouldn't be doing any work around the farm, Dona Caterina won't allow us to let them out of their field in the morning, or lock them away at night; both actions that would help her and save her time. Subsequently, whenever Fernando hasn't arrived early and we're going out in the car, the flock gathers at the fence bordering the car park to watch us intently, expectation evident on each of their faces. Instead of letting them out, as they hope, we simply wave at them and wish them a "*bom dia*". It freaks them out. One will look at another, blink, then turn back to us with a "what does that mean?" expression, before repeating the sequence. If we're not actually there to release them from their field, they must wonder what *our* purpose on the farm is. What do we add to their lives?

As we sip our *Porto tónico* the sheep complete the last of their many circuits, pausing at the section of fence which lies directly behind our terrace. They do this every single night; stop at the same spot and simply stand there staring at us for a while. And every night we wave at them, prompting a mass bout of "what does this mean?" expressions.

"It's a strange, pointless life they lead isn't it?" I mumble. "Just doing the same thing every day, never changing their route." We watch the sheep watching us for a few moments.

"Perhaps the sheep think the same thing," Andy muses. "Maybe that's why they stop at the same spot each night, to look at us whilst pondering 'what a strange, pointless life these two lead. Every night doing exactly the same thing at the same time.' From their perspective we might not seem that different."

She has a point. It's not only farm animals whose routines never vary from one day to the next. For our part, over the last few months we have become gradually and imperceptibly assimilated into the routine of daily life at the farm. We feel as settled as the sheep.

DEPARTURE

Ropes are unhooked from metal bollards on the pontoon pier and our vessel gently eases sidewards and away from the dock.

Departure.

A year ago, almost to the day, we watched the port of Santa Cruz recede into the distance not knowing what lay ahead. This time it's Setúbal's port which is doing the receding. Just like the May day twelve months ago, the weather is glorious with not one cloud breaking an intensely blue sky. However, unlike the Santa Cruz ferry, there's no lively reggaeton soundtrack nor dancing girls to mark the occasion, just the low thrum of the ferry's engines and the faint swish of lines being cast by fishermen on the promenade next to the ferry terminal. The catamaran creates V-shaped ripples on the surface of the Sado Estuary; a millpond today, as it is on many days. The morning has barely reached its stride, yet the sun's rays are fierce enough to warrant the wearing of broad-brimmed hats. Veteran commuters shun the sun, staying cool below deck, but first-timers like us want to soak up the 360 degree scenery from the deck of the little, lime-green ship. Behind us, the busy port with its juggernaut cargo ships morphs into the old town which itself secedes to Arrábida Natural Park at the star-shaped *Forte de São Filipe*. In the sharp morning light, Arrábida is a splendid sight, worthy of the description 'where the mountains melt into the sea' even if the verdant bumps in an otherwise flat land are more hills than mountains; 'where the green, green hills dip their toes in azure waters' isn't quite as dramatically poetic. Mountains or not, Arrábida is an eye magnet. From the ferry's deck, the narrow mouth of the Sado doesn't really stand out, instead Arrábida melts into the blight at the tip of the Troia Peninsula where there's an unsightly small resort with a handful of apartment blocks. Without them the thin strip of land would be a wild-looking enigma. They dilute the natural beauty, but

only a smidgens. Most of our view from the bow is taken up by
a low-lying band of shrubs separated from the cerulean Sado
by a sliver of a golden strip which stretches south for miles and
miles into the morning haze. From a distance, Troia has the
appearance of a coral atoll. In a way it looks more West African
than Southern European. This notion is aided and abetted by the
small fleet of rowing boat-sized fishing craft which populate
the water between us and our destination. A police patrol boat is
moored alongside one; we pass so close I can see the crumpled
documents being checked by officers in sky-blue uniforms. It's a
20 minute ferry journey between Setúbal and Troia and a world
of difference. Troia is a finger of salt marshes, dunes and stone
pines where gennets and marsh harriers patrol the forest whilst
white herons step purposefully through the shallow waters of sea
lagoons, feasting on fish darting in and out of the rusting hulks
of crumbling shipwrecks. There are treasures in this cut-off slice
of Alentejo; an endless beach made famous when Madonna
rode her horse along part of it; a fishermen's shanty town with
a network of rickety jetties stretching into the water where the
Sado curves eastward; the ruins of a Roman settlement, once the
largest *garum* factory in all Europe. It's only 20 minutes away
but, in the course of nearly eight months, we haven't got around
to actually visiting it, until today.

We lean lazily on the railings, transfixed by the desert island-
like strip of land drawing ever closer. Our year in Portugal is
up. In one way it has whizzed past at rapid download speed. In
another, it seems impossible to think only a mere 12 months
have passed since we sailed from Santa Cruz de Tenerife not
knowing whether Portugal would be a good fit or for how long
we'd stay. We've travelled the country from its southernmost
point to its northern border with Spain; walked on beaches lining
Portugal's western coastline and negotiated smugglers' paths on
its eastern frontier; and pounded city streets in Porto, Lisbon,
and Coimbra. In a year we've experienced far more of the
country than we could ever have anticipated.

Obviously we've discussed our future plans on an ongoing
basis. The long-term objective was to spend a year or two in

different European countries, starting with Portugal. When we initially hatched these fluid plans, a year seemed like a decent amount of time. Now...

We have an ongoing list of pros and cons concerning living at Quinta Novesium. The cons include rarely having any privacy; the potential unreliability of fundamentals (water, electricity, internet - not always as speedy as we thought. Because of our work, having unreliable ADSL is a deal-breaker); rent, which is too high for the size of house and facilities (shared washing machine, a temperamental fridge which on a whim decides to freeze everything in it, even at its lowest setting). The pros include it being the most delightful place to live in an ideal location, and being part of a small, friendly community which gives us access to insights we wouldn't otherwise have. Even the downsides act as a reminder of simpler times before materialism became an epidemic in some countries; although, we'd already materialistically detoxed during our time on Tenerife.

Portugal itself has exceeded expectations and continues to throw up surprise after surprise. In a way it's like a larger scale version of Tenerife. When writing about Tenerife, we'd regularly describe it as being a location that millions have visited and thought they knew but which few people actually knew at all. Portugal is similar. Many people know the Algarve, Lisbon, Porto and a handful of other places. Beyond those, much of the country remains unknown to a significant number of non-Portuguese; 18 months ago we didn't know Setúbal existed. There is an annual competition in Portugal to find the 'best of' something. That 'something' can be regional gastronomic specialities, pastries, beaches, historic towns etc. When we read the ten nominations which were chosen for the finals of the country's prettiest villages, we hardly knew any of them despite having visited towns which we declared as being among the most picturesque we'd seen anywhere. The more you get to know about a place, the more you discover you don't know. The year hasn't sated our appetite for Portugal, it has whetted it.

Up to a point, the decision about 'should we stay or should we go' has already been made for us. At the start of May James

Keane, our pal from Inntravel, paid us a whirlwind visit to see for himself whether Arrábida Natural Park had enough of the requisite ingredients that make up an Inntravel holiday. Over two days, we strolled Sesimbra Castle's battlements; devoured a seafood platter on the town's promenade; pored over military maps trying to find tracks to link various towns by walking routes; explored dirt tracks and dusty paths leading deep into the heart of Arrábida, at one point skirting a hidden lake in a forest filled with spring flowers in bloom; ate *presunto* and Azeitão cheese inside the walls of Palmela Castle; and drank thyme-flavoured craft beer as we bounced ideas and logistics off each other, debating whether a walking holiday in Arrábida might actually work. The outcome was we were all enthused and excited by the prospect of creating a walking holiday in an area of natural beauty, bursting with historical and gastronomic riches, which remained below the radar of every other specialist holiday company in Europe.

"Well, we can't leave until we've pulled the Arrábida holiday together," Andy says, transfixed by the sun dancing across fallen stars sparkling on the surface of the water.

"Yup, that does pretty much seal it," I watch fishermen in a rowing boat haul at a net, trying to see what they've caught. "That will take months to achieve. Anyway, there's still a lot around Setúbal we haven't done yet, like this visit the Troia Peninsula. Next time we can take the car ferry and embark on a mini road trip to get back home." Although it's 20 minutes by boat, it's one hundred kilometres by road.

"Or explore the Costa da Caparica," Andy adds.

"Of course, there's a huge sea lake there I want to walk around," I'd forgotten about the Costa da Caparica on the west coast of the Setúbal Peninsula. "Plus we've never even visited the Cristo Rei on the south bank of the Tagus, and that's no distance away."

"We've hardly spent any time in Alcácer do Sal; it's lovely there," Andy throws in another 'to do'.

"And we've still to visit JMF and Bacalhôa's *adegas* in Azeitão," the list is rapidly gaining momentum.

"These are only the places a short drive away, what about those farther afield? All those fabulous looking places we've seen on Portugal's 'best of' competitions that we didn't even know existed."

Suddenly we're overwhelmed by what we *haven't* done.

"Jeez, what have we been doing with ourselves?" I'd been feeling smug about all the things we've notched up over the year. We've barely scratched the surface. "You know what? We haven't even managed to order anything from the baker who delivers bread and pastries to the farm. That's pathetic."

The village's baker leaves freshly made goodies on the *quinta's* gate first thing in the morning. Susanna the estate agent had told us this on our very first visit. Despite asking Dona Catarina how the process actually works - you leave a note saying what you want with some money, he leaves the bread and change - we've never tried it out; mainly because we don't know what to ask for. Dona Catarina reels off a list of types of bread in Portuguese whenever we ask, but we haven't a clue how to spell them.

"There's no way we can leave until after we have successfully picked up a warm bag of freshly made bread from the gate," another thought occurs to me. "And I'm definitely not leaving Portugal until I get a photo of that bizarre naked-man orchid."

"Another year it is," Andy turns her face toward the sun and smiles. "… or possibly two. And then what?"

And then what? Three words filled with the promise of adventure and new experiences hidden just around the next corner of life's path. And then what indeed. Now we've jumped on that seventh wave and broken free from the Canary Islands it feels like we can go anywhere at anytime.

ABOUT THE AUTHOR

In 2003 Jack Montgomery stepped away from a job he loved in the North West of England to live in the middle of a banana plantation in the north of Tenerife.

A case of mistaken identity shortly after arriving in the Canary Islands was the catalyst for the launch of a new career as a travel writer. Along with his wife Andrea, he started writing about the 'real Tenerife', the one that existed beyond the resorts. Over 14 years of recounting experiences which provided an insight into a world largely ignored in travel writing, both gained reputations as specialists for the Canary Islands, writing travel articles for numerous travel and airline magazines (Easyjet, Wizz, Traveller, Norwegian Air, GEO), newspapers (The Independent, The Telegraph) and websites, whilst contributing their expertise to guidebooks (Rough Guides, Dorling Kindersley), and producing their own guides.

In the last few years, Jack and Andrea widened their scope to include the European mainland, becoming Slow Travel specialists, writing travel guides for off the beaten track destinations in France, Slovenia, Greece, Spain, Germany, Austria, and Portugal. Their experiences are also chronicled in their award-winning, online travel magazine Buzztrips.co.uk.

In between discovering more off-the-beaten-track locations in Portugal, and around Europe, Jack is currently putting the finishing touches to a book about a Machiavellian cat, as well as continuing to hone his skills as a scorpion removal specialist.

If you want to keep up to date with what's happening in Jack's world of Slow Travel follow him on facebook (BuzzTrips.co), Twitter (@JACtravelwriter), or Instagram (@ jackbuzztrips).

Printed in Great Britain
by Amazon